THE CHILD CARE PROBLEM

THE CHILD CARE PROBLEM

An Economic Analysis

David M. Blau

Russell Sage Foundation / New York

The Russell Sage Foundation

The Russell Sage Foundation, one of the oldest of America's general purpose foundations, was established in 1907 by Mrs. Margaret Olivia Sage for "the improvement of social and living conditions in the United States." The Foundation seeks to fulfill this mandate by fostering the development and dissemination of knowledge about the country's political, social, and economic problems. While the Foundation endeavors to assure the accuracy and objectivity of each book it publishes, the conclusions and interpretations in Russell Sage Foundation publications are those of the authors and not of the Foundation, its Trustees, or its staff. Publication by Russell Sage, therefore, does not imply Foundation endorsement.

Library of Congress Cataloging-in-Publication Data

Blau, David (David M.)
  The child care problem : an economic analysis / David M. Blau.
    p.   cm.
  Includes bibliographical references and index.
  ISBN 0-87154-101-7
    1. Child care—Economic aspects—United States.   2. Child care services—Economic aspects—United States.   I. Title.

  HQ778.63 .B53 2001
  362.71'2'0973—dc21   2001041786

RUSSELL SAGE FOUNDATION
112 East 64th Street, New York, New York 10021
10 9 8 7 6 5 4 3 2 1

To Janet, Kathryn, and Michael

Contents

About the Author   ix

Acknowledgments   xi

PART I   **INTRODUCTION AND OVERVIEW**

Chapter 1   **WHAT IS THE CHILD CARE PROBLEM?**   3

Chapter 2   **AN OVERVIEW OF THE CHILD CARE MARKET IN
THE UNITED STATES**   17

Chapter 3   **ECONOMIC MODELS OF CHILD CARE**   47

PART II   **ANALYSIS OF THE CHILD CARE MARKET**

Chapter 4   **THE DEMAND FOR CHILD CARE AND THE LABOR
SUPPLY OF MOTHERS**   67

Chapter 5   **THE SUPPLY OF CHILD CARE**   86

Chapter 6   **EQUILIBRIUM PRICE AND QUALITY IN THE CHILD
CARE MARKET**   104

Chapter 7   **THE DETERMINANTS AND EFFECTS OF CHILD
CARE QUALITY**   125

PART III   **CHILD CARE POLICY**

Chapter 8   **CHILD CARE SUBSIDIES**   149

Chapter 9   **CHILD CARE REGULATIONS**   173

Chapter 10   **WHAT SHOULD WE DO ABOUT THE CHILD CARE PROBLEM?**   208

Notes   233

References   247

Index   261

About the Author

DAVID M. BLAU is professor of economics at the University of North Carolina at Chapel Hill, and a fellow of its Carolina Population Center.

Acknowledgments

Much of the material in this book is drawn from published articles and unpublished manuscripts, including several co-authored by Alison Hagy, Naci Mocan, and Philip Robins. I am grateful to my co-authors for their collaboration, and appreciate the opportunity to use our joint work here. Three anonymous reviewers provided very helpful and detailed comments on an early draft of the book. The initial development of the ideas in the book was supported by the Russell Sage Foundation during a year I spent as a visiting scholar at the Foundation. Much of the research on which the book is based was supported by a grant from the National Institute of Child Health and Human Development. I am grateful for the support of these institutions. The ideas and opinions in the book are my own, and should not be attributed to these institutions or any other individuals.

Part I

INTRODUCTION AND OVERVIEW

Part I

INTRODUCTION AND OVERVIEW

Chapter 1

What Is the Child Care Problem?

Child care in the United States is a problem. This is the message of many newspaper and magazine articles and reports by think tanks, government agencies, and conferences. Depending on whom you ask, the child care problem endangers the well-being of children, causes financial hardship and stress for families, makes it next to impossible for low-income families to work their way off welfare, causes substantial productivity losses to employers, and prevents many mothers from maintaining productive careers in the labor force. What is the nature of the child care problem? Why does it exist? What is being done to solve the problem, and what more can and should be done about it?

This book addresses these issues from an economic perspective. The price, cost, demand, and supply aspects of child care fall naturally into the domain of economics. Other important aspects of child care, such as the determinants and consequences of the quality of child care, are considered the domain of developmental psychology and are generally ignored by economists. I believe that an economic perspective can contribute to an understanding of these issues as well, so a substantial portion of the book is devoted to issues of child care quality. I take seriously the perspective of developmental psychologists on child care quality: I use their measures of quality and discuss and critique their research.

This book is based on the results of my own research on child care over the past decade as well as that of others. Much of this research has been published in scholarly journals and is addressed primarily to an audience of economists. My purpose here is to synthesize these economic analyses of child care issues in the United States and present the research results in a way that is intelligible and useful to other social scientists and to non-academic readers. I hope that this straightforward and nontechnical economic analysis of child care is helpful to all readers in thinking about the child care problem and alternative solutions to it.

Most of the book is devoted to description and analysis: discussion of conceptual issues, models, data, and empirical results. I try to put aside the opinions and biases I bring to the subject and present the pros and cons of alternative ways of thinking about the issues. In the last chapter, I put forward my policy proposals on how to deal with the child care problem in the United States, being as explicit as possible about their social and economic objectives. These ideas are strongly influenced by the results of my research, but they also reflect my value judgments about the issues.

CHILD CARE PROBLEMS AND THEIR CONSEQUENCES

There are several commonly cited problems with child care in the United States: much of it is of low quality; some types of child care are unavailable; high-quality child care is expensive and in short supply; child care providers receive low earnings and consequently experience high turnover; consumers lack knowledge and awareness of important aspects of child care; and child care costs are a major barrier to escaping welfare for low-income families. Let's consider each of these problems in turn.

Low Quality

> *Child care at most centers in the United States is poor to mediocre, with almost half of the infant and toddler rooms having poor quality. Only one in seven centers provides a level of quality that promotes healthy development.*
>
> —Helburn 1995, 1

Suzanne Helburn (1995) and her colleagues measured the quality of care in a sample of four hundred day care centers by spending two to three hours observing rooms in the centers and rating them on the Early Childhood Environment Rating Scale (ECERS), a quality scale with well-established reliability (for a detailed description, see Clifford and Harms 1980). The quality rating scale covers a wide range of factors related to safety and health, facilities, materials, toys, developmentally appropriate activities, and interactions between staff and children. The results of this study, which appear to be reliable and have been widely cited, confirm in a systematic way what many child care experts have been saying for a long time: from a child development perspective, the typical day care center in the United States provides care of mediocre quality. A good example of the type of care that would probably be rated as barely adequate or mediocre was described in the *New York Times* on April 27, 1998:

> At the three Houston centers, workers seem to see their role more as managing children than interacting with them. If a child was not having a problem, not in need of feeding or diapering or nose wiping, no one was likely to engage that child. In one room at Educare recently, Shirley Arceneaux was responsible for 15 children, most of them recently turned 3. . . . Although it was noisy and some children wandered around aimlessly, there was no fighting and no crying. Mrs. Arceneaux monitored the group, reminding children

who knocked things over to pick them up, and making sure they shared. But she never joined the play, or discussed what the children were doing . . . what child care experts call "teachable moments" were often overlooked.

What about the quality of other forms of child care? There is less information about the quality of family day care homes and relatives, but the available data suggest that on average quality is also low. In their study of the quality of about two hundred family day care homes and relatives providing child care, Susan Kontos and her colleagues (1995, 206) concluded: "Only 9% of the providers were observed to be providing good quality care, whereas 35% were rated as providing inadequate quality care. The remaining providers (56%) were rated as providing adequate or custodial quality care. . . . The vast majority of providers offering inadequate care are nonregulated (82%), and the relative providers are the largest group (46%)."

Why is the quality of child care so low on average in the United States? Do parents realize that their children are receiving low-quality care? Do parents use the same criteria to evaluate the quality of child care that child development professionals use? Should they?

We can gain insight into these issues by thinking of child care as a service that is bought and sold in "markets." As in the markets for most other goods and services, there is a wide range of quality available and higher-quality care generally has a higher price. Consumers of child care can usually find the quality of care they prefer *if* they are willing to pay the price for such care. Providers can offer high-quality care if they choose, incurring high costs but also commanding the high price that goes with such care, or they can offer lower-quality care, at lower cost, and receive a lower price.

Chapter 2 presents descriptive information on the quality of child care in the United States, and chapters 4 and 5 provide empirical analyses of the demand for and supply of quality in child care. The main findings of the analysis are that, despite wide variation in the quality of care available in most child care markets, the cost to providers of offering higher-quality care is not exorbitant. Nevertheless, child care is of low average quality in the United States because consumers appear unwilling to pay what is needed to cover the higher cost of higher-quality care.

The most important question about the quality of child care is how it affects the development of children. One authoritative review of the child development literature (Love, Schochet, and Meckstroth, 1996, iii) answers this question as follows:

Extensive research in child care and early childhood education conducted over the past 20 years has clearly demonstrated strong, positive relationships between a variety of quality measures and various dimensions of children's development and well-being. Across a wide range of settings, from center-

/ 5

based care to family child care homes, research shows that higher levels of quality are associated with enhanced social skills, reduced behavior problems, increased cooperation, and improved language in children.

"Poor-quality care, more than any single type of program or arrangement, threatens children's development, especially children from poor and minority families" (Hayes, Palmer, and Zaslow, 1990, xii).

I discuss this research in detail in chapter 7. Much of it seems unreliable to me, and an inadequate basis for these conclusions, but there are a few studies that do seem reliable enough to support these claims. Thus, despite the overall weakness of the evidence, I am inclined to believe these assertions. The low average quality of child care and the harmful effect of low-quality care on the development of children provide compelling arguments that we should try to use public policy to improve quality in the child care market. However, identifying the existence of a problem does not guarantee that a viable public policy that could solve it can be found. Two problems stand in the way of identifying policies to improve the quality of child care. First, as pointed out by John Love and his colleagues (1996, iii), "At this stage in the evolution of research on child care quality, we do not know enough to be able to guide policy by specifying the point at which lower levels of quality are clearly detrimental to children's well-being."

Second, even if such thresholds of quality can be identified in future research, it is not obvious how to design policies to ensure that such thresholds are achieved. There is a large developmental psychology literature on how to "produce" high-quality child care, but as I argue in chapter 7, most of this literature is flawed. I present my own analysis of the "quality production process" and conclude that there is considerable uncertainty about whether the approach to producing high-quality care advocated by development psychologists will be successful if applied nationally.

Lack of Availability

Definite shortages [of child care] exist in specific areas; for infant and school-age care; for children with disabilities or for children who are ill; for children in rural areas; and for those who need care during non-standard hours.

—Raikes 1998, 10

The phones ring, the mothers plead and May-Roline Charles shakes her head as she flips through her list of available child care centers in Manhattan. "I can tell you right now there are no infant day care centers available for children under 2," says Mrs. Charles. . . . The state, which used to exempt mothers of children under 3 from work programs, narrowed that exemption this year to women with children younger than 3 months. For each parent who needs help, city rules require welfare caseworkers to find two openings in a licensed day care center or in the home of a professional

baby sitter—known as a family day care provider—who has registered with the health department. . . . But finding these vacancies is another story.
—New York Times, April 14, 1998

Most observers do not believe that there are widespread shortages of child care in the United States, but these recent reports suggest that some forms of care are perceived to be difficult to find or are simply unavailable. Does this indicate a failure of the child care market? Are the laws of supply and demand suspended when dealing with the care of young children? A simple way to think about this issue in economic terms is to ask: *"At what price is child care difficult to find or unavailable?"* As the *New York Times* report illustrates, some "shortages" appear to be caused by government rules, a fact that will not surprise most economists. In this case, the government requires mothers of infants to join the labor force but probably does not provide enough reimbursement to cover the cost of expensive infant care. Economics textbooks are full of examples of the unintended consequences of government policies that impose restrictions on the behavior of market participants.

The High Expense and Short Supply of High-Quality Child Care

We now know how critical children's earliest years are to their development, but the type of care that optimizes early physical, intellectual and emotional growth is in short supply—and far beyond the reach of most families. It may be more accurate to say that, as a whole, we're just not willing to pay for quality.
—Raleigh News and Observer,
November 24, 1997, "The Child Care Crunch" [editorial]

The lives of women like Mrs. Garrett are ruled by hard economic facts. "If my finances permitted, I'd love to stay home," said Mrs. Garrett, whose husband, Rod, works in a factory making hospital curtains. Her husband takes home about $250 a week. . . . When it comes to child care, Mrs. Garrett, who is 36, has almost no choices. She would like to put her children . . . in her church day care center and preschool, Holy Temple Christian Academy, but at $180 a week—$90 less than what most licensed day care centers in Fort Lauderdale charge for three children—it is beyond her reach.
—New York Times, November 25, 1997

High-quality child care is expensive to any low-income family. It is probably beyond the reach of most such families unless subsidized by the government. On the other hand, the great majority of families in the United States are not poor. They could afford high-quality child care as easily as they could afford a nice car. Chapter 4 analyzes how the price of child care, family income, and other characteristics of families influence the quantity and quality of child care they purchase. We do not yet have the data to accept or reject definitively the assertion that "we're just not willing to pay for quality," but the evidence strongly suggests that high-quality child care is not a high-priority item for many households.

Low Earnings and High Turnover of Child Care Providers

Across the country the quality of early childhood programs is being adversely affected by serious problems in recruiting and retaining qualified staff. For years, early childhood staff have subsidized the provision of early childhood programs by accepting compensation far below the value of their work.

—Willer 1987, 42

On average, workers in child care centers earn less than bartenders. How's that for having our priorities straight?

—*Raleigh News and Observer,*
November 24, 1997, "The Child Care Crunch" [editorial]

Full-time teachers in day care centers (97 percent of whom are women) earn less than half the amount earned by other women on average: $14,506 versus $30,344 per year for those with at least a bachelor's degree in 1994.[1] One-third of all teachers in day care centers leave their jobs each year, a rate that is about three times higher than the average for all women. Family day care providers earn substantially less than teachers in day care centers, and unregulated family day care providers earn on average only $5,132 per year after expenses.[2]

Why are child care wages so low? Are coldhearted day care center owners making profits by exploiting women who would like to take care of children for a living? This would not explain why self-employed family day care home operators earn even less than day care center employees. Who is exploiting them? Basic economic reasoning suggests that there must be many women who are willing to take care of children for very low wages. Naturally, they would prefer higher earnings. But the fact that they are willing to supply their labor for such low compensation, despite the fact that higher-wage jobs are available in other sectors, suggests that there may be some nonpecuniary rewards to being a child care provider. Chapter 5 explores this issue by analyzing the supply of child care. The evidence shows that the willingness of many women to work as child care providers for low wages is indeed an important part of the explanation for low child care wages. Another important factor is a steady increase in the number of women who are willing to work in child care, possibly owing to increased illegal immigration of low-skilled women.

Consumers' Lack of Knowledge and Awareness of Important Aspects of Child Care

Child care, in fact, is not a perfect economic market; it is a mixture of family and marketplace services, paid and unpaid, about which consumers know relatively little because the children experience the child care—while their parents make the decisions.
—Mitchell, Cooperstein, and Larner 1992, 21

There is little public understanding of the importance of early childhood and the characteristics that determine quality programs for young children.
—Willer 1987, 42

These two studies portray consumers as doubly ignorant: they cannot tell the difference between low-quality and high-quality care if they see it, and they don't see it anyway because they just drop their children off and head to work. Is this a realistic view? Is consumer ignorance the underlying source of most problems in the child care market? If so, how can such ignorance be remedied so that consumers will make well-informed choices in the child care market? Chapter 8 presents an extensive discussion of the information problems in the child care market and the role that public policy could play in dealing with their consequences. My own proposal for dealing with information problems in the child care market appears in chapter 10.

Child Care as a Barrier to Escaping Welfare

I was told that they're only going to pay for child care for 12 months. There's a one year limit. All three of my kids are in child care. That would take more than half my income to pay. I'm going to have to stay home with my kids because there's no way I can afford to pay child care.
—working mother formerly on welfare, quoted in Fuller et al. 2000, 51

State child care subsidy programs are so underfunded that they cut off eligibility at family income levels far below what is allowed by federal law and what is needed by families—with the result that families earning as little as $20,000 a year for a family of three are not eligible for help in many states. . . . Yet even with low income cutoffs, many states face demand they simply cannot meet. As of January 1998 about half the states had to turn away eligible working low-income families or put them on waiting lists for help.
—Adams, Schulman, and Ebb 1998, 3–4

National data show that child care costs take up over one-quarter of the income of families in poverty who pay for child care (Smith 2000). And it is estimated that only 15 percent of children eligible for a subsidy under the main federal block grant to states for child care are actually receiving a subsidy (Administration for Children and Families 1999). How can welfare reform succeed in its goal of moving low-income families from dependence on cash assistance to employment in view of the high cost of child care? What are the consequences for children and their families of being squeezed off welfare while facing a strong risk of going without a child care subsidy? Is this really a child care problem, or is it a problem with the basic approach to welfare reform? I discuss these issues in chapter 8 and present my own views in chapter 10.

THE CHILD CARE PROBLEM: MARKET FAILURE

Most of the problems identified here can be summarized in one phrase: market failure. A market is said by economists to have failed when the amount of the service provided in the market is too low (or too high) compared to the amount that would be optimal from society's perspective. In this case, the market is providing too little high-quality child care and child care for infants, low-income families, school-age children, children who have disabilities or are ill, children in rural areas, and children who need care during nonstandard hours, or all of the above.

Either explicitly or implicitly, most non-economists and many economists assert that the child care market fails in some important ways, and that government intervention to improve the market is justified. Sometimes the assertion is explicit, as in this 1993 policy statement of the Child Care Action Campaign, "Child Care and Education: The Critical Connection":

> Child care is fragmented, poorly financed and hard to find. Its quality has declined over the past decade. Individual providers are isolated and do not see themselves as part of a common effort committed to achieving a national goal. Parents are faced with a confusing and chaotic array of choices. . . . There is neither a comprehensive system of governance for child care nor any reliable source of financing for it.

The New Republic was even blunter in its TRB column of November 17, 1997, "The Parent Trap":

> As one House Republican staffer put it, "This is the kind of stuff that drives Republicans nuts. Here's a huge problem that affects zillions of people where the market has been a complete failure. What are Republicans supposed to say? That everything's hunk-dory with day care?"

I would like to tell you that this book will resolve the question of whether and how the child care market fails, and that the remedies proposed here for where it does fail will be successful. Unfortunately, direct evidence for or against market failure is very difficult to find, since a failed child care market would be one that produces less than the socially optimal amount of the service. But what is the socially optimal amount, and how do we know that the market is failing to provide it? I present a considerable amount of evidence about the quantity and quality of child care that is actually provided in the United States. But neither I nor anyone else can present reliable evidence on the quantity and quality of child care that would be optimal from society's perspective, because there is no such evidence. There are plenty of *opinions* on this issue, including my own. The only claim that might be asserted with any degree of confidence is that the average quality of child care in the United States is probably too low relative to the social optimum. How much below the social optimum is anyone's guess (or opinion). This assertion is based on evidence on the impact of the quality of child care on the development of children (discussed in chapter 7). But even this assertion is controversial: it depends on one's view of how children *should* develop.

The main thesis of this book is that the child care market functions much better than is commonly believed. Shortages are uncommon, and those that do exist are often caused by government policy and are limited to small segments of the market. Child care workers receive low wages because they are willing to work for low wages, not because they are exploited by center owners or forced to subsidize consumers. If fewer women were willing to accept low wages to provide child care, then wages would rise. The main problem in the child care market is low quality. Child care quality is low on average because the market responds to the demands of consumers, and the average consumer demands low-quality care. That is, the average consumer is unwilling to pay enough for high-quality care to cover the cost of providing it.

If low-quality child care harms child development, and if the consequences of suboptimal child development are felt by society at large, not just by the parents who are unwilling to pay for high-quality care, then there is indeed a market failure. Similarly, if parents lack the information needed to recognize high-quality child care when they see it or to understand its benefits, there is a market failure. The failure in this case is not due to some defect in the *internal* workings of the child care market. For example, it is not caused by market power being concentrated in the hands of a few providers who are able to extract excess profits from consumers by restricting supply. Rather, it is caused by an *externality:* market participants—in this case, parents—either do not bear all of the costs of their child care decisions, or they make these decisions without understanding their consequences, or both.

In general, economists argue against meddling with the market itself to remedy a market failure caused by an externality or an information problem. Rather, they recommend providing appropriate information to market participants so that they can make well-informed decisions, and finding a way to internalize the externality by inducing parents to consider all of the consequences of the choices they make about the quality of child care. In chapters 8 and 9, I evaluate current child care policy from this perspective by asking how well it does in these respects. The proposals I offer in chapter 10 are based on my view that society should care about the quality of child care even if parents are unwilling to pay much for high-quality care.

A recurring theme in the book is the tension between two objectives of child care: facilitating the employment of parents and enhancing the development and well-being of children. Child care of mediocre quality may serve the former objective quite well and fail at the latter. The converse is true for high-quality child care. For example, high-quality preschools and Head Start programs often provide only part-day care and require parent participation. In principle, a given child care arrangement could serve both objectives, but in practice there is usually a trade-off, since higher-quality child care is more costly in both monetary terms and in the time input required of parents. A given amount of money spent on child care buys more hours of care if the care is of low quality than if the care is of high quality, resulting in a quality-quantity trade-off.

This tension between employment and child development also exists in U.S. child care policy. Some child care subsidies are explicitly employment-related: employment is required for eligibility, but there are few restrictions on the quality of care that can be purchased. Other subsidies are explicitly development-related: there is no employment requirement, but the child care must be of high quality.

This trade-off is especially stark in the case of child care subsidies targeted at low-income families. The central goal of the welfare reform of 1996 was moving low-income families off cash assistance welfare programs and into the workforce. This goal obviously cannot be achieved without child care, and welfare reform revamped child care subsidy programs for the poor and increased funding for them. It is notable that the reformed child care subsidy program, the Child Care and Development Fund (described in chapter 8), is almost exclusively employment-related, in line with the major goal of welfare reform. There are few restrictions on the quality of child care that can be purchased with subsidies, and there is no emphasis on improving the development of low-income children. Other government programs that provide child care for low-income children, such as Head Start and Title I-A of the Elementary and Secondary Education Act, are explicitly development-oriented. There is a very real sense in which every dollar devoted to an employment-related child care subsidy program is a dollar that is not available for a development-related child care subsidy.

I argue in the final chapter that employment-related child care subsidies are a misguided approach to child care policy. The main problems with the child care market cited earlier are related to quality, not employment. The market failure stems from low demand for quality, not from some inherent flaw in the ability of the market to provide the quality of care demanded. The remedy for suboptimal quality in the child care market is not an employment-related policy but a policy that deals directly with this problem. There is no getting around the trade-off in child care policy between facilitating employment and enhancing child development, especially for low-income families. Hence, I am very explicit about my recommendations: employment-related child care subsidies should be replaced with quality-related subsidies and information provision, both for low-income families and other families.

A ROAD MAP TO THE BOOK

Part I of this book provides an introduction and overview of the U.S. child care problem. As this chapter has made clear, understanding the child care market is central to my analysis, which begins with a description in chapter 2 of the main features of that market. It contains summary information on prices, quantity, quality, and the characteristics of consumers and providers in the child care market and documents the tremendous increase in the employment of mothers of young children in the last few decades.

This change has been the main cause of the dramatic expansion of the child care market in the United States. As the market has grown, it has increasingly shifted from unpaid child care by relatives and family to paid child care in centers and family day care homes. Nevertheless, the market remains predominantly "informal": over two-thirds of preschool-age children of employed mothers are cared for in homes rather than centers while the mother works. Despite the rapid growth of the child care market, the price of child care has increased at a modest pace. The supply of child care has grown rapidly, keeping pace with growth in demand and dampening any tendency for large price increases.

Chapter 3 presents economic models of the child care market and explains how economists think about the behavior of consumers and producers in a market for a service such as child care. Basic models of demand, supply, and price determination are described. The nature of equilibrium in a market in which quality matters is discussed, and the models are used to illustrate the consequences of government interventions such as subsidies.

I devote an entire chapter to economic models of child care because such models may be unfamiliar to non-economist readers. A useful model makes assumptions that simplify a problem in order to understand its essence. Without simplifying assumptions, models would be too complex to be useful, and without useful models, we might be able to describe a problem but we could not analyze it. The crucial questions about any model are whether the model is too simple and whether it provides useful insight. The models I describe in chapter 3 are not the only possible basis for analyzing child care. Other models could be constructed based on alternative assumptions, including models based on non-economic approaches to thinking about child care. I do not claim that the models in chapter 3 are "right," but I do believe they are useful.

Part II presents empirical analysis of the main aspects of child care: demand, supply, price, and the determinants and consequences of child care quality. Chapter 4 analyzes jointly the demand for child care and the supply of labor by mothers, since these two aspects of family behavior are closely related. This chapter discusses the results of empirical analyses of the effects of the price of child care, family income, and other family characteristics on the type, quantity, and quality of child care used by families, and on the employment of mothers.

One of the main findings is that a higher price of child care causes the quantity of child care demanded to decline. Consumers are moderately sensitive to the price of child care: a higher price of care leads to modest reductions in hours of care per week and in the use of paid child care. Another important finding is that consumers appear to view the quality and quantity of child care as substitutes: quality tends to be higher when quantity (hours) of care is lower. And consumer willingness to pay for higher-quality child care increases very little as income rises. The findings indicate that the employment decisions of mothers are not very sensitive to the price of child care, but that low-income mothers are more sensitive. Overall, the analysis suggests that on average consumers are unwilling to pay for high-quality child care.

Chapter 5 analyzes the supply of child care. Provider behavior in the child care market is analyzed, including the relationship between cost and quality and the effect of price on the supply of quality. The behavior of child care workers is analyzed in order to understand the causes of low wages in the child care market. The main findings are that both the quantity and quality of child care are quite responsive to increases in the price of care. An increase in demand that tends to drive up the price of care induces a substantial increase in the quantity of child care supplied, thus dampening any tendency for large price increases. The cost of improving the quality of care offered in day care centers is modest, given the current relatively low level of quality. Day care centers can and do improve quality when the price of care rises.

Chapter 6 analyzes the relationship between price and quality, using data from samples of day care centers and regulated family day care homes. The results indicate that the price-quality relationship varies substantially across states and even within states. In some markets, higher-quality care commands a much higher price than lower-quality care, while in other markets the relationship between price and quality is much weaker. On average, the price-quality relationship is relatively weak. This reflects consumers' low willingness to pay for higher-quality care.

Chapter 7 studies the determinants and consequences of child care quality. Literature from the field of developmental psychology on two important issues is reviewed: how does the quality of child care affect child development, and how does one "produce" high-quality child care? If government policy is to be designed effectively to improve quality in the child care market, we need to understand the benefits of high-quality care for children, and the inputs that are most productive in affecting quality. I evaluate the large literatures on both subjects and discuss my own analyses of some of these relationships as well. A main finding from my analysis is that group size and staff-child ratio do not have significant positive effects on the quality of child care. Recent training in early childhood education does have a positive effect on child care quality, but less recent training, education, and experience are not associated with child care quality. The other main finding is that child care quality is positively associated with child development.

In part III on child care policy, chapter 8 analyzes child care subsidy policy in the United States. Child care subsidies are an important part of government child care policy in the United States. It is important to understand the goals and rationales for the current child care subsidy system in order to determine whether it is sensible and how it should be reformed. One major conclusion of the chapter is that there is little sound basis for child care subsidies that are conditioned on the employment of the parents. The empirical analysis examines the effects of child care subsidies on employment and child outcomes. The results show that employment-related child care subsidies encourage the employment of mothers of young children. High-quality child care provided by subsidies that are not employment-related has beneficial effects on the development of low-income children, but there is little evidence on how employment-related child care subsidies affect child care quality and child outcomes.

Chapter 9 analyzes child care regulation policy, the other main type of child care policy in the United States, and the effects of regulations on aspects of the child care market: the regulated items, price, and quality. The evidence suggests that regulations have small effects on the price and quality of child care and on the wages and supply of child care workers. This low impact may be due in part to relatively lax regulations and lack of vigorous enforcement.

In chapter 10, I propose a new child care policy. I first summarize the lessons learned from the analysis in previous chapters and set out principles that I believe should guide child care policy. Child care policy should be made as rational as possible in light of what we know about how the child care market works. But child care policy inevitably reflects a set of values and opinions, and I try to make mine as explicit as possible. I then discuss the problems with existing child care policy in light of these principles. After discussing proposals for reform made by other authors, I finally

THE CHILD CARE PROBLEM

present my own proposal: to provide both a child allowance that can be used to defray any expenses of families with children and a child care voucher that is worth more if it is used for higher-quality child care. I also propose a systematic effort to inform consumers of the benefits of high-quality child care and to assist providers in their efforts to improve quality.

My proposal represents a fairly radical shift in U.S. child care policy, away from employment-based subsidies and toward quality-based subsidies. I believe such a change is warranted, however, by the findings presented in this book and by the evidence that high-quality child care has important benefits for child development, especially for low-income children. I invite readers to give serious consideration to this proposal and to join the discussion of its political feasibility.

Chapter 2

An Overview of the Child Care
Market in the United States

How many American children are cared for on a regular basis by adults other than their parents? What are the characteristics of these children and their families? Who provides the child care, and where is the care provided? What are the characteristics of the providers? How much do parents pay for child care? What is the quality of care provided? This chapter provides an overview of child care in the United States by addressing these questions.

Economic models of a market are not very useful unless they are solidly grounded in the basic facts about the market, and my intention here is to highlight those facts, not to present an in-depth statistical portrait of the market. The issues studied in any empirical analysis depend in part on the specific questions of interest, but those questions are usually shaped by the basic facts about the subject. Thus, the description in this chapter serves as the basis for the models developed in chapter 3 and for the empirical analyses presented in subsequent chapters.

I define child care as the care of a child on a regular basis during non-school hours by someone other than the child's parents, or by the mother or father while the mother is at work. The majority of child care is used to facilitate the employment of the mother, so we would like to know who cares for the child while the mother works. As documented later, often it is the father or the mother herself who provides care while the mother works—hence, the inclusion of parental care while the mother works. The definition is broad, including part-day preschool arrangements that are used mainly for child development purposes, unpaid child care by a relative, and full-time care by a nonrelative while the mother is employed.

I do not claim that this is the only useful or interesting definition of child care. For example, the focus on the child care arrangement while the mother works, rather than while both the mother and father work, might strike some as unnecessarily restrictive. I would certainly not discourage anyone from studying child care from this angle, or any other angle, using other definitions as appropriate. The main issue of interest in this book, however, is the trade-off between child care policies that encourage mothers to be employed and those that encourage families to use high-quality care. To analyze this issue, it seems not only reasonable to ignore the employment status of the father but important to include child care provided while the mother is both at work and not at work.

CHILD CARE DEMAND

Labor Force Participation by Mothers of Young Children

Child care is an issue of interest today because of the tremendous growth in labor force participation by mothers of young children. Figure 2.1 illustrates this growth for the half-century from 1948 to 1998. In 1948, 11 percent of married mothers of preschool-age children (ages zero to five) were in the labor force (employed or actively seeking employment). As recently as 1966, fewer than one-quarter of mothers of preschool-age children were in the labor force. In 1998, 63.7 percent of such mothers were in the labor force. Today it is much more common for the mother of a young child to be employed than not. This is the main reason that child care, especially for infants and toddlers (ages zero to two), has become so much more prominent a public issue than in the past. By 1985 more than half of married mothers of infants and toddlers were in the labor force. There is no published time series on the labor force participation rate of mothers of children under one year of age. But the rate was 60.0 percent in March 1999 (computed from the Current Population Survey [CPS]), so we can certainly say that it has grown very rapidly as well.

The shorter available time-series for single mothers of preschool-age children shows a much slower rate of increase of labor force participation from 1975 to 1992, followed by a dramatic increase through 1998. In 1992 the labor force participation rate for single mothers of young children was twelve percentage points lower than for married mothers. In 1998 the rate for single mothers was four percentage points *higher* than for married mothers. The biggest increase, from 1996 to 1997, coincided with a major reform of the welfare system that emphasized moving welfare recipients into employment.

Labor force participation by married mothers of school-age children (ages six to seventeen) has grown rapidly as well, and today more than three-quarters of such mothers are in the labor force. This growth has also contributed to the expansion of the child care market, because younger school-age children may require before-school or after-school child care. But school itself occupies children for the bulk of the day, so child care demand for school-age children is of much less importance than for preschool-age children. And it is easier to arrange work schedules so that a family member is available to provide child care outside of school hours than it is to arrange for full-day child care.

Figure 2.1 / Labor Force Participation Rate of Mothers, 1948 to 1998

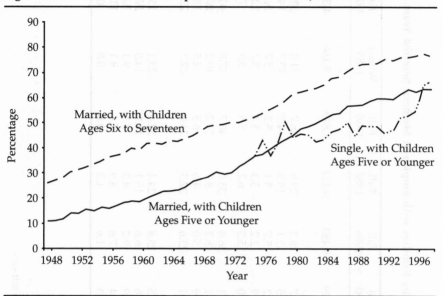

Source: U. S. Department of Labor, various years; Jacobs 1999, 132.

The Number of Children in Child Care and the Type of Care

The federal government began collecting data on child care regularly in 1985 as part of the Survey of Income and Program Participation (SIPP). In this stratified random sample of the U.S. population, households are surveyed every four months for two and a half years. A special module on child care is included in one or two of the survey waves. Child care data are currently available from the SIPP for 1985 to 1995. The SIPP child care module was redesigned in 1995, and the published data for 1995 are for the most part not directly comparable to the data for earlier years. I therefore use the 1995 data sparingly, that is, only with respect to those items for which it is comparable to earlier years.[1] I also use a onetime Current Population Survey supplement on child care from 1977 to provide a longer time series, though the CPS is not strictly comparable to the SIPP. Except for 1995, the SIPP data cover only mothers who are employed, so later in the chapter I use an alternative source for information on child care used by children of non-employed mothers.

Table 2.1 shows trends in the number of preschool-age children of employed mothers and their child care arrangements over the period 1977 to 1994. During this seventeen-year period, the number of preschoolers with an employed mother more than doubled, from 4.4 million to 10.3 million.

Table 2.1 / Primary Child Care Arrangements Used for Preschoolers by Families with Employed Mothers: Selected Years, 1977 to 1994

Type of Arrangement	Fall 1994	Fall 1993	Fall 1991	Fall 1990	Fall 1988	Fall 1987	Fall 1986	Winter 1985	Fall 1977[a]
Number of children (in thousands)	10,288	9,937	9,854	9,629	9,483	9,124	8,849	8,168	4,370
Care in child's home (percentage)	33.0	30.7	35.7	29.7	28.2	29.9	28.7	31.0	33.9
By father	18.5	15.9	20.0	16.5	15.1	15.3	14.5	15.7	14.4
By grandparent	5.9	6.5	7.2	5.2	5.7	5.1	5.2	5.7	NA
By other relative	3.5	3.3	3.2	2.9	2.2	3.3	3.4	3.7	12.6[b]
By nonrelative	5.1	5.0	5.4	5.0	5.3	6.2	5.5	5.9	7.0
Informal care in another home	31.3	32.1	31.0	35.1	36.8	35.6	40.7	37.0	40.7
By grandparent	10.4	10.0	8.6	9.1	8.2	8.7	10.2	10.2	NA
By other relative	5.5	5.5	4.5	5.9	5.0	4.6	6.5	4.5	18.3
By nonrelative (FDCH)	15.4	16.6	17.9	20.1	23.6	22.3	24.0	22.3	22.4
Formal organized child care facilities	29.4	30.1	23.0	27.5	25.8	24.4	22.4	23.1	13.0
Day–group care center	21.6	18.3	15.8	20.6	16.6	16.1	14.9	14.0	NA
Nursery school–preschool	7.8	11.6	7.3	6.9	9.2	8.3	7.5	9.1	NA
Mother cares for child at work[c]	5.5	6.2	8.7	6.4	7.6	8.9	7.4	8.1	11.4
Other arrangements[d]	1.1	1.1	1.6	1.3	1.6	1.3	0.8	0.8	0.6

Source: Casper 1997.

NA Not available.

[a] Data only for the two youngest children under five years of age.

[b] Data for 1977 includes grandparents.

[c] Includes mothers working for pay at home or away from home.

[d] Includes children in kindergarten–grade school, other school-based activities, and self-care.

In 1994, 33.0 percent of these children were cared for in their own home, very close to the 33.9 percent cared for at home in 1977. Another 31.3 percent were cared for in another home in 1994, down from 40.7 percent in 1977. About half of these arrangements were in a relative's home, and the other half were in a nonrelative's home, which I refer to as a family day care home (FDCH). For brevity, I refer to home-based child care arrangements, regardless of the provider and of whether the provider is paid, as *informal*. The other main form of child care takes place in organized child care facilities, a category that includes day care centers, nursery schools, and preschools. I refer to these as *formal* child care arrangements. Formal arrangements accounted for 29.4 percent of child care for preschool children of employed mothers in 1994, up from 13 percent in 1977. Some mothers care for their children while they are at work (including mothers who work at home): 5.5 percent in 1994, down from 11.4 percent in 1977.[2]

The major change in the child care market during this period, aside from the increase in its size, has been the shift away from care in another home and care by the mother while at work and toward formal arrangements. The 16.4-percentage-point increase in the use of formal care is mostly accounted for by the 9.4-percentage-point decline in care in another home and the 5.9-percentage-point decrease in care by the mother while at work. Most of the decline in care in another home is due to the decrease by 7.0 percentage points in the use of family day care homes. Most of the increase in formal child care (all of the increase since 1985) is in day care centers rather than nursery schools and preschools. Chapter 4 analyzes the determinants of the type of child care arrangement chosen by families, focusing on the effects of both economic factors, such as price and income, and noneconomic factors, such as the age of the child and the education of the mother.

Despite the growth in formal child care, in 1994 about two-thirds of child care took place in a home, and the child care market remains predominantly home-based to this day. The evidence presented in chapter 4 suggests that this reflects the preferences of consumers, not a failure of the formal sector to keep up with growing demand. Families make a variety of home-based child care arrangements for preschool children of employed mothers: fathers accounted for 18.5 percent of child care for this population in 1994, up from 14.4 percent in 1977; grandparents provided 16.3 percent, about the same as in 1985; other relatives accounted for 9 percent, similar to 1985; and family day care homes and baby-sitters provided 20.5 percent of child care in 1994, down from 29.4 percent in 1977 and 28.2 percent in 1985.

Table 2.2 shows how child care arrangements in 1994 varied by the mother's employment schedule. Formal child care accounted for about one-third of all care for mothers employed full-time or working a day shift, versus only about 21 percent for mothers working part-time or a non-day

Table 2.2 / Primary Child Care Arrangements of Preschoolers with Employed Mothers, by Mother's Employment Schedule, Fall 1994

Type of Arrangement	All Preschoolers	Full-time	Part-time	Day Shift[a]	Non-Day Shift[a]
Number of children (in thousands)	10,288	6,705	3,582	6,048	4,240
Care in child's home (percentage)	33.0	26.1	45.3	24.5	44.8
Care in provider's home	31.3	35.4	23.6	34.4	26.7
Organized child care facility	29.4	33.5	21.6	35.5	20.5
Mother cares for child at work[b]	5.5	3.9	8.5	4.2	7.3
Other[c]	1.1	1.0	1.0	1.2	0.8

Source: Casper 1997.
[a]Calculations based on mother's principal job only.
[b]Includes women working for pay at home or away from home.
[c]Includes preschoolers in kindergarten and school-based activities.

shift. Child care in the provider's home was also more common when the mother was employed full-time or on a day shift, accounting for about 35 percent of care versus 24 to 27 percent for mothers working part-time or a non-day shift. Care in the child's home and by the mother while at work were correspondingly less common when the mother was employed full-time or on a day shift. Part-time and non-day-shift employment provide more opportunities for families to arrange their schedules so as to facilitate informal child care arrangements, if they prefer such arrangements. On the other hand, some families may choose such employment schedules for the mother precisely in order to take advantage of the increased opportunities for informal arrangements.

Table 2.3 shows how child care arrangements varied by child and family characteristics in 1994. Compared to whites, blacks used less care by fathers, baby-sitters in the child's home, family day care homes, and the mother while at work, and they used more care by relatives and formal care. These differences may reflect the much lower rate of marriage of black mothers compared to white mothers.[3] Hispanics used much less formal care and much more relative care than did non-Hispanics. Hispanic mothers were slightly less likely to be married than non-Hispanic mothers, but the preference of Hispanic mothers for informal care persisted, even controlling for differences in marital status and other characteristics. Married mothers used much more care by the father than did nonmarried mothers, and less care by relatives. This no doubt reflects the availability of the father as a provider during at least some of the mother's work hours.

Table 2.3 / Primary Child Care Arrangements of Preschoolers with Employed Mothers, by Child and Family Characteristics, Fall 1994

	Mother While at Work	Father[a]	Relative	Baby-Sitter	FDCH	Organized Facility[b]
Race						
White	6.0%	19.4%	23.1%	5.6%	15.9%	30.1%
Black	2.6	11.4	36.3	1.7	12.3	35.7
Hispanic	2.2	16.9	38.9	5.7	15.0	21.3
Marital status						
Married	6.3	22.3	20.0	5.6	15.7	30.0
Not married	2.5	5.4	42.4	3.4	14.6	31.7
Mother's age						
Fifteen to twenty-four	4.1	19.2	38.5	2.5	13.1	22.8
Twenty-five to thirty-four	5.5	19.6	22.6	5.0	16.3	31.0
Thirty-five and over	6.5	15.0	21.5	7.3	14.9	34.8
Child's age						
Zero	6.5	20.6	28.4	7.0	18.9	18.4
One	4.5	20.8	28.6	5.0	16.8	24.3
Two	4.3	17.7	27.3	5.1	17.6	28.1
Three	6.8	16.7	25.0	5.3	13.8	32.5
Four	5.5	17.0	17.4	3.4	10.7	46.1
Mother's education						
Less than twelve years	5.3	23.6	34.5	3.8	12.2	20.6
Twelve years	5.1	17.4	30.9	3.2	16.0	27.4
Thirteen to fifteen years	6.4	20.8	21.5	4.3	14.2	32.8
Sixteen years and more	5.1	15.5	17.2	8.9	17.1	36.3
Monthly family income						
Less than $1,200	5.5	16.5	32.9	4.1	15.1	25.9
$1,200 to $2,999	6.0	22.1	28.7	3.2	13.0	27.1
$3,000 to $4,499	5.7	18.8	25.4	3.8	17.9	28.4
$4,500 and more	4.6	15.0	18.9	8.5	16.0	37.0
Region						
Northeast	5.5	25.4	24.0	6.2	11.9	26.9
Midwest	6.2	19.4	24.1	4.3	17.6	28.4
South	4.5	12.6	26.9	4.1	14.0	37.6
West	5.9	20.1	23.9	6.7	17.6	24.9

(Table continues on p. 24.)

Table 2.3 / *Continued*

	Mother While at Work	Father[a]	Relative	Baby-Sitter	FDCH	Organized Facility[b]
Type of area						
Central city	4.6	19.2	26.3	5.6	13.8	30.3
Suburb	6.3	19.8	23.5	5.8	14.1	30.7
Nonmetropolitan	4.7	14.7	27.4	2.9	20.3	29.7

Source: Casper 1997.
[a]Includes only care by the father in the child's home.
[b]Includes preschool, nursery school, and school.

Younger mothers used less formal care and nonrelative care and more relative care than did older mothers.

The use of formal care rose rapidly with the age of the child, from 18.4 percent for infants under age one to 46.1 percent for four-year-old children. More-educated and higher-income mothers used more formal and nonrelative care than did less-educated and lower-income mothers. Formal care was used by 36.3 percent of mothers who were college graduates versus 21.6 percent of mothers who were high school dropouts, and nonrelative care (baby-sitter and FDCH) was used by 26 percent and 16 percent of the two groups, respectively.

Formal child care was used by 37.6 percent of families in the South, versus a maximum of 28.4 percent in any other region of the country. Most of this difference is accounted for by lower use of father care in the South. This may reflect the higher full-time employment rate of mothers in the South compared to other regions.[4] Family day care homes were more widely used in nonmetropolitan areas than in cities and suburbs, with most of the difference accounted for by less use of father care in nonmetropolitan areas. Most of the differences by age, education, income, and location persist in multivariate analysis in which other variables are controlled. Hence, they seem to reflect fundamental differences in the preferences of parents.

In 1990 the National Child Care Survey collected data on child care from a representative sample of households with children under age thirteen, regardless of the mother's employment status. This was a onetime survey, unlike the SIPP, so it is not possible to track trends, and the data are more than a decade old. Nevertheless, they are the best available data on the use of child care by families in which the mother is not employed.[5]

Table 2.4 shows the distribution of primary child care arrangements for children ages zero to twelve by the mother's employment status and the child's age, covering 8.6 million children of employed mothers and 7.0 mil-

Table 2.4 / Distribution of the Primary Child Care Arrangement of the Youngest Child, by Employment Status of the Mother and Age of the Child, 1990

	Organized Facility	Parent	Other Relative	FDCH or Baby-Sitter	Other[a]
Mother employed					
All ages (zero to twelve)	20.5%	30.5%	21.2%	15.9%	11.9%
Under one	13.6	37.7	24.0	23.8	0.9
One to two	22.7	28.6	20.5	25.6	2.5
Three to four	42.8	20.7	16.3	18.9	1.3
Five	31.9	23.5	16.0	15.6	13.0
Six to nine	15.0	35.4	22.3	11.3	16.0
Ten to twelve	3.2	33.1	24.7	4.7	34.3
Mother not employed					
All ages (zero to twelve)	9.3	62.7	12.8	4.6	10.6
Under one	2.2	74.1	12.5	7.9	3.3
One to two	7.2	70.0	14.2	5.8	2.8
Three to four	29.6	54.0	7.9	2.4	6.1
Five	19.3	52.7	14.5	1.5	12.0
Six to nine	1.6	58.8	13.4	4.0	22.1
Ten to twelve	2.9	46.5	15.1	1.0	34.5

Source: Hofferth et al. 1991, tables 2.14, 2.16.
[a]Consists mainly of lessons for children age five and over. For school-age children, the arrangement is the primary one other than school.

lion children of non-employed mothers. Families with a non-employed mother were less than half as likely to use formal child care than were families with an employed mother, slightly more than half as likely to use relative care other than a parent, and only about one-quarter as likely to use a family day care home or baby-sitter. Families with a non-employed mother were more than twice as likely as families with an employed mother to use care by a parent as the primary child care arrangement. This is not surprising. What may be somewhat surprising is that formal care was the primary child care arrangement used by a substantial proportion of families with non-employed mothers, especially for children ages three to four: 29.6 percent of children of non-employed mothers compared to 42.8 percent of children of employed mothers in the same age range.

The formal arrangements used for children of non-employed mothers are mainly preschools and nursery schools, and these children are enrolled for fewer hours per week than the children of employed mothers (Blau and Hagy 1998, table 2). Nevertheless, in 1990 about 850,000 preschool-age children of non-employed mothers were in formal child care, accounting for one-quarter of all formal child care arranged for preschool children.

FAMILY EXPENDITURE ON CHILD CARE

Table 2.5 shows trends in the weekly amount paid by families with an employed mother for child care for all of their children from 1985 to 1995. On average, slightly more than one-third of such families paid something for child care during the 1985 to 1995 period. Of the families who did pay for care, the average weekly payment rose from $58.50 to $85.00 (adjusted for inflation), an increase of 3.7 percent per year on average. The average share of family income spent on child care among those paying for care rose from 6.3 percent to 7.4 percent during this period. The table shows that families in poverty were less likely to pay for care than other families, and that they paid less per week than other families on average if they did pay. But poor families who paid for care spent 34.8 percent of their income on child care in 1995 (up from 21.1 percent in 1993) compared to only 7.0 percent for other families. These data do not suggest that the cost of child care is a major burden for most families, but they show that for the half a

Table 2.5 / Weekly Child Care Costs for All Children in Family Under Fifteen Paid by Families with Employed Mothers, 1985 to 1995

Date of Survey	Number of Mothers (In Thousands)	Percentage Making Payments	Weekly Expenses (Constant 1995 Dollars)[a]	Percentage of Monthly Income Spent on Child Care[b]
Fall 1995	19,907	40.5%	$85.00	7.4%
Below poverty	1,734	32.9	75.30	34.8
Above poverty	18,173	41.2	85.70	7.0
Fall 1993	19,798	35.3	73.80	7.3
Below poverty	1,802	27.3	58.01	21.1
Above poverty	17,996	36.1	74.88	7.0
Fall 1991	19,180	34.5	70.60	7.1
Below poverty	1,642	24.1	66.44	26.6
Above poverty	17,537	35.5	70.66	6.9
Fall 1990	18,938	38.0	68.70	6.9
Fall 1988	18,843	39.9	69.00	6.8
Fall 1987	18,501	33.3	64.60	6.6
Fall 1986	18,305	31.4	61.60	6.3
Winter 1985	15,706	33.7	58.50	NA

Source: Smith 2000, table 14; Caspar 1995, table C2.
[a]Weekly expenditures among persons making child care payments.
[b]Derived from the ratio of average monthly child care payments (prorated from weekly averages) to average monthly income.

million poor families who paid for care in 1995, the cost of child care was clearly a major burden.[6]

Table 2.6 provides a more detailed breakdown of child care expenditures in 1993 and 1995 for families with a preschooler and an employed mother. The table shows that the proportion of families paying for care and average child care expenditures among those who paid for care rose with family income, but that the percentage of income spent on child care fell sharply with family income. Eighty-nine percent of families with an employed mother and a preschool-age child who used formal day care in 1993 paid for care, 92 percent of families who used family day care homes paid for care, 84 percent of families using a baby-sitter paid for care, and only 17 percent who used relatives paid. The proportion of families who paid for care rose with the age of the youngest child from zero through three years, then fell for four-year-old children, while average expenditure followed the opposite pattern. The average expenditure was about two-thirds higher for families with two or more preschoolers than for families with only one young child.

Table 2.7 shows that a smaller proportion of families with a non-employed mother pay for child care than do families with an employed mother. This finding, which is true even within types of child care, suggests that many families with non-employed mothers are receiving subsidies for the use of preschools or have children enrolled in Head Start. Families with a non-employed mother who do pay for care pay more per hour on average than families with an employed mother, for each type of child care.

CHILD CARE SUPPLY

The Current Population Survey

The data collected on providers of child care is less systematic than the data collected on users, and thus it is difficult to provide a clear picture of the supply side of the market. The only source of information that covers the entire child care market, not just the formal sector, is the annual demographic supplement to the March Current Population Survey. Employed individuals in the CPS are asked to report their occupation and industry, and this information can be used to identify child care workers. The information that can be extracted from the CPS covers only the workers themselves, not characteristics of the establishments that employ them. This limits the usefulness of the CPS for studying the supply side of the child care market, but it is the only source with information on a substantial sample of informal-sector child care workers and with consistent information over a long period of time.

The most useful piece of information on child care from the CPS is the

Table 2.6 / Child Care Expenditures for Preschoolers by Families with Employed Mothers, by Selected Characteristics, Fall 1993 and Fall 1995

Characteristics	Number of Families (In Thousands)[a]	Percentage Paying for Child Care	Weekly Child Care Expenses[b]	Expenditure as a Percentage of Family Income
Fall 1993				
All families	8,076	55.6%	$74.15	7.55%
Number of pre-schoolers				
One	6,515	56.7	66.48	6.81
Two or more	1,561	51.2	109.63	10.87
Monthly family income				
$1 to $1,200	927	39.4	47.29	25.14
$1,200 to $2,999	2,667	48.6	60.16	11.98
$3,000 to $4,499	2,091	56.9	73.10	8.46
$4,500 and over	2,391	68.7	91.93	5.67
Child care arrangement				
Organized facility	3,268	89.4	63.58	NA
FDCH	1,797	91.9	51.52	NA
Baby-sitter	621	84.3	68.31	NA
Relative	5,216	17.0	42.04	NA
Child's age				
Zero	1,492	52.0	87.43	8.73
One	1,959	54.2	79.03	8.28
Two	1,599	56.7	72.55	7.23
Three	1,592	62.6	63.83	6.54
Four	1,435	52.5	69.19	7.05
Fall 1995				
All families	7,936	65.7	96.69	8.66
Monthly family income				
Less than $1,500	1,087	61.3	66.41	29.36
$1,500 to $2,999	2,162	56.6	83.51	15.38
$3,000 to $4,499	1,820	67.8	89.80	10.56
$4,500	2,867	72.9	118.12	6.23

Source: Casper 1995; Smith 2000.
[a]Excludes families reporting no income in the last four months.
[b]Average for families making payments for any child under age five.

Table 2.7 / Child Care Expenditures in Families with Preschool-Age Children, by Employment Status of the Mother, 1990

	Employed		Not Employed	
	Percentage Paying for Care	Average Expenditure per Hour	Percentage Paying for Care	Average Expenditure per Hour
All	56%	$1.56	14%	$2.38
Organized facility	90	1.67	57	1.89
FDCH	94	1.35	83	2.20
Baby-sitter	93	2.30	94	2.08
Relative	36	1.11	12	—[a]

Source: Hofferth et al. 1991.
[a] Sample size too small for reliable estimate.

average hourly earnings of child care workers.[7] Child care is highly labor-intensive: in the formal sector, labor accounts for about 70 percent of all costs (Helburn 1995), and labor's share of informal child care costs is probably much higher. Thus, changes over time in the wages of child care workers provide a reasonably good index of changes in the cost of providing child care.

Figure 2.2 shows trends in the real average hourly earnings of three groups of female child care workers that can be identified consistently in the CPS over the period 1977 to 1998. (Fewer than 3 percent of child care workers are male.) Private-household child care workers provide child care in a home, either their own or the child's. Non-household child care workers provide care in an institutional setting, such as a day care center. Some individuals identify themselves as "pre-K" (prekindergarten) teachers, which is probably the equivalent of preschool teachers. For comparison, average hourly earnings of women who are not child care workers are shown in the figure as well.

The wages of private-household child care workers have been rising fairly steadily in real terms since 1984, at an average annual rate of 4.3 percent. Wages of non-household child care workers trended downward from 1977 through 1992, at an average annual rate of 2.4 percent. The wages of this group, though they have grown by 3.3 percent per year on average since 1992, were about one dollar per hour lower in 1997 than in 1977, adjusted for inflation. Wages of pre-K teachers rose by a very small amount from 1983 to 1997. (The samples are too small for reliable estimates before 1983.) Averaged over all child care workers, wages were roughly constant over most of the period, with a slight upward trend in the last few years (not shown in the figure). The wages of other women workers grew slowly over this period, mainly after 1982, with an average annual growth rate of about half a percent over the entire period.

Figure 2.2 / Average Hourly Earnings of Child Care Workers and Other Female Workers, 1977 to 1998

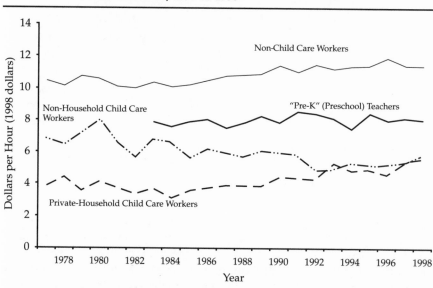

Source: Tabulations from the Current Population Survey.
Note: Figures are deflated to a 1998 basis using the consumer price index.

It is not surprising that women's wages grew slowly during this period. The biggest change in the overall distribution of wages in the United States during the last quarter-century was an increase in the inequality of the distribution around a stagnant or slowly growing average. But it is quite surprising that the wages of child care workers grew so little. This was a period of tremendous growth in demand for child care, with an increase of more than four and a half million in the number of preschool-age children of employed mothers in nonparental care. One would expect such a large increase in demand to drive up the wages of child care workers as they become increasingly scarce relative to the number of children in care.

That this did not occur suggests that the supply of child care labor is highly elastic: as demand grows, the quantity of labor supplied expands along with it, dampening the tendency for the demand increase to drive up wages. This could occur only if many additional women are attracted to the child care sector as demand grows, or if existing child care workers substantially increase the number of hours they are willing to work. Chapter 5 presents an analysis of the supply of child care labor, with results that also suggest a fairly elastic supply. A possible alternative explanation for the failure of child care wages to rise faster is that child care providers hired less-qualified staff during this period. The CPS data have limited information on staff qualifications—years of education is the best available measure. The data show no evidence that the average education of child care workers declined over this period, but this does not rule out the possibility of a decline in other dimensions of staff qualifications, such as experience and training.

The other notable feature of figure 2.2 is that the wages of child care workers are low compared to the wages of other women. Pre-K teachers average about $1.80 per hour less than other women over the whole period, non-household workers average $5.30 less, and private-household workers average about $7.00 less. These are large gaps, and they strongly suggest that women do not become child care providers mainly for the money.

Table 2.8 shows that these wage gaps are pervasive throughout the child care market. The gaps are especially large for highly educated women. Unlike in most other sectors of the labor market, education is not highly rewarded in child care. The ratio of the average wage of a college graduate to the average wage of a high school graduate is 1.48 for non–child care workers, 1.32 for pre-K teachers, 1.14 for non-household workers, and 1.21 for private-household workers. This suggests that women who enter the child care profession have strong nonpecuniary motivations for choosing an occupation that provides low returns to education.

Wages also rise more slowly with age in the child care sector than in other sectors (except for pre-K teachers). It is interesting to note that black women earn higher wages as child care workers than white women, while in other sectors of the economy black women earn less than white women on average. Black child care workers may have more education and experience than their white counterparts. Hispanic child care workers earn more than non-Hispanics only in the private-household child care sector.

The wages of private-household and non-household child care workers steadily converged over the two-decade period shown in figure 2.2. During the late 1970s the non-household child care wage exceeded the household child care wage by about three dollars per hour on average, but by the late 1990s the gap had vanished. This suggests that within the child care market private-household child care labor became increasingly scarce relative to non-household child care labor.

Table 2.9 compares women child care workers with other women workers and non-employed women. Child care workers are younger than other women, especially in the private-household sector. Private-household workers have a low level of education, averaging 11.5 years of schooling. Non-household workers average 12.7 years, and pre-K teachers 14.2, compared to 12.9 for all women workers and 11.4 for non-employed women. Blacks are underrepresented in the private-household sector, and somewhat overrepresented in the other child care sectors, compared to their distribution in the population. Hispanics are overrepresented in child care compared to their share of the population.

/ 31

Table 2.8 / Average Hourly Earnings of Child Care Workers and Other Working Women, by Worker Characteristics, 1977 to 1998

	Private-Household Child Care Worker	Non-Household Child Care Worker	Pre-Kindergarten Teacher	Other Women Workers
Race				
White	$3.91	$5.46	$7.93	$10.88
Black	5.43	6.36	8.20	10.06
Other	4.88	5.74	9.17	11.12
Hispanic				
No	4.01	5.57	8.04	10.94
Yes	4.50	5.56	7.67	9.59
Education				
Less than twelve years	3.87	4.96	6.33	7.64
Twelve years	3.85	5.45	6.76	9.64
Thirteen to fifteen years	4.82	5.80	7.86	11.06
Sixteen years	4.65	6.21	8.94	14.30
Seventeen years or more	5.36	7.19	10.86	17.11
Age				
Under twenty	3.87	5.64	6.04	6.83
Twenty to twenty-nine	3.97	5.72	7.25	9.92
Thirty to thirty-nine	4.20	5.40	8.33	11.74
Forty to forty-nine	4.46	5.60	8.89	11.91
Fifty to fifty-nine	4.21	5.49	9.38	11.44
Sixty and over	4.20	5.68	8.08	11.38

Source: Tabulations from the March Current Population Survey.
Note: Figures are deflated to a 1998 basis using the consumer price index.

Child care workers have more young children than other women workers, and about the same number as non-employed women. They have more older children than other women. Private-household child care workers are less likely to be married than other child care workers, while the latter are more likely to be married than are other workers. The total family income of child care workers is about $10,000 less per year than for other women workers, but about $3,300 higher than for non-employed women. The earnings of women child care workers account for only 10.1, 16.8, and 20.5 percent of family earnings for private-household, non-household, and pre-K child care workers, respectively, compared to 35.2 percent for other women workers. This is partly explained by the fact that child care workers work fewer hours per week, and fewer weeks per year, than other

Table 2.9 / Characteristics of Child Care Workers and Other Women Age Fifteen to Sixty-Four, 1977 to 1998 (Average)

	Child Care Workers				Other Women Workers	Non-Employed Women
	Private-Household	Non-Household	Pre-K Teacher	All		
Age (years)	31.6	33.7	33.6	33.0	35.8	40.3
Education (years)	11.5	12.7	14.2	12.6	12.9	11.4
Race						
Black	0.089	0.112	0.109	0.104	0.098	0.119
White	0.874	0.854	0.854	0.861	0.862	0.838
Hispanic	0.137	0.129	0.098	0.126	0.099	0.160
Number of children						
Age zero to five	0.40	0.44	0.33	0.41	0.24	0.42
Age six to seventeen	0.67	0.87	0.82	0.79	0.61	0.68
Married	0.48	0.63	0.69	0.59	0.58	0.68
Total family income	$34,808	$41,754	$50,156	$41,001	$51,127	$37,688
Hours worked per week	29.1	33.9	31.0	31.7	35.6	—
Weeks worked per year	29.6	38.1	39.7	35.5	43.1	—
Annual hours worked	927	1,389	1,297	1,212	1,581	—
Annual earnings	$3,524	$7,001	$10,299	$6,447	$18,009	—
Sample size	4,595	6,114	2,605	13,314	14,683	6,064

Source: Tabulations from the March Current Population Survey.

women workers, but the bulk of the difference is explained by lower wages.

A final feature of the child care labor force that can be documented with the CPS is the rate of turnover. Child care workers have a higher propensity to change employers than the average worker, perhaps as a result of low wages and benefits. Lack of stability in the child care profession is thought to be detrimental to the quality of care, because secure attachment between children and their caregivers is an important aspect of quality. The CPS does not identify job changes, but it does identify changes in occupation and employment status between the longest job held during the previous calendar year and the job, if any, held at the survey date in March.

Table 2.10 tabulates these changes and confirms that child care is a relatively unstable occupation. On average, only 55 percent of the women who were private-household child care workers in their longest job in the calendar year preceding the March survey week remain in that occupation as of the survey week. The corresponding figures for non-household child care workers and pre-K teachers are 68 and 76 percent, respectively, while 82 percent of women in other occupations remain employed in a non–child care occupation. Private-household child care workers are also much more likely than other women to exit the labor force, while non-household child care workers are only a bit more likely to do so, and pre-K teachers substantially less likely, than other women. Thus, as a whole, the child care profession is clearly less stable than the average profession for women, with private-household child care workers much more unstable than other child care workers.

THE PROFILE OF CHILD CARE SETTINGS

The Profile of Child Care Settings (PCS) surveyed samples of day care centers and regulated family day care homes in 1990. The PCS is still the most recent source of systematic information about these sectors of the child care market, despite being more than a decade old.

The sample is representative of the population of day care centers and regulated family day care homes in the United States, but not of the population of all family day care homes. Most states exempt very small family day care homes from regulations, and the vast majority of family day care is unlicensed and unregulated, either as a result of this exemption or because such providers evade the registration requirement (Hayes et al. 1990, 151). The PCS used state and county licensing lists to draw its sample, so unregistered family providers were not included in the sample frame. The PCS sample represents about 80,000 day care centers with a licensed capacity of 5.33 million children, and 118,000 regulated day care homes with a capacity of 860,000 children (Kisker et al. 1991). Table 2.11 describes several features of the PCS data.

Table 2.10 / Turnover Rates of Child Care Workers and Other Women Between the Longest Job in the Previous Year and the Survey Week, 1977 to 1998

Previous Year	Private-Household Child Care	Non-Household Child Care	Pre-Kindergarten Teacher	Other Occupation	Not Employed
Private-household child care	55.5	0.2	0.1	10.2	33.9
Non-household child care	0.8	67.9	0.4	11.7	19.1
Pre-kindergarten child care	0.2	0.3	76.5	11.3	11.7
Other occupation	0.1	0.1	0.1	81.8	18.0
Not employed	0.3	0.2	0.1	7.0	92.3

Source: Tabulations from the March Current Population Survey.

Table 2.11 / **Characteristics of Day Care Centers and Regulated Family Day Care Homes, 1990**

	Day Care Centers			Regulated Family Day Care Homes
	All	For-Profit	Non-Profit	
Number	80,072	—	—	117,995
Licensed capacity	5,333,067	—	—	859,506
Auspice[a]	100.0%	35.3%	64.7%	—
Chain	—	5.9	—	—
Independent	—	29.4	25.2	—
Head Start	—	—	9.0	—
Religious-sponsored	—	—	14.9	—
Public-school–sponsored	—	—	7.7	—
Other-sponsored	—	—	7.9	—
Capacity (number of children)	—	65	60	—
Percentage of children on public assistance[b]	17.0%	8.0%	21.0%	5.0%
Average teacher wage rate (per hour)[a]	$7.49	$6.15	$8.84	$4.04
Average group size[c]	16	—	—	7
Infants only	7	8	9.1	7/4[d]
One-year-olds only	10	10.2	10.7	7/4
Two-year-olds only	12	13.2	14.4	7/4
Three-to five-year-olds only	17	15.5	16.8	8/4
Average child-staff ratio[c]	9	—	—	6
Infants only	4.0	4.5	4.2	5.9/3.8
One-year-olds only	6.2	6.2	5.7	6.2/3.9
Two-year-olds only	7.3	7.8	7.2	6.2/3.9
Three- to five-year-olds only	9.9	9.8	8.9	6.5/4.0
Average hourly fee[c]	—	$1.51	$1.63	$1.61
Annual rate of teacher turnover	25.0%	29.0%	22.5%	—
Percentage of centers with any turnover	50.0	54.5	46.6	—
Turnover rate in centers with turnover	50.0	52.5	50.0	—
Average percentage of teachers with				
At least a college degree	47.0	33.0	50.0	11.0
Some college	39.0	—	—	44.0
High school degree or GED	13.0	20.0	8.6	34.0

Source: Kisker et al. 1991.
[a]Excluding programs that serve primarily handicapped children and programs that do not serve three- to five-year-old children.
[b]Excluding programs that serve primarily handicapped children, programs that do not serve three- to five-year-old children, and public-school-based programs.
[c]Excluding programs that serve primarily handicapped children.
[d]The first figure for group size by age is average maximum group size. The second figure is average full-time-equivalent group size, equal to total hours of care for all children divided by the number of hours the provider cares for children.

The table shows that about two-thirds of day care centers were nonprofit and one-third were for-profit in 1990. Most of the for-profits were independent; only 17 percent of for-profits (6 percent of all centers) were part of a national or local chain. The most common type of nonprofit was independent, followed by religious-based. Many characteristics of centers differed substantially by profit status. For-profits were larger on average, served fewer children of low-income families, and paid lower wages than nonprofits. Perhaps surprisingly, for-profits had smaller group sizes on average than nonprofits, but they also had fewer staff per group, resulting in higher child-staff ratios than nonprofits had. For-profits and nonprofits that charged any fee charged about the same fee on average. For-profits were more likely to experience teacher turnover, though the rate of turnover was similar among those for-profits and nonprofits that experienced any turnover. The annual teacher turnover rate among centers that experience any turnover was strikingly high: 50 to 52 percent. Overall, turnover was 25 percent. Day care center teachers were well educated on average: only 13 percent had not attended college, and there were virtually no high school dropouts among them.

Regulated family day care providers were much less well educated; only 51 percent attended college, and about 10 percent were high school dropouts. The average hourly fee in regulated family day care was about ten cents higher than in centers, but family day care providers earned only about four dollars per hour of providing care, before expenses. Thus, family day care had much lower monetary compensation than center care, though family providers were able to work in their own homes, many while caring for their own children as well. Group size and child-staff ratios tended to be smaller than in centers, especially when computed on a full-time-equivalent child basis.

The PCS data can also be compared with an earlier survey of centers collected as part of the National Day Care Study (NDCS) in 1976–77 (Ruopp et al. 1979) in order to provide some measure of growth in the industry. It is estimated that in the thirteen- to fourteen-year period between the two surveys, the number of day care centers in the United States tripled, and enrollment more than quadrupled. The percentage of teachers with at least a college degree increased from 29 to 42 percent, average group size increased from 13.5 to 15.7, and the average child-staff ratio rose from 6.8 to 8.5. These figures show a large increase in the size of the industry, with mixed trends in quality-related characteristics. Average teacher wages and average fees remained roughly constant in real terms.[8]

THE CENSUS OF SERVICES

Every five years a census of the service sector conducted by the U.S. Census Bureau provides a series of snapshots of the day care industry.

Table 2.12 presents selected data from the 1982 to 1997 censuses. In the terminology of the census, an "establishment" is a specific day care center or family day care home, while a "firm" is a legal entity that may own more than one establishment. Establishments or firms that are for-profit are subject to the federal income tax, while nonprofits are exempt from the income tax. Establishments with no payroll have no employees and are run by their owner. Most such establishments are probably family day care homes.

According to the table, the number of for-profit establishments with payroll increased by 143 percent, from 18,086 to 43,955, between 1982 and 1997. Receipts and payroll increased by factors of 3.6 and 3.8 in real (inflation-adjusted) terms, while the number of paid employees increased by a factor of 3.2. The nonprofit sector expanded at a much slower rate, with the number of establishments increasing by 43 percent, from 12,676 to 18,099, receipts and payroll by factors of 2.3 and 2.0 in real terms, and the number of paid employees by 77 percent.

These figures suggest that the for-profit sector is much more responsive to increased demand for child care than the nonprofit sector. Nonprofit day care centers often rely on donated space and volunteer labor and therefore cannot easily expand in response to increased demand. The number of establishments without payroll rose by 120 percent during the five-year period from 1987 to 1992, and the receipts of these establishments increased by 108 percent in real terms. (1997 data on these items have not been released.) Most firms in the day care industry own a single establishment, but the relatively small number of multi-establishment firms account for about one-third of all employment. The four largest for-profit firms alone account for close to 15 percent of receipts in the for-profit sector.

CHILD CARE QUALITY

Developmental psychologists have devoted considerable effort to studying the determinants of child care quality and the effects of child care quality on child development. I discuss this literature in chapter 7. Here, I describe one of the best-known measures of child care quality and present descriptive statistics on this measure from two samples of day care centers.

The measures of the quality of child care devised by developmental psychologists are based on instruments that rate child care arrangements on a large number of features and then average or summarize the ratings of the individual features. Trained observers spend several hours observing the arrangement and completing the rating scale. The ratings are objective in the sense that different observers who are trained sufficiently well in using the instruments produce independent ratings of the same arrangement that are highly correlated.

The developmental psychology approach to defining and measuring

Table 2.12 / Summary Data on Day Care Establishments from the Census of Services, 1982 to 1997

	1982	1987	1992	1997
Establishments with payroll subject to federal income tax (for-profit)				
Number	18,086	26,809	35,327	43,955
Receipts (millions of dollars)	2,338	4,160	6,029	8,419
Payroll (millions of dollars)	1,024	1,847	2,732	3,948
Number of paid employees	123,130	199,666	282,675	388,731
Percentage of receipts from				
private payers	—	94.0	89.0	—
Establishments with payroll exempt from federal income tax (nonprofit)				
Number	12,676	13,822	15,970	18,099
Receipts (millions of dollars)	2,544	3,155	4,224	5,766
Payroll (millions of dollars)	1,478	1,751	2,221	3,015
Number of paid employees	135,269	155,402	185,253	239,981
Percentage of receipts from				
private payers	—	34.5	31.0	—
Establishments without payroll (FDCHs)				
Number	—	221,880	489,054	—
Receipts (millions of dollars)	—	1,893	3,933	—
Firms with payroll subject to federal income tax (for-profit)				
Number	15,844	23,265	30,290	37,905
Percentage with more than one				
establishment	3.5	3.0	4.2	3.6
Percentage of paid employment accounted for by firms with				
more than one establishment	29.9	28.1	32.8	33.1
Percentage of receipts accounted				
for by four largest firms	—	19.2	17.8	14.9
Firms with payroll exempt from federal income tax (nonprofit)				
Number	10,201	11,105	12,241	12,998
Percentage with more than one				
establishment	10.9	10.7	12.4	13.3
Percentage of paid employment accounted for by firms with				
more than one establishment	32.9	33.0	36.8	41.9
Percentage of receipts accounted				
for by four largest firms	3.4	2.6	3.9	2.8

Source: U.S. Bureau of the Census, Census of Services 1997.
Notes: Dollar figures were adjusted for inflation using the consumer price index (CPI-U) with 1997 as the base year. A few establishments with payroll may be family day care homes, but most family day care homes have no paid employees.

quality is not the only possible approach. Consumers can be asked what features they believe determine the quality of child care. The quality of a child care arrangement from the perspective of the adults who provide the care can also be measured. I believe the developmental psychology approach is the most appropriate one to use, however, because it claims to measure quality from what seems to me to be the most important perspective: how it affects children. This is not to say that other concepts of child care quality are unimportant; for example, parents are likely to make child care decisions based on their own concepts of quality. But the developmental psychology approach is reasonably objective and can be quantified. If quality as defined by developmental psychologists does influence child development as claimed, then it warrants our attention.

Many instruments have been designed to measure child care quality. I focus here on the Early Childhood Environment Rating Scale (ECERS) and its infant-toddler counterpart, the Infant-Toddler Environment Rating Scale (ITERS) (Harms and Clifford 1980; Harms, Cryer, and Clifford 1990). They are widely used, and there are data sets with reasonably large samples that can be used to describe the distribution of quality. I cannot evaluate how this instrument compares to others that are available, but it seems to me quite reasonable as a measure of child care quality from the perspective of the development of children.

The ECERS is designed to assess quality in day care center classrooms serving preschool-age children (two and a half to five), and the ITERS does the same for classrooms serving younger children. The ECERS consists of thirty-two items covering personal care routines, furnishings and display, language-reasoning experiences, fine and gross motor activities, creative activities, and social development. Additional items assess the needs of the adults providing care. Each item is rated on a scale from 1 to 7, with 1 representing the lowest score and 7 the highest (see this chapter's appendix for a list of the ECERS items).

Raters are given detailed instructions on what to look for when rating each item. For example:

	Inadequate		Minimal		Good		Excellent
Item	1	2	3	4	5	6	7
Under-standing language	Few materials present and little use of materials to help children understand language (for example, no scheduled daily story time).		Some materials present, but not regularly available or used for language development.		Many materials available for free choice and supervised use. At least one planned activity daily.		Everything in 5, plus teacher provides good language model throughout the day (for example, gives clear directions, uses words exactly in descriptions).

Continued

Item	Inadequate		Minimal		Good		Excellent
	1	2	3	4	5	6	7
Art activities	Few art materials available; regimented use of materials (for example, mostly teacher-directed).		Some materials available for free choice, but major emphasis on projects that are like an example shown.		Individual expression and free choice encouraged with art materials. Few projects that are like an example shown.		Variety of materials available for free choice. Attempt to relate art activities to other experiences

These instructions seem well designed to measure aspects of child care arrangements that matter for child development. I think of the ECERS as formalizing what a well-educated parent might look for when observing a day care center. The descriptors listed above the numerical ratings reflect the judgments of the instrument designers about the quality of care from the perspective of child development.

Table 2.13 presents descriptive statistics on the ECERS and ITERS from two samples of day care centers, the Cost, Quality, and Outcomes Study (CQOS) and the National Child Care Staffing Study (NCCSS). These samples are not nationally representative but are intended to be representative of the areas in which the samples were drawn. In both samples the average rating is about 4, which is halfway between minimal and good according to the ECERS-ITERS descriptors. Care of such quality has been referred to as "mediocre" by the investigators of one of the studies (Helburn 1995, 126).

There is substantial variation in average quality across locations, with California and New England centers offering the highest-quality care and centers in the South offering the lowest-quality care. These differences are large: in the CQOS the difference between average quality in California and North Carolina is about one standard deviation, and in the NCCSS the difference between Boston and Atlanta is also about one standard deviation. There is also considerable variation within states between the average quality offered in nonprofit and for-profit centers, and in infant-toddler and preschool classrooms. In most cases nonprofit quality is higher than for-profit quality, with especially large differences observed in North Carolina, Atlanta, Boston, and Phoenix. Quality in preschool classrooms is almost always higher than quality in infant-toddler rooms—again, substantially so in some sites (California and North Carolina). The ECERS and ITERS instruments are not identical, so it is possible that this difference is due to differences in the rating scales rather than true differences in quality.

/ 41

Table 2.13 / The Distribution of Child Care Quality in Day Care Centers, as Measured by the ECERS and the ITERS, 1989 and 1993 (Mean and Standard Deviation)

		For-Profit		Nonprofit	
	All Centers	Preschool	Infant-Toddler	Preschool	Infant-Toddler
Cost, Quality, and Outcomes Study (1993)					
All sites	3.99 (1.07)	4.07 (0.99)	3.33 (1.02)	4.41 (0.96)	3.57 (1.07)
California	4.36 (0.96)	4.27 (0.88)	3.86 (0.70)	4.66 (0.97)	3.60 (1.07)
Colorado	3.94 (0.95)	4.09 (0.85)	3.40 (0.89)	4.25 (0.89)	3.66 (1.04)
Connecticut	4.24 (1.05)	4.46 (1.02)	4.00 (1.07)	4.33 (0.99)	3.85 (1.13)
North Carolina	3.44 (1.08)	3.28 (0.83)	2.54 (0.60)	4.31 (0.95)	3.29 (1.02)
National Child Care Staffing Study (1989)					
All sites	3.92 (0.99)	3.59 (0.90)	3.43 (0.98)	4.39 (0.97)	4.09 (1.07)
Atlanta	3.57 (0.96)	3.32 (0.84)	3.04 (0.86)	4.30 (0.87)	3.89 (1.05)
Boston	4.44 (0.72)	3.66 (0.86)	3.16 (0.57)	4.72 (0.61)	4.51 (0.72)
Detroit	3.96 (1.24)	4.23 (1.04)	3.86 (1.37)	4.14 (1.40)	3.69 (1.45)
Phoenix	4.09 (0.90)	3.74 (0.75)	3.84 (0.83)	4.79 (0.89)	4.48 (0.97)
Seattle	3.62 (0.84)	3.30 (0.86)	3.37 (1.06)	3.99 (0.73)	3.63 (0.96)

Source: See Cryer et al. (1995) for a description of the CQOS, and Whitebook et al. (1989) for a description of the NCCSS.

Notes: Sample size is 731 classrooms in 401 centers for the CQOS and 665 classrooms in 227 centers for the NCCSS. The public release data set from the NCCSS does not include the scores on the individual ECERS and ITERS items or the average score. Rather, it includes two summary measures derived from factor analysis of the underlying items. I present the unweighted average of the two summary measures here. This has the same scale as the ECERS and ITERS scores from the CQOS but was derived differently, so comparisons between the CQOS and NCCSS should be made with caution.

The overall message of the data in table 2.13 is that day care center quality is medium on average and highly variable. The total number of centers in the two samples is only 667, and as noted earlier, the samples are not nationally representative. It is also important to recall that centers account for only about 30 percent of all nonmaternal child care. There is little comparable data for other types of care, and there are no large national samples of centers or longitudinal samples that would allow comparisons over time. Thus, the basis for drawing inferences about the quality of child care in the United States is quite limited.

Nevertheless, there is little reason to think that the results of these two studies underestimate average child care quality. In fact, if anything, they may overestimate it. The response rates in the studies were relatively low (55 percent in the CQOS, 61 percent in the NCCSS), and there is some indication that the centers that refused to participate may have had lower quality than participating centers (Whitebook, Howes, and Phillips 1990, 18). A study of family day care homes and relative care that used similar quality ratings concluded that "family child care is, on average, just adequate, and almost identical to quality in centers" (Kontos et al. 1995, 204).

Developmental psychologists argue that in order to provide high-quality child care it is important to care for children in relatively small groups with a high ratio of adult caregivers to children, and with caregivers who are trained in early childhood education and development. In chapter 7, I review the evidence on this issue. Here I present descriptive statistics from the CQOS on these "structural" features of day care centers. Table 2.14 shows that the average staff-child ratio is 0.19 (about one adult per five children), the average group size is 13.4, and the most common level of staff training is at least one college course in early childhood education and development. The average staff-child ratio is much higher and average group size is much lower in infant-toddler rooms, sometimes by as much as a factor of two. Despite this, quality as measured by the ECERS-ITERS is generally much lower in infant-toddler rooms, as noted earlier. There is considerable variation in the averages across states, but the high-quality states are not always the high-ratio and low-group-size states. For example, California has both relatively high quality according to table 2.13 and relatively high group size according to table 2.14. Nonprofit centers have higher staff-child ratios than for-profit centers in every state for both types of rooms, but only about half the group size comparisons favor nonprofits over for-profits.

The bottom panel of table 2.14 indicates that the modal level of training in North Carolina is one level below that of the other states, and the modal level of training in nonprofit Connecticut centers—a B.A. or B.S. degree in early childhood education or child development—is substantially higher than in other sectors.

SUMMARY AND CONCLUSIONS

The child care market has expanded dramatically in the last few decades, by any measure. This expansion was driven by the huge increase in the labor force participation of mothers of young children. In addition to increasing in size, the market has increasingly moved away from informal home-based care and toward formal child care arrangements. Nevertheless, the child care market remains predominantly informal.

About two-thirds of families with an employed mother and a preschool-age child that use nonparental child care pay for care. The percentage of

Table 2.14 / The Distribution of Classroom Structure in Day Care Centers, 1993 (Mean and Standard Deviation)

	All Centers	For-Profit Preschool	For-Profit Infant-Toddler	Nonprofit Preschool	Nonprofit Infant-Toddler
Staff-child ratio					
All sites	0.19 (0.14)	0.14 (0.06)	0.26 (0.13)	0.19 (0.12)	0.31 (0.13)
California	0.18 (0.15)	0.12 (0.04)	0.36 (0.20)	0.17 (0.08)	0.38 (0.22)
Colorado	0.20 (0.15)	0.15 (0.06)	0.27 (0.12)	0.21 (0.22)	0.29 (0.14)
Connecticut	0.22 (0.13)	0.16 (0.08)	0.32 (0.13)	0.22 (0.10)	0.35 (0.12)
North Carolina	0.15 (0.10)	0.12 90.08)	0.18 (0.12)	0.15 (0.10)	0.26 (0.10)
Group size					
All sites	13.4 (6.4)	14.0 (8.1)	7.88 (3.4)	13.4 (5.5)	8.33 (2.9)
California	13.9 (7.0)	14.4 (6.6)	7.30 (3.2)	14.7 (6.3)	9.20 (5.3)
Colorado	12.8 (8.4)	13.7 (10.5)	7.70 (3.5)	13.0 (5.7)	6.80 (2.0)
Connecticut	11.8 (6.5)	13.2 (8.3)	7.20 (2.8)	11.5 (4.1)	8.30 (3.4)
North Carolina	12.3 (5.7)	14.7 (7.2)	8.60 (3.7)	14.3 (5.9)	8.70 (2.1)
Teacher training in early childhood education (mode)					
All sites	6	—		—	
California	—	6		6	
Colorado	—	6		6	
Connecticut	—	6		9	
North Carolina	—	5		5	

Source: Helburn 1995, tables 6.9, 6.10, 6.12, 6.13, 6.14.
Notes: Staff-child ratio and group size are the values recorded by observers at midmorning (around 11 o'clock). Training is reported by the center director. The training values are the mode of the distribution of the following codes: 1, no training; 2, in-service training at the center; 3, workshops in the community or at professional meetings; 4, courses in high school or vocational school; 5, Child Development Associate training; 6, College courses; 7, AA degree in early childhood education or child development; 8, RN degree; 9, B.A. or B.S. in early childhood education or child development; 9, graduate courses; 10, graduate degree in early childhood education or child development.

income spent on child care by those families who do pay is relatively small on average, 7 to 8 percent in 1995. But child care expenditures can be a great burden for the poor. Despite the expansion of the child care market, the wages of child care workers and family expenditures on child care have increased only modestly in the last fifteen to twenty years. The largest source of growth in the more formal sector of the industry has been the for-profit sector, which seems to be more responsive to increased demand than the nonprofit sector. Day care center quality is medium on average and highly variable.

This description of the child care market highlights key features for which the theoretical and empirical models developed in subsequent chapters must be able to account. There is no guarantee that past trends and current features of the market will persist in the future. In this sense it is risky to use a model that can explain past trends and current features as a device for predicting the effects of alternative policies. But a good model must be based on an understanding of the main features of the market, and the description in this chapter provides a basis for the analysis that follows.

The following specific features seem especially important and are emphasized in the analysis in subsequent chapters:

- Many families have access to and use informal child care, much of it unpaid. These families have a choice between formal and informal care, and choose informal.

- Employment is the dominant factor in child care choices, but child care is also used for reasons other than facilitating employment.

- Child care providers are very heterogeneous; the most dynamic sector is the for-profit day care center sector, but this sector also has relatively low quality among formal providers.

APPENDIX

An (I) following one of the thirty-two child-related ECERS items listed here indicates that it is also part of the Infant-Toddler Environment Rating Scale.

1. Greeting/departing (I)
2. Meals/snacks (I)
3. Nap/rest (I)
4. Diapering/toileting (I)
5. Personal grooming (I)
6. Furnishings (routine) (I)
7. Furnishings (learning) (I)
8. Furnishings (relaxation) (I)
9. Room arrangement (I)
10. Child-related display (I)
11. Understanding language
12. Using language
13. Reasoning
14. Informal language (I)
15. Fine motor

16. Supervision (fine motor)
17. Gross motor space
18. Gross motor equipment
19. Gross motor time
20. Supervision (gross motor)
21. Art (I)
22. Music/movement (I)
23. Blocks (I)
24. Sand/water (I)
25. Dramatic play (I)
26. Schedule (creative)
27. Supervision (creative)
28. Space to be alone
29. Free play
30. Group time
31. Cultural awareness (I)
32. Tone

Additional items included in the ITERS are: health practice, active physical play, health policy, peer interaction, safety practice, adult-child interaction, safety policy, discipline, books and pictures, schedule of daily activities, and eye-hand coordination.

Chapter 3

Economic Models of Child Care

This chapter describes simple economic models of the behavior of child care consumers, producers, and the resulting market outcomes. A model focuses attention on the essential aspects of a problem and provides a framework for interpreting the results of empirical analysis. Suggesting hypotheses that can be tested empirically, a model is not "right" or "wrong"; it is either useful in accomplishing these objectives if it is thoughtfully constructed, or it isn't.

Sometimes a problem is so simple to understand (though not necessarily to fix) that the discipline of formulating and deriving the implications of a formal model is unnecessary. In other cases a formal model can draw attention to subtle but important aspects of a problem that might have been missed had the modeling been more informal. A formal model does not have to be expressed mathematically, though doing so can help identify the exact consequences of each assumption. The important requirement is to state explicitly our assumptions about the environment faced by the actors in the model and about their behavior given the environment they face. A useful model is simple, assuming away many aspects of a problem in order to focus on those of interest. We can thus see clearly the consequences of a given set of assumptions.

The economic approach to modeling the child care market is not the only possible approach. We could build models based on the principles of sociology, psychology, political science, or other disciplines. However, in practice students of child care in these disciplines rarely specify explicit behavioral models. They may have a model in mind that guides their thinking about child care, but few of them spell it out explicitly and clearly derive its implications. This is a strength of the economic approach—we may not like the assumptions of the model, but they are clearly stated and we can put a finger on exactly what we don't like about them. And in my view, we must explicitly model the behavior of actors in the child care market if we hope to understand the market's outcomes. Otherwise, we risk engaging in fuzzy, shortsighted, and wishful thinking about the problems we see in the market.

The models described in this chapter provide the conceptual basis for the empirical and policy analyses described in the following chapters.

However, the models discussed here are not as rich in detail as the empirical models used in subsequent chapters. This is a deliberate choice. The goal in this chapter is to provide an overview of what can be learned by thinking about child care from an economic perspective. This is best accomplished in the simplest possible framework. To meet the goals of subsequent chapters—providing empirical analyses that are useful for policy purposes—we must pay attention to details that are not crucial to an overview. I discuss in turn models of the behavior of child care consumers and child care providers and models of the child care market. In each case I give examples of how the models can be used to analyze the impact of alternative government policies in the child care market.

A MODEL OF CONSUMER BEHAVIOR IN THE CHILD CARE MARKET

The child care market offers parents many options for the type, location, schedule, quality, reliability, and cost of child care. The labor market offers parents employment options that vary by the number of hours of work required, flexibility in scheduling work, work shift, work location, pay, and benefits. Some child care options would preclude certain employment choices, and vice versa. For example, a particular child care arrangement might be available at hours that differ from the work schedule required by a given employer. The employment choices of the mother and other family members and related adults might be coordinated so as to facilitate child care arrangements. It is important to model child care and employment decisions jointly since they are typically closely interrelated.

Consider first the simplest possible model that can capture the interrelationship between child care and employment. (For related models, see Blau and Hagy 1998; Blau and Robins 1988; Connelly 1992a; Michalopoulos, Robins, and Garfinkel 1992; Ribar 1995.) For simplicity, I refer to the mother as the decisionmaker in the model, but in a two-parent family we can imagine the decisions being made jointly by the parents. The model is deliberately oversimplified, ignoring some crucial features of child care in order to bring out as clearly as possible the key child care–employment connection. I make the model more realistic later. For now its key features are the following:

- The mother cares about three things: her *leisure time*, defined as all of her time other than the hours she spends at work; the amount of money available to the family after paying child care expenses, which I refer to as *net income*; and the *quality of care* her children receive. Other things being equal, she prefers more leisure and net income to less, and higher-quality child care to lower-quality care.

- The mother divides her time between employment and leisure. Each hour spent in employment adds to family income but subtracts from leisure.

- There is at least one young child in the family who requires continuous care by an adult. Care is assumed to be provided by the mother during all hours in which she is not employed. During the mother's work hours, child care must be purchased in the child care market. No unpaid child care is available. Child care is purchased only for the hours in which the mother is employed.

- The quality of care provided by the mother and the quality of care available in the child care market are both fixed and given. The overall quality of care, which is what the mother cares about, depends on the quality of her care and the quality of purchased care, weighted by the amount of time spent by the children in each source of care.

- The mother can work as many or as few hours as desired at a fixed wage rate per hour of work. Nonwage income from assets and the husband's earnings, if any, is also available, in amounts that do not depend on how much the mother works.

- The mother chooses her allocation of time between work and leisure to maximize the satisfaction she receives from the three things she cares about (leisure, net income, and the quality of child care), subject to the time and budget constraints she faces. A job with the desired number of hours can always be found at the given wage rate, and the desired number of hours of child care can always be purchased at the given market price.

In this model every hour of work by the mother requires an hour of paid child care. If the mother's hourly wage rate is W and the market price of an hour of purchased child care is P, then her net wage from an hour of work is $W-P$. An increase in P (or a decrease in W) reduces the incentive to be employed. A testable hypothesis implied by the model is that mothers who face a higher price of child care (or a lower wage rate) are less likely to be employed, other things being equal. An increase in the price of child care has ambiguous implications for the number of hours the mother works and purchases child care, if she remains employed following the price increase. The price increase makes work less financially rewarding and induces substitution of work hours with leisure hours. But the higher price reduces the mother's net income, and she may want to work more hours to make up this loss. A policy implication of the model is that a child care subsidy that defrays some or all of the mother's child care expenses increases the incentive to be employed. This implication holds in more realistic models as well, but it is easiest to see the basis for it in this very simple model in which paid child care and employment are closely connected.

/ 49

The model is useful for bringing out the key (and obvious) point that a higher price of child care reduces the incentive for a mother to be employed. But the model is clearly too simple to serve as a basis for realistic policy analysis. Two critical elements that are missing from the model are informal child care and the variable quality of purchased child care. Adding these elements complicates the model, but these are crucial features of the child care market that cannot be ignored in a policy-relevant analysis. To deal with these features, consider the following modifications of the model.

- An informal child care provider, such as the children's grandmother or another relative, is available. The informal provider does not have the option of being employed; she divides her time between leisure and caring for the mother's children. The quality of care she provides is fixed and given. The mother cares about the relative's leisure time; other things being equal, she prefers that the relative have more leisure because that is what the relative prefers.

- Only one of the three sources of child care (mother, relative, market) is used for any given hour of the child's time, but the different sources of care can be used in any combination as long as the child receives continuous care.

- Child care of any desired quality can be purchased in the market. The price per hour of care has a fixed component and a component that is proportional to the quality of care purchased. To be concrete, suppose the price per hour of purchased child care is given by $P = \alpha + \beta Q$, where Q is the quality of the purchased care chosen by the parents, α is the fixed component of the price (independent of quality), and βQ is the variable component. There is no particular reason to expect a linear price-quality relationship, but it keeps the analysis simple. Later I use other examples as well.[1]

In this version of the model, if the mother works, the family faces two trade-offs: whether to use informal or market child care, and the quality of market child care, if she uses any such care. Informal child care by the relative has no monetary cost but requires the relative to give up some of her leisure. Lower-quality purchased care is cheaper than higher-quality care but reduces the satisfaction of the mother, presumably because of the harmful effects of lower-quality care on child development. The model can be used to analyze the effects of two types of child care subsidies: those that are independent of quality and can be interpreted as reducing α; and those that provide higher subsidies for higher-quality care and can be interpreted as reducing β.

To understand the implications of the model, consider the following combinations of discrete yes or no choices that can be made according to the model (see table 3.1):

Table 3.1 / Child Care and Employment Choices

Choice	Mother Works	Relative Provides Child Care	Child Care Is Purchased
One	No	No	No
Two	Yes	Yes	No
Three	Yes	No	Yes
Four	Yes	Yes	Yes

Source: Author's configuration.

These four choices are mutually exclusive and exhaustive: according to the model, a given family will be in one, and only one, of these categories. The family chooses the option from among these four alternatives that provides the greatest level of satisfaction. Choice 1 is likely to be favored by traditionalist parents: the mother provides all child care and does not work outside the home. In choices 2, 3, and 4, the mother works, so child care must be provided by a relative or purchased in the market for the hours during which she is employed. In choice 2, only informal care is used, in choice 3 only purchased care is used, and in choice 4 both are used (though not at the same time).

In addition to these discrete choices, the mother chooses the number of hours of care by the relative or the market or both, if those options are relevant; the number of hours she works; and the quality of purchased care if any is used. These choices are also made to maximize utility, conditional on the combination of discrete choices made.

The main testable implications of the model are:

1. An increase in the price of child care as a result of increases in either of the parameters of the price equation, α or β, reduces the likelihood of using purchased care (choices 3 and 4).

2. An increase in α or β reduces or leaves unchanged the probability of employment.

3. An increase in the mother's wage rate increases the likelihood that she works (choices 2, 3, and 4).

These hypotheses can be tested empirically, and such tests are reported in chapter 4. It is worth noting some predictions that the model does not make. The model says nothing about how changes in either α or β affect the quality or quantity of the purchased care demanded. It also says nothing about how the mother's wage rate affects the quantity and quality of care demanded, or how changes in α or β affect the hours that the mother works. All of these effects depend on the nature of preferences. This means that the model is flexible enough to be consistent with many different patterns of effects, but at the same time the model does have testable implica-

/ 51

tions: there are some patterns that could be observed in the data that would be inconsistent with the model.

This model serves three purposes. First, it highlights the trade-offs faced by families making child care and employment decisions and provides a way to analyze how child care subsidies affect consumer decisions. Second, it suggests a set of explanatory variables that should be included in empirical models to explain variation between families in child care and employment choices: the wage rate of the mother; nonwage income; the price of child care; the quality of care provided by the mother and other relatives; the availability of care by another relative; and determinants of preferences. The model also draws attention to a key issue that any empirical study of child care demand must confront: the price of child care paid by the family is a choice variable, since it depends on the quality of the purchased care chosen by the family. Hence, it is important to find a source of variation in price that is independent of the quality chosen by the parents. For example, α and β may vary across households in different geographic child care markets. This approach is used in the empirical analysis in chapter 4. Third, the model has testable implications. If these implications turn out to be consistent with the data, it gives us some confidence that the model is useful for policy purposes, though such consistency does not guarantee that the model is "right" or that a better model could not be constructed.

The model could be expanded in many dimensions at the cost of greater complexity. Allowing the father to be a caregiver during the mother's work hours, at the monetary or psychic cost of coordinating their work schedules, could be an interesting extension. Quality of child care could be modeled more realistically as multidimensional. Dynamic considerations could be incorporated by allowing for the possibility that choices made by the parents today have consequences in the future. Distinctions could be made among types of purchased child care, such as day care centers, family day care, and baby-sitters. Child care could be purchased during nonwork hours for the purpose of enhancing child development. The availability of cash assistance from welfare and child care subsidies from means-tested child care programs could be incorporated for low-income families. The price of child care could be modeled as fixed in weekly instead of hourly terms, regardless of the number of hours of care used per week. Several of these extensions are incorporated in the empirical analysis in chapter 4.

The three most critical assumptions of the model are that quality can be represented by a single index (Q), that any level of quality is available to be purchased in the market if the family is willing to pay the market price for the desired level of quality, and that informal care is readily available.

Regarding the first assumption, quality might be multidimensional in reality, consisting of many different items to which each family might attach different weights. It is possible to construct a model based on this approach, but it would be too complex to provide useful insights. The assumption that the quality of child care can be represented by a single index such as the ECERS makes the model simple enough to yield useful insights. For this assumption to be a useful basis for a model, parents must be at least roughly in agreement that the items included in the index are aspects of quality. It is not necessary to assume that every family places the same weight on quality in their preferences, just that they more or less agree on what constitutes quality. The important phrase in the second key assumption is *if the family is willing to pay the market price.* Some families might have strong preferences for high-quality care but feel "priced out" of the market for such care because it is so expensive. Economists do not describe such an outcome as a lack of availability. It may be a social problem, but it does not indicate that the market has failed. I think it is a reasonable simplifying assumption, and I describe evidence in chapter 4 to support it.

Finally, the model assumes that a relative is available to provide informal unpaid child care. This is obviously true for many families, since we observe them using such care, but how do we know it is true for the families who are not using such care? Maybe they are not using it because it is not available. In the model, they are not using it because the quality of such care is too low or the opportunity cost is too high (the relative's leisure has a high value). If we knew whether informal care was available to a family, we could simply delete it as an option for those families for whom it is unavailable. But we cannot observe this information in most data sets. Because of the absence of such information, I assume in the empirical analysis in chapter 4 that every family has access to informal care. I attribute the failure to use it when it is available to either low quality, high opportunity cost, or both. One source of informal care is the children themselves, an option that is rarely chosen because of its presumably very low quality.

The economic approach is not the only theoretical framework that could be used as a basis for modeling child care and employment decisions. But I believe it is the most natural approach given its emphasis on constraints and choices. It is flexible enough to allow for variation in preferences across families, so that non-economic variables can play a role in the model. The key testable prediction of the model is that an increase in the price of market child care causes a reduction in the likelihood that child care is purchased and a decrease or no change in the likelihood that the mother is employed.

A MODEL OF CHILD CARE PROVIDERS

I have developed a simple model of the behavior of child care providers that charge a fee for child care. Such providers include most day care centers, family day care homes, and baby-sitters.[2] Providers that charge a fee have two general motivations for being child care providers: earning money, and the satisfaction derived from working with young children. The key assumptions of the model are:

- All providers have these two motivations, but different types of providers may place different emphasis on pecuniary versus nonpecuniary motivations. The nonpecuniary motivation is modeled as a desire to provide high-quality care: the provider's satisfaction increases with the quality of care provided. The relative weight that the provider puts on profit versus quality in her decisions can range from zero (the provider does not care about profit at all) to one (the provider cares only about profit; higher-quality care does not increase the provider's satisfaction at all).[3]

- Providers choose the quality of care by choosing the amounts of *labor input* of different skill levels to employ, and by choosing the amounts of other inputs used in providing care. Workers who are better educated and trained in early childhood development are more skilled and provide higher-quality care, but they also cost more per hour employed. Care provided in smaller groups is of higher quality but costs more to provide because more staff hours are required per child. Increasing the staff-child ratio by, for example, using a teacher and an aide in each group instead of just a teacher increases the quality of care but also increases cost.

- The price per hour of care that a provider can charge depends on the quality of care offered. Providers face the same price function as consumers: $P = \alpha + \beta Q$, where P is the price a provider can charge per hour of care, and Q is the quality of care offered by the provider.

- The quality chosen by the provider determines the provider's revenue and costs and therefore profit. Providers choose the level of quality to maximize their satisfaction as a function of the profit they earn and the quality of care they provide.

As in most service industries, providers do not choose the quantity of the service to provide. Rather, they choose the quality of their service, the price is then determined by the market price equation, and the quantity of service is determined by the number of consumers who prefer the price-quality combination offered by the provider to others available in the market. An important assumption implicit in this approach is that a provider can expand capacity at a constant average cost in the long run to provide service for all customers who are willing to pay the market price for the provider's chosen level of quality. This assumption is known as "constant returns to scale." A day care center with one facility could, for example, double the number of children cared for at no increase in average cost per child by constructing another facility just like its original one and staffing it with teachers of the same skill level as those in the original facility.

This might be a reasonable assumption to make about for-profit day care centers (as shown in chapter 2, firms that own more than one center are an important part of the industry), but it is less plausible for nonprofit centers, family day care homes, and baby-sitters. Many nonprofit day care centers rely heavily on donated space and could expand capacity only by purchasing or renting additional space at a much higher cost than they pay for their current space. Family day care homes are similar in that they essentially rely on space that is "donated" by the provider's family. Buying or renting another home next door or across the street in order to expand capacity would substantially increase the average cost of care. Also, family day care homes often use unpaid labor provided by family members, and such labor is not inexhaustible in supply.

Put differently, I have assumed away the possibility of permanent shortages of child care. A family who wants to purchase care of a specified quality and is willing to pay the market price for such care can always find it eventually. This assumption does not rule out the possibility of temporary shortages of child care of certain types. For example, an unexpected increase in demand for infant care in day care centers may cause centers to reach their full capacity for infants in a particular market. The assumption rules out the possibility that such shortages would persist indefinitely. New centers would eventually enter the market, and existing centers would expand their capacity for infant care, because they could increase their profit by doing so.

The plausibility of this assumption ultimately boils down to one question: What is quality? If quality is thought of as a measure like the ECERS, then the assumption is reasonable. There are many for-profit day care centers that provide high-quality care at a high price and at least in the long run can presumably take on all the customers who are willing to pay the price. A family might prefer to place a child in a family day care home or a nonprofit center, but if such an arrangement offering the quality desired by the family is not available, and if quality is equivalent to a measure like the ECERS, then the family can always find the same quality of care in a for-profit day care center. On the other hand, if quality is idiosyncratic, then the assumption is less plausible. For example, a certain type of quality might be provided by a nonprofit preschool on the local college campus, and a different type of quality might be provided by a family day care home located in the same neighborhood as the family seeking care. The care provided by a for-profit day care center simply may not be able to replicate the types of quality found in these settings, no matter how high the ECERS score of the for-profit center. If this is the way consumers think of quality, then long-run shortages are more plausible. I prefer to use the quality-equals-ECERS approach, however, because it is analytically simple and has powerful predictions.

The predictions of the model are:

- An increase in the market reward to quality (β) causes the provider to increase the quality of care, by hiring more skilled labor or upgrading the skills of existing staff.

- An increase in the fixed component of price (α) causes the provider to increase the quality of care if the provider values quality at all for its own sake. But a profit-maximizing provider that does not care at all about quality except as it affects profit will leave quality unchanged in response to an increase in α.

- An increase in the hourly wage rate of any type of labor employed by the provider will cause the provider to reduce the level of quality.

- Both a profit-maximizing provider that does not care about quality and a quality-maximizing provider that does not care about profit but is constrained to break even in order to stay in business, will leave quality unchanged in response to an increase in the number of customers.

- Providers that place some weight on quality and some on profit may raise or lower quality in response to an increase in demand.

These predictions follow straightforward logic. An increase in β raises the return to quality but does not affect the cost of providing a given level of quality, so a provider will benefit both in terms of profit and satisfaction by increasing quality. Even a profit-maximizing provider will respond by raising quality. An increase in α raises the price that can be charged independent of the level of quality, so a profit-maximizing provider has no incentive to increase quality since it will get higher profit without incurring the increased cost of raising quality. A provider that cares about quality will sacrifice some of the additional profit resulting from an increase in α by increasing quality, since the provider values quality for its own sake. An increase in the cost of labor or any other input raises the cost of quality without raising the return, so all providers will be forced to reduce quality, even a quality-maximizing provider that does not care about profit at all but must break even in order to remain in business. An increase in the quantity of services demanded does not affect the level of quality supplied by a profit-maximizing provider in the long run because under constant returns to scale the provider can expand capacity without affecting average cost and was already supplying the profit-maximizing level of quality before the increase in demand. The same logic applies to a quality-maximizing provider subject to a break-even constraint: it was already supplying the highest level of quality consistent with breaking even prior to the increase in demand and can expand capacity to meet the increased demand at the same level of quality without a change in cost, subject to the qualifications about the supply of child care in nonprofits discussed earlier. If nonprofits can expand only at a substantial increase in average cost, then the for-profit providers are the *marginal* providers that will expand and contract as the number of customers fluctuates. The model of child care supply developed here treats child care providers as firms that sell a service in order to make a profit. The model allows for the possibility of a nonpecuniary motivation to provide child care as well. As shown in chapter 2, the for-profit child care sector has grown much faster than the nonprofit sector in recent years. For-profit firms may have nonpecuniary motivations as well as profit motives, but it seems likely that to survive in a competitive market, for-profit providers must focus heavily on profit. Two key points brought out by the model are that for-profit firms can provide high-quality care if the market price of such care is high enough to cover their costs, and that for-profit firms can expand to meet increased demand for high-quality child care, while nonprofit firms are less likely to be able to do so. A specific prediction of the model is that a government subsidy for high-quality child care (equivalent to an increase in β) will induce for-profit firms to increase the quality of child care offered. The model is consistent with temporary shortages of certain types of child care but implies that in the long run the quantity supplied of any type of child care will equal the quantity demanded *if* consumers are willing to pay a price high enough to cover the cost of producing child care of the specified type.

EQUILIBRIUM IN THE CHILD CARE MARKET

The models described so far characterize the behavior of individual actors in the child care market: consumers and providers. The final model developed in this chapter takes the analysis to the level of the market as a whole and characterizes market outcomes.

What is a child care market? It consists of all consumers and providers that might conceivably engage in a child care transaction. There is no precise way to operationalize this notion, since we can observe the market transactions that take place but not those that might have taken place but did not. The simplest way to think about a child care market is in geographic terms: a particular market consists of all potential consumers and providers of child care within a well-defined area, such as a county. This is imprecise because there is nothing to prevent transactions from taking place across county lines. At the level of abstraction in this chapter, such precision is unnecessary, but we will need it when we turn to the empirical analysis in chapter 6.

The outcomes of interest in the child care market are the distributions of price and quality. In a market in which quality matters, we do not observe just one price and quality but rather many prices and qualities. Hence, we would like to be able to characterize how many consumers pay each price and receive each level of quality of care: the distribution of consumers and providers among prices and qualities. The key concept used here to characterize these market outcomes is *equilibrium*. A market is in equilibrium when the distribution of price and quality is such that it will remain unchanged unless disturbed by some outside force. For this to be the case, each consumer must have found a child care arrangement that maximizes her satisfaction given her budget and time constraints, and each provider must be offering the level of quality that provides it with the maximum possible satisfaction (profit or quality or some combination) subject to the constraints imposed by the prices of inputs, the technology of providing quality, and the price-quality relationship. In a market in which quality matters, the equilibrium will be a price-quality relationship: the price of each level of quality of care must be such that the quantity of child care supplied at each level of quality equals the quantity demanded at that quality.

The concept of equilibrium is central to economic models of markets. Thus, it is important to understand what it means and how it is used to characterize market outcomes and make predictions about the effects on the market outcomes of outside forces such as changes in subsidies and regulations, changes in consumer preferences for quality, and changes in knowledge about producing high-quality child care. When we observe the child care market or any other market at a particular moment, it may not be in equilibrium. Economists believe that "market forces" tend to push markets toward equilibrium, but the market equilibrium is itself continually changing as a result of outside forces. These outside forces are events that affect the child care market but are not caused by factors within the market. A new equilibrium arises in response to an outside force hitting the child care market. Market forces then cause the market to adjust toward its new equilibrium distribution of price and quality.

To illustrate the nature of these market forces, consider the example of a family day care provider withdrawing from the market owing to the "outside force" of her husband being transferred to a job in another city. The children she cared for must now be placed in alternative arrangements. As these families seek new arrangements, they increase the quantity of services demanded from other providers offering the desired level of quality. This leads to upward pressure on the price associated with that level of quality; in response, some providers may start to offer that level of quality because it is now more profitable to do so. The pressure on price also might lead some consumers to shift to a lower level of quality because the price of the quality of care they were using increased. This process continues until a new equilibrium is reached at which each consumer and each provider is again maximizing satisfaction subject to their constraints, including the new price-quality relationship. In practice, some other outside force may hit the market before it has completely adjusted to the new equilibrium, and this sets off another round of adjustments to yet another equilibrium.

The concept of equilibrium is clearly an abstraction that we will not observe in practice in most cases. But it is a powerful conceptual tool that can help us understand the market outcomes we do observe. We cannot use the concept of equilibrium to predict what the actual distribution of price and quality will be in a particular child care market at a particular time in the future. We do not know what new and unforeseen outside forces will impinge on the market between now and then. But if we have the data we need to construct a solid quantitative model of the market, we can use the concept of equilibrium to address counterfactual policy-related questions. For example, if the government increases the reimbursement rate of a child care subsidy by 10 percent, and no other outside factors change, by how much would the average price and quality of child care observed in the market change between the old equilibrium and the new equilibrium?

If quality in the child care market were uniform, then standard supply-demand analysis could be used to characterize the market equilibrium. It is useful to begin with this assumption because, though highly unrealistic, it helps illustrate the key idea that carries over to a more realistic model. So suppose for the moment that only one level of quality is available in the child care market. In this case the equilibrium "distribution" of price and quality collapses to a single point, as illustrated in figure 3.1. The market demand curve D_1 represents the willingness of consumers to purchase child care at alternative prices, for given levels of income and preferences. The quantity demanded is relatively low at high prices because, as predicted by the theory described earlier, some consumers do not find it worthwhile to sacrifice the income needed to finance child care expenses when the price is high. They opt out of the formal market and use informal care instead, or perhaps the mother withdraws from the labor force or works part-time instead of full-time. Other consumers still find the sacrifice worthwhile at high prices, so the quantity demanded does not necessarily fall to zero. The market supply curve S_1 represents the willingness of providers to supply child care at alternative prices, for given values of teacher wages and other input costs. The quantity supplied is higher at higher prices because expanding quantity drives up costs, and firms will only expand capacity if the price rises by enough to cover the increased cost.[4]

The market demand and supply curves for child care are derived from the underlying behavior of the consumers and providers, which act according to the models described earlier in this chapter. The location and shape of the market demand curve depends on consumer preferences, income, wage rates, and the other factors discussed earlier. The location and shape of the market supply curve depends on input prices and technology. The

Figure 3.1 / A Child Care Market with Uniform Quality

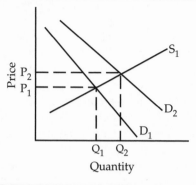

Source: Author's configuration.

market is in equilibrium when the price of child care is such that all consumers who wish to purchase care at the market price are able to do so, and all providers that wish to offer child care at the market price are able to find customers. Given the positions of the supply curve at S_1 and the demand curve at D_1, the only price for which this is true is the price at which the curves intersect, P_1. Any other price results in a shortage or an excess supply and is not an equilibrium because market forces will tend to cause the price to move toward equilibrium even in the absence of any outside force.

If the market is in equilibrium and an outside force causes a change in demand or supply, then the original equilibrium price is no longer the equilibrium. For example, if the demand curve shifts from D_1 to D_2 as a result of an increase in the number of families with young children, then the new equilibrium is at a price of P_2 and market forces will tend to drive the price up toward its new equilibrium level.

Now let us take a small first step toward introducing variation in quality and price in the market. Suppose two levels of quality are available in the market instead of only one, and that each has its own price. Call the two types of care high-quality and low-quality. Such a situation is depicted in figure 3.2. Each family chooses whether to seek high-quality or low-quality care (or neither: informal care and full-time mother care are options as well), depending on their preferences for quality relative to other goods and on the price of each type of care. This gives rise to the market demand curves shown in the two parts of figure 3.2. The demand curve labeled D_H (P_{L1}) in part A shows the willingness of consumers to purchase high-quality care at alternative prices *given a particular price of low-quality care:* all points along this particular demand curve for high-quality care correspond to a price of P_{L1} for low-quality care. The demand curve $D_H(P_{L2})$ shows

Figure 3.2 / A Child Care Market with Two Levels of Quality

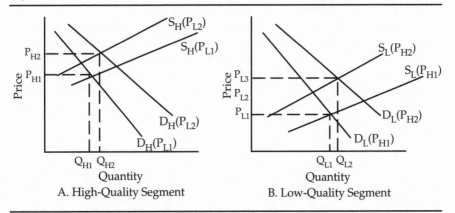

A. High-Quality Segment

B. Low-Quality Segment

Source: Author's configuration.

another demand curve for high-quality care, this one conditional on a price of low-quality care of $P_{L2} > P_{L1}$. This high-quality-care demand curve lies everywhere above the other high-quality-care demand curve because the price of the low-quality alternative is greater, and some consumers switch out of low-quality care into high-quality care. The demand curves for low-quality care shown in part B have similar interpretations, with $P_{H2} > P_{H1}$.

The supply curve in part A labeled $S_H(P_{L1})$ shows how much high-quality child care would be provided at alternative prices for high-quality care, holding the price of low-quality care constant at P_{L1}. The other supply curves have similar interpretations. $S_H(P_{L2})$, for $P_{L2} > P_{L1}$, shows a smaller amount of high-quality care supplied at any given price P_H, because the higher price of low-quality care induces firms to shift toward providing low-quality care. Many more supply and demand curves could be depicted in each panel; only two are presented in order to avoid cluttering the diagram.

Two different candidates for equilibrium are shown in each part of figure 3.2 (and many others could be shown): P_{H1} and P_{H2} for high-quality care, and P_{L1} and P_{L3} for low-quality care. In this case the equilibrium *distribution* of prices is P_{H1} for high-quality care and P_{L1} for low-quality care. At a price of low-quality care of P_{L1}, the quantity of high-quality care demanded equals the quantity supplied at a price of P_{H1}. And at a price of high-quality care of P_{H1}, the quantity of low-quality care demanded equals the quantity supplied at a price of P_{L1}. This is an equilibrium distribution because the quantity demanded equals the quantity supplied in *both* segments of the market.

In contrast, P_{H2} and P_{L2} is not an equilibrium distribution: at a price of low-quality care of P_{L2}, the quantity of high-quality care demanded equals the quantity supplied at a price of P_{H2}, but at the price of P_{H2} the quantity of low-quality care demanded equals the quantity supplied at a price of P_{L3}. Thus, P_{H2} and P_{L2} cannot be an equilibrium distribution because the quantity supplied does not equal the quantity demanded in both segments of the market at these prices. As illustrated, the equilibrium has the price of high-quality care greater than the price of low-quality care, and the quantity of low-quality care demanded greater than the quantity of high-quality care demanded. This configuration is not a prediction of the theory but seems like a plausible outcome.

The final step in the analysis of the market is to generalize beyond two levels of quality. This can be done by adding another diagram for each additional level of quality, but doing so becomes very awkward because each curve in each diagram would depend on the price of all other possible levels of quality. And in reality, quality is continuous—it does not come in discrete steps. In effect, what is needed is a three-dimensional diagram depicting the relationships between price, quantity, and quality. Though feasible, such a diagram would not be easy to work with, so I take a short-cut and use a two-dimensional diagram to depict the equilibrium price-quality distribution. Some examples are shown in figure 3.3.

The curve depicting the relationship between price and quality shown in each of the four parts is to be interpreted as an equilibrium distribution: at each price-quality combination on the curve, the quantity of care supplied at that quality and price equals the quantity demanded at that quality and price. Unlike in figures 3.1 and 3.2, the quantities are not shown in the diagram but must be imagined. The curve shown in part A is deliberately drawn to be wiggly to emphasize the point that there is no reason why the equilibrium distribution should have a particularly simple shape. In fact, the only implication of the theory for the shape of the curve is that it should not be downward-sloping. If consumers were unwilling to pay anything at all for higher-quality care, or if higher-quality care could be supplied at no additional cost to providers, then the curve would be horizontal. In this case there would be no price premium for higher-quality care, but there would also be no reason for higher-quality care to have a price below that of lower-quality care.

An example of an equilibrium price-quality relationship of the shape assumed earlier in this chapter is shown in part B. It is linear and upward-sloping with an intercept of α and a slope of β ($P = \alpha + \beta Q$). It should be clear now that there is no particular reason to assume such a shape, other than the analytic simplicity that it provides.

Part C of figure 3.3 shows an example of how the equilibrium price-quality distribution might change in response to outside forces. The original equilibrium distribution is labeled E_1. Suppose reliable evidence that high-quality child care improves the school readiness of children is widely publicized. Even if no new consumers enter the market, demand shifts

Figure 3.3 / Alternative Equilibrium Price-Quality Distributions in a Child Care Market with Continuous Quality

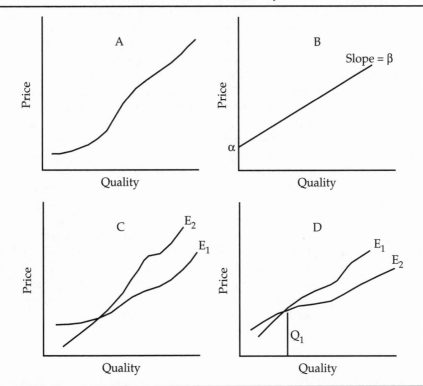

Source: Author's configuration.

away from lower-quality care toward higher-quality care. We might expect the new equilibrium to look something like E_2. In the new equilibrium the price-quality relationship is steeper because of the demand shift away from lower quality and toward higher quality. Referring back to the simpler example in figure 3.2, one can imagine the demand curves for high-quality care shifting up and the demand curves for low-quality care shifting down, resulting in a wider price spread between low- and high-quality care, a higher equilibrium quantity of high-quality care, and a lower equilibrium quantity of low-quality care. As similar forces occur throughout the quality distribution, we get a new equilibrium like that depicted in E_2 in part C of figure 3.3, in which the price premium for higher-quality care has increased. The exact level of quality at which the two curves cross depends on the perception of consumers about the level of quality at which the school readiness benefits become important.

Another example of an outside force that changes the equilibrium is a government subsidy designed to defray the costs of providers that meet a designated quality standard. Let the original equilibrium be depicted in part D of figure 3.3 by the curve labeled E_1, and suppose the designated quality threshold for eligibility for the subsidy is Q_1. A subsidy to providers is equivalent to a reduction in their cost of providing the service. Providers respond to this by increasing the supply of the service. With demand unchanged, this leads to a lower equilibrium price for care that meets or exceeds the quality standard (despite the lower market price, providers will have higher profits than before as a result of the subsidy). Some providers that were previously offering care of quality lower than the threshold Q_1 will now find it worthwhile to improve their quality in order to become eligible for the subsidy. Thus, the supply of lower-quality care will decline. The net effect is a flatter price-quality relationship, as illustrated in curve E_2 in part D. Because the government is picking up some of the additional cost of higher-quality care, consumers can now upgrade to higher quality at a smaller increase in price than in the absence of the subsidy. Referring to figure 3.2 again, imagine the supply curves for high-quality care shifting out and the supply curves for low-quality care shifting in, resulting in a narrower market price spread between low- and high-quality care (but a higher spread to firms, accounting for the subsidy for providing high-quality care), a higher equilibrium quantity of high-quality care, and a lower equilibrium quantity of low-quality care.

CONCLUSIONS

Economic theory provides a powerful organizing tool for thinking about markets and how they are affected by government policy. The models described in this chapter illustrate the basic forces at work in the child care market. They can be elaborated in many ways to analyze specific issues of interest. Some illustrations of how the models can be used to analyze policy issues were given for the case of subsidies. The impact of other policies such as regulations can be analyzed in the context of these models as well (see chapter 9). Economic models also give us a straightforward way to incorporate externalities into the analysis, by allowing for consumer demand for high-quality child care to fail to reflect the total benefits to society and the child from high-quality care.

The next step is to fill in the framework with empirical evidence. All of the analysis in chapters 4 through 9 is based on the models developed here, and these models serve as a guide to specifying the empirical analysis and interpreting the results.

Part II

ANALYSIS OF THE CHILD CARE MARKET

Chapter 4

The Demand for Child Care and the
Labor Supply of Mothers

This chapter describes the results of empirical analyses of consumer behavior in the child care and labor markets. As described in chapter 3, the supply of labor by mothers of young children is closely related to the demand for child care, and it makes sense to analyze them together. I discuss results from empirical estimates of demand for the quantity, quality, and type of child care, and the labor supply of mothers. Most of the results discussed are from my own analyses, but I also compare my results to others in the literature.

The model of consumer behavior developed in chapter 3 provides the conceptual basis for the analysis. The major questions of interest are:

1. How does an increase in the price of child care affect the use of paid child care, the type of child care chosen, the quantity and quality of child care used, and the employment and hours worked of mothers?

2. How does an increase in the mother's wage rate affect these choices?

3. How does an increase in family income from sources other than the mother's earnings affect these choices?

The effects of price, wage, and other income are the main focus of the analysis for two reasons: the economic model developed in chapter 3 makes predictions about their effects, and these are the key variables through which government policy affects consumer behavior. A child care subsidy to consumers can be interpreted as reducing the effective price of child care to consumers, so the effects of the price of child care are of direct interest for policy.

The Earned Income Tax Credit (EITC) might be an alternative to a child care subsidy as a policy to encourage employment. From a consumer's perspective, the EITC is equivalent to a change in the wage rate (and in some cases, nonwage income). Another alternative to a child care subsidy is a tax credit for children, which is equivalent to an increase in nonwage income. So the effects of wages and nonwage income are also of direct interest from a policy perspective.

The analyses presented here are of two types. One examines consumer choices between discrete alternatives, including whether to use paid child care, what type of child care is used, and whether the mother will work. The second examines demand for specific features of child care, such as hours of care used per week, group size, child-staff ratio, and quality (as measured by the Early Childhood Environment Rating Scale), as well as the number of hours worked per week. These are complementary analyses, revealing different facets of consumer behavior. After discussing the data and results, I summarize the implications of the findings for child care policy. The findings reported here play a major role in my proposal for redesigning child care policy.

DATA

Most of the results reported in this chapter were estimated using data from the National Child Care Survey (NCCS) and the Profile of Child Care Settings (PCS). The NCCS collected data by telephone from a stratified random sample of 4,392 households with at least one child under age thirteen in one hundred sites around the United States, between October 1989 and May 1990. The PCS collected data by telephone from a sample of 2,089 day care centers and 583 registered family day care homes in the same one hundred sites as the NCCS, during the same time period. These surveys make it possible to match households to the child care prices they face in the geographic market in which they live and presumably purchase child care. Each of the one hundred sites is a county or group of counties.

I focus on explaining the behavior of households with at least one preschool-age child not yet enrolled in school at the time of the survey. Data on the attributes of care were collected only for the youngest child, so I analyze the quantity, type, and attributes of the youngest child's primary child care arrangement. The sample used in the analysis contains 2,426 households with complete data on the outcomes of interest: type, weekly hours, and attributes of care, and mother's employment and weekly hours worked. The sample includes both married and unmarried mothers. The main drawback of these data is that they do not contain a direct measure of the quality of child care, such as the ECERS. Attributes of child care such as group size, staff-child ratio, and teacher training may influence quality, but they are not direct measures of quality. For this reason, in the latter part of the chapter I use another data source, the Cost, Quality, and Outcomes Study (CQOS), to analyze consumer demand for quality.

I classify child care arrangements into four types: center, family day care, other nonparental care, and parental care. Other nonparental care includes baby-sitters in the child's home, relatives in the child's home or the relative's home, and miscellaneous, little-used types such as self-care. Parental care includes all cases in which either the father or the mother is the primary care provider, regardless of the mother's employment status. I further classify each child care arrangement by whether a payment was made for the arrangement. Finally I classify each household by whether the mother was employed. Allowing for the fact that parental care is unpaid, this yields a fourteen-way classification of each household's child care and employment outcomes by type, payment, and mother's employment status. This approach allows the data to reveal the ways in which employment, payment for child care, and types of child care choices are interrelated without imposing strong assumptions.

This classification scheme does not correspond exactly to the model discussed in chapter 3. That model did not distinguish purchased child care by type or incorporate care by a child's father, and it did not account for mothers who provide care during their working hours. These features were not important for deriving the basic implications of the model, but they are important in practice. In the case of parental care, I do not distinguish which parent provides care because this is not essential for policy analysis. I distinguish between center and family day care because attributes of child care and the employment behavior of mothers differ substantially across these types of care. I combine care by relatives and baby-sitters to avoid adding another type of care (baby-sitters) that is used infrequently. This classification scheme is consistent with the model in chapter 3 but expands the model in ways that are of empirical and policy interest.

Table 4.1 describes the distribution of the sample by type of child care and shows the percentage of families with a working mother and the percentage using paid care within each type. Forty-five percent of households use parental care, and 55 percent use nonparental care as the primary care arrangement of the youngest child. Among households using nonparental care, 39 percent each use center care or other nonparental care, and 22 percent use family day care. The mother is most likely to be employed in families using family day care (92.5 percent), center care (76.4 percent), or other nonparental care (62.4 percent), and least likely to be employed in families using parental care (34.2 percent). Paying for care is most common among families who use family day care (94.5 percent) and centers (84.3 percent) and much less common among those who use other nonparental care (39.5 percent). Family day care is apparently used almost exclusively to care for children while the mother works, while the other types are sometimes used even when the mother does not work, for purposes such as stimulating child development or freeing the mother for non-employment activities.

For households using any form of nonparental care, I estimate a model to explain hours of care per week. And for households using center or family day care, I estimate models of the attributes of the arrangement used, including group size, staff-child ratio, and whether the provider has any training in early childhood education. These models are estimated

Table 4.1 / Employment and Use of Paid Child Care, by Type of Care

Type of Care	Mother Employed	Using Paid Care	Percentage of Total	Percentage of Types 1, 2, and 3
Center	76.4%	84.3%	21.5%	39.1%
Family day care	92.5	94.5	12.1	22.0
Other nonparental	62.4	39.5	21.4	38.9
Parental	34.2	0.0	45.0	—
All	56.4	38.0	100.0	—

Source: Blau and Hagy 1998.
Notes: Other nonparental care includes relatives, baby-sitters, and self-care by the child. The percentage using paid care among users of types 1, 2, or 3 is 69.1.

jointly with the discrete choice model, accounting for the possibility that demand for these attributes depends on the same unobserved factors as the discrete choices.[1] Finally, for employed mothers I estimate a model explaining the number of hours worked per week. The effects of the price of care and the mother's wage rate are allowed to vary depending on the type of care and the payment status and employment status of the mother. Group size is the number of children in the youngest child's primary care arrangement who are cared for in the same group, and the staff-child ratio is the number of teachers and aides assigned to that group divided by group size. Training is a binary indicator of whether the person primarily responsible for caring for the youngest child has been trained in the care and education of young children.

Descriptive statistics for these outcomes are shown in table 4.2 by type of child care. Average group size is highest in centers, much lower in family day care, and lower still in other nonparental care. The mean staff-child ratio varies from about one staff member per five children in centers to about one provider per two children in family day care. Provider training is more than twice as common in centers than in family day care homes. Average weekly hours of care is highest when family day care is used, somewhat lower when centers are used, and substantially lower in other nonparental care. Average hours of work per week of employed mothers are very similar across types of care at thirty-six to thirty-seven hours, except for parental care, where the average is twenty-seven hours per week.

As discussed in chapter 3, the price per hour of child care paid by a family is directly affected by the quality of care it chooses. Hence, the price paid by a family itself is not a suitable explanatory variable in a model intended to explain the family's child care and employment choices. Furthermore, we do not directly observe the price that would have been paid by a family who does not use paid care. An approach that deals with both of these problems is to use the market-level determinants of price, α and β

Table 4.2 / Attributes and Hours of Child Care and Mother's Hours of Work
by Type of Care (Mean and Standard Deviation)

Type of Care	Group Size	Staff-Child Ratio	Provider Has Training[a]	Hours of Care per Week	Mother's Hours of Work per Week[b]
Center	13.2 (7.8)	.21 (.13)	.87 (.33)	31.1 (16.2)	36.8 (10.9)
Family day care home	3.8 (3.1)	.52 (.40)	.40 (.49)	35.5 (13.7)	37.0 (9.4)
Other nonparental care	1.3 (0.9)	.90 (.23)	—	23.7 (18.2)	36.2 (13.3)
Parental care	—	—	—	—	27.7 (16.1)
Sample size[c]	1,247	1,247	719	1,085	1,281

Source: Unpublished results from Blau and Hagy 1998.
[a]Training is not available for other nonparental care.
[b]Only for mothers who are employed.
[c]Sample sizes vary by cell.

in the example from chapter 3 ($P = \alpha + \beta Q$), as the explanatory variables. These parameters are determined in the child care market, as explained in chapter 3, and are not influenced by the behavior of individual families. The PCS did not measure quality using an observational instrument such as ECERS. Instead, the PCS collected extensive data on attributes of the care provided, such as group size, staff-child ratio, teacher training, and program goals and philosophy. These are determinants of quality, but they are not measures of quality. So the best that can be done with this data set is to estimate a price equation that includes the determinants of quality as explanatory variables, rather than quality itself. This approach provides an estimate of the intercept of the price equation (α), but not the quality slope (β), and does so only for centers and registered family day care homes.

I used the PCS data to estimate the parameters of equations explaining the price of care charged by day care centers and family day care homes, as a function of the attributes of the care provided. I estimated separate equations for centers and family day care homes to allow for the possibility that the determinants of price differ in these two sectors. In order to allow for geographic variation in the estimated intercept of the equations, I estimated a different intercept for each of the sites in the sample, while restricting all other parameters to be the same across sites. This restriction was imposed because there were not enough observations per site to allow all parameters to vary by site. After estimating this equation for centers and family day care homes by least squares regression, I used the estimated coefficients to construct a measure of price to include in the demand functions of interest. I used the overall sample means of the explanatory variables in constructing the price measure, so that the only source of variation in the price measure is the site-specific intercept. This procedure can be thought of as providing a "quality-adjusted" measure of price. All households in a particular site are assumed to face the same quality-adjusted price.[2]

This method could not be used for other nonparental care, because the PCS did not include relatives in its sample of providers. The only way to construct a price measure for this type of care was to use data from the NCCS on those households that used this type of care and paid for it to estimate a regression equation like the one already described. The difference is that the explanatory variables included household characteristics rather than provider characteristics. Site-specific intercepts are included in the regression, and the method described earlier is used to construct an estimate of the site-specific average price for this type of care, using only variation in the intercepts.

The other explanatory variables included in the model are the mother's estimated wage rate,[3] her spouse's annual earnings,[4] the age of the youngest child, the number of children by age, whether the mother is married, the number of other adults in the household, the mother's age, race, and education, the spouse's education, the kind of neighborhood in which the family lives (urban, suburban, rural), and the region of the country (South, West, North Central, Northeast). Descriptive statistics on these variables are shown in the appendix to this chapter.

RESULTS

Price Effects

Table 4.3 shows estimates of the effect of the price of child care on the discrete child care and employment choices. A statistical test rejected the hypothesis that the effect of price was the same for employed and non-employed mothers. The estimated price coefficient when the mother is employed is −.30, and .03 when the mother is not employed. This indicates that the demand for child care is much more sensitive to price when the mother is employed than when she is not employed. The price coefficient estimate for non-employed mothers is actually of the wrong sign (we expect a negative sign: demand curves are downward-sloping), but the hypothesis that it equals zero is not rejected at the 5 percent level of statistical significance. Because of the categorical nature of the dependent variable, the magnitude of the price coefficient does not have a simple interpretation. Table 4.3 therefore provides estimates of various elasticities[5] derived from the coefficient estimates and also reports the results of some simulations using the estimates.

The price elasticity of demand for care in day care centers is estimated to be −.24. This means that, for example, a 1 percent increase in the price of

Table 4.3 / Price Effects on Type of Child Care, Use of Paid Care, and Mother's Employment

Type of Care	Price Elasticity	Simulations: Absolute (and Percentage) Changes in the Proportion of Families Caused by Cutting the Price from $1.50 to $0.00 for			
		Centers	Family Day Care	Other Non-Parental Care	All Types of Child Care
Center	−.24	.047 (22.0)	−.013 (−6.1)	−.007 (−3.4)	.026 (11.8)
Family day care	−.34	−.010 (−8.5)	.045 (37.0)	−.004 (−3.2)	.028 (22.6)
Other nonparental care	−.12	−.014 (−6.7)	−.011 (−5.2)	.023 (10.8)	−.003 (−1.6)
Parental care	−.07	−.022 (−4.9)	−.021 (−4.6)	−.011 (−2.5)	−.050 (−11.0)
Pay for care	−.34	.034 (8.7)	.030 (7.9)	.016 (4.2)	.073 (19.3)
Mother works	−.20	.026 (4.6)	.020 (3.5)	.012 (2.2)	.073 (19.3)

Source: Blau and Hagy 1998.

Note: Price coefficients are −.30 (standard error .05) when the mother works and .03 (standard error .023) when she does not work. The elasticities are computed for each family as the percentage change in the use of each type of care resulting from a 1 percent increase in the price of care. The simulations are computed by using the model estimates to calculate the predicted proportion of families who would use each type of child care, first assigning a price of $1.50 to each family, and again assigning a price of $0.00 to each household. The differences in these proportions are shown in the table. See Blau and Hagy (1998) for further details.

care in day care centers, holding prices of other types of care constant, would be expected to result in a .24 percent decrease in the proportion of families using center care. A 10 percent price increase would cause a 2.4 percent decrease in usage, and so forth. The corresponding figures for family day care and other nonparental care are − .34 and − .12. Thus, use of family day care is the most price-sensitive type of care, and other non-parental care is the least price-sensitive. The price elasticity of demand for paid care overall is − .34, indicating that an across-the-board 10 percent increase in the price of all types of paid care would lead to a 3.4 percent reduction in the use of paid child care of all types. The latter figure is especially useful for analysis of the effect of child care subsidies. As shown in table 4.1, many families prefer to use unpaid child care. A child care subsidy would not affect their decision unless it induced them to switch from unpaid to paid care. The − .34 estimate for the price elasticity of use of paid care indicates that families are only moderately sensitive to the price of child care. A subsidy that results in a large cut in the price of child care would have only a modest impact in inducing families to switch to paid child care. Finally I estimate a modest price elasticity of employment of − .20: a 10 percent increase in the price of care would lead to a 2 percent decrease in the employment rate of mothers of young children.[6]

The simulation results shown in table 4.3 provide another way to gauge the magnitude of the estimated price effects. Each column shows the estimated impact of cutting the price of a particular type of care from $1.50 per hour for every household to $0.00 for every household.[7] Cutting the price of each type separately results in increases in the proportion of families who would use the type of care by 0.047 for centers (a 22 percent increase), 0.045 for family day care (a 37 percent increase), and 0.023 for other nonparental care (a 10.8 percent increase). These same price cuts would increase the use of (what would have been) paid child care by 4.2 to 8.7 percent. Cutting all prices to $0.00 jointly (shown in the last column of table 4.3) leads to increases of 11.8 percent in the use of day care centers and 22.6 percent in the use of family day care homes, a decrease of 1.6 percent in the use of other nonparental care, and a decrease of 11.0 percent in the use of parental care. This suggests that in some sense parents feel most "priced out" of center and family day care and would prefer these types over other nonparental care and parental care if all were equally cheap.

Making all child care completely free would lead to only a 19.3 percent increase in the use of (what would have been) paid arrangements, and a 9.5 percent increase in the employment rate of mothers. This suggests that many families strongly prefer care by a relative or parent even when more formal child care is fully subsidized. Child care subsidies may not be a very effective policy for encouraging mothers to work if they fail to induce many mothers to take advantage of them and use formal care. This implication of the estimates is discussed in more detail in chapter 8.[8]

Table 4.4 shows the estimated effects of the price of child care on the other outcomes of interest. With the exception of training, these models are all linear, so the price coefficients are easy to interpret. Consider the price effect on hours of child care demanded per week, allowing it to differ by type of care and the mother's employment status. Five of the six estimates are negative, as predicted by the theory in chapter 3. They indicate that a price increase of $1.00 per hour would cause families in which the mother works and the child is cared for in a day care center to use 5.79 fewer hours of child care per week on average. If the mother does not work and the child is in a center, 3.69 fewer hours of care per week would be used. The estimates for family day care are −2.0 and −10.7 for working and nonworking mothers, respectively, and −5.43 and 0.33 for other nonparental care. Averaging across the six estimates and expressing the result as an elasticity yields a price elasticity of demand for hours of child care of −.21. Thus, on average a 10 percent price increase would cause a 2.1 percent decrease in hours of child care demanded.

We might wonder how a family cuts back hours of child care if the mother is required by her employer to work a fixed number of hours. Some mothers might switch from a full-time to a part-time job, and parents might rearrange their schedules so that the primary child care arrangement is used for fewer hours and secondary arrangements are used for more hours. (Recall that only the primary arrangement is analyzed here.) The results in table 4.4 show that a $1.00 increase in the price of child care causes a decrease of 1.77 hours of work per week for mothers using other nonparental care, while the effects for center and family day care users are positive. This illustrates that cutting back on hours of paid care in response to a price increase does not necessarily lead to cutting back the mother's hours of work by the same amount.

The estimates in table 4.4 indicate that a $1.00 price increase for center care leads to higher-quality care in the form of a decrease in group size of 2.18 for employed mothers and 4.41 for non-employed mothers. The effects of a price increase on staff-child ratios and the use of trained providers are positive for center care, again indicating that a higher price is associated with the use of child care with higher-quality attributes. These results imply that a child care subsidy that *reduces* the price of care would lead to the use of *lower*-quality center care, as measured by group size, staff-child ratio, and provider training. The corresponding effects for family day care are positive for group size and negative for staff-child ratio, the opposite of the results for centers. The training effects for family day care are positive, similar to the results for centers. Thus, the results for family day care do not follow the same pattern except for provider training.

Overall, the results indicate that quantity of child care in centers is substituted for quality when the price falls: a lower price leads to more hours of center care but a lower quality of care. One possibility suggested by this

Table 4.4 / Price Effects on Attributes and Hours of Child Care (Coefficient Estimates and Standard Errors)

	Center Care		Family Day Care		Other Nonparental Care	
	Mother Employed	Mother Not Employed	Mother Employed	Mother Not Employed	Mother Employed	Mother Not Employed
Group size	−2.18 (.39)*	−4.41 (.49*)	2.16 (.43)*	0.62 (.56)	—	—
Staff-child ratio	0.01 (.014)	0.02 (.025)	−0.06 (.03)*	−0.26 (.04)*	—	—
Provider has training	0.26 (.06)*	2.08 (.07)*	0.56 (.06)*	2.2 (.07)*	—	—
Hours of care per week	−5.79 (.89)*	−3.69 (1.27)*	−2.01 (1.26)	−10.7 (1.65)*	−5.43 (1.18)*	0.33 (1.03)
Mother's hours of work per week	1.32 (.82)	—	1.98 (1.16)	—	−1.77 (.93)	—

Source: Blau and Hagy 1998.

Notes: The training coefficients are from binominal logit models. The implied price elasticity of training is .24: a 1 percent increase in price leads to a .24 percent increase in the use of trained providers.

*The hypothesis that the coefficient estimate equals zero can be rejected at the 5 percent level of significance.

pattern is that it is more difficult to provide high-quality care for long hours than for shorter hours. Another possibility is that parents do not place much value on the quality of child care, at least as measured by inputs such as group size, staff-child ratio, and training. The results do not permit a definitive conclusion on this point, but I discuss it further later in the chapter.

WAGE AND INCOME EFFECTS

Table 4.5 presents coefficient estimates, elasticities, and simulation results for the effects of the mother's wage rate and other family income (as measured by the spouse's earnings). A statistical test rejects the hypothesis that wage effects were the same for paid and unpaid care. The wage coefficient for paid care is 1.20, and −.61 for unpaid care. An increase in the mother's wage rate has a relatively strong positive effect on the use of paid care: the estimated wage elasticity of paying for care is .67. The wage elasticities of demand for center and family day care are positive, while the wage elasticities of demand for other nonparental and parental care are negative. And as predicted by economic theory, a higher wage increases the employment rate, with an elasticity of .17. These results indicate that paid child care arrangements in centers and family day care homes are relatively attractive to higher-wage mothers, most likely because such arrangements are more conducive to employment than less formal arrangements. The simulated impact of increasing the mother's wage rate from $8.00 to $15.00 per hour is a 48.6 percent increase in the likelihood of using paid care. This hypothetical wage increase also leads to a 55.5 percent increase in the use of family day care, a 28.9 percent increase in the use of center care, and a 15.4 percent increase in the employment rate.

The results in table 4.5 show that the income elasticity of demand for center care is .10, while the income elasticity of demand for the other types of care is negative. Thus, as family income increases, families tend to switch to center care from the other types. They also increase their use of paid child care, as indicated by the income elasticity of .03. These are small effects, a finding reinforced by the simulation results, which show that doubling the spouse's annual earnings from $20,000 to $40,000 is predicted to increase the proportion of families using center care by only .01 (4.7 percent). These findings indicate that many parents prefer a specific type of child care and that even when income rises substantially, they are reluctant to change to another type of care. The only nontrivial effect of income is on the employment of the mother. The income elasticity of the mother's employment rate is −.18, with a $20,000 increase in the spouse's earnings estimated to cause a 9.5 percent decrease in the mother's employment rate. This result is consistent with the findings of many other studies and indi-

Table 4.5 / Wage and Income Effects on Type of Child Care, Use of Paid Care, and Mother's Employment

| | Elasticity | | Simulations: Absolute (and Percentage) Effects on the Proportion of Families Caused by Increasing | |
| | | | Mother's Wage Rate from $8 to | Spouse's Earnings from $20,000 to |
Type of Care	Wage	Income	$15 per Hour	$40,000 per Year
Center	.44	.10	.058 (28.9)	.010 (4.7)
Family day care	.61	−.09	.064 (55.5)	−.005 (4.4)
Other nonparental	−.05	−.02	−.011 (5.2)	−.003 (1.4)
Parental	−.47	−.02	−.110 (23.5)	−.001 (0.3)
Pay for care	.67	.03	.173 (48.6)	.000 (0.0)
Mother works	.17	−.18	.085 (15.4)	−.054 (9.5)

Source: Blau and Hagy 1998.

Notes: Wage coefficients are 1.20 (standard error .056) when the household pays for care, and −.61 (standard error .062) when the household does not pay for care. The elasticities are computed for each family as the percentage change in the use of each type of care resulting from a 1 percent increase in the wage rate or other family income. The simulations are computed by using the model estimates to calculate the predicted proportion of families who would use each type of child care, first assigning a wage rate of $8 per hour to each mother, and again assigning a wage rate of $15 per hour. The differences in these proportions are shown in the table. The same approach is used for other family income. See Blau and Hagy (1998) for further details.

cates that the mother's nonwork time is a "normal" good—something that families prefer more of to less as income rises.

Table 4.6 shows that a higher wage rate is associated with a larger group size and fewer staff per child in centers. The table also shows that higher-wage mothers who use center care work more hours per week and use more hours of child care. This indicates that the mother's hours of work and child care quality are substitutes: a higher wage rate increases the quantity of labor supplied and decreases the quality of child care demanded in centers. This is another illustration of the quantity-quality substitution described earlier: factors that induce longer hours of work and care also induce lower quality of care, at least in centers. The wage effect on staff-child ratios is also negative for family day care, but the group size effect is negative. Wage effects on the demand for trained providers are negligible for both types of care. The wage effect on hours of care is small and positive for centers, .327, implying that a $1.00 per hour increase in the wage would cause an increase of about twenty minutes per week in child care. The wage effects on hours of care are negative, but of negligible magnitude for the other two types of care shown.

The estimated effects of the spouse's earnings on group size and staff-

Table 4.6 / Wage and Income Effects on Attributes and Hours of Care (Coefficient Estimates and Standard Errors)

	Mother's Wage (Dollars per Hour)			Spouse's
	Center	Family Day Care	Other Nonparental Care	Earnings ($10,000 per Year)
Group size	.156 (.038)*	−.106 (.022)*	—	−.45 (.10)*
Staff-child ratio	−.0036 (.0008)*	−.011 (.001)*	—	.006 (.002)*
Provider is trained	−.003 (.006)	.002 (.005)	—	−.026 (.043)
Hours of care per week	.327 (.093)*	−.093 (.077)	−.141 (.100)	−.39 (.26)
Mother's hours of work per week	.156 (.078)*	.015 (.062)	.033 (.077)	−.75 (.24)*

Source: Blau and Hagy 1998.
Notes: The training coefficients are from binomial logit models. The implied wage elasticity of demand for training is .002: a 1 percent increase in the wage rate causes a .002 percent increase in the use of trained providers. The implied income elasticity of demand for training is −.02: a 1 percent increase in other family income causes a .02 percent decrease in the use of trained providers.
*The hypothesis that the coefficient estimate equals zero can be rejected at the 5 percent level of significance.

child ratios are negative and positive, respectively, as one would expect if parents value these attributes. That is, if quality of care is a "normal" good (people want more of it as their income increases), and low group size and high staff-child ratios are productive inputs, then as income rises we would expect higher demand for these inputs. However, the effects are very small: a $10,000 increase in the spouse's earnings would cause a decrease of .45 in group size and an increase of .006 in staff-child ratio. Income effects on training and hours of care are very small as well.[9]

EFFECTS OF SELECTED OTHER VARIABLES

Table 4.7 summarizes the effects on the discrete child care choices of several of the other explanatory variables. (The complete list of explanatory variables is shown in the appendix.) The effects of these variables are of less interest from a policy perspective than the effects of price, wage, and income, since the latter can be affected by policy while the former cannot. But it is useful to examine their effects in order to put the effects of the economic variables in perspective. For example, the effect of child age is large: use of center care increases by 126.7 percent as children move from age zero to one, by another 59.8 percent from age two to three, and de-

Table 4.7 / Effects of Selected Other Variables on Type of Child Care, Use of Paid Care, and Mother's Employment

| | Simulated Absolute (and Percentage) Effects on the Proportion of Families Caused by Changing | | | | | |
| | Child Age from | | | Marital Status from Single to Married | Race from White to Black | Education from Twelve to Sixteen Years |
Type of Care	Zero to One Year	Two to Three Years	Five to Six Years			
Center	.08 (126.7)	.11 (59.8)	−.12 (30.2)	−.11 (36.4)	.05 (22.0)	.04 (21.2)
Family day care	.01 (9.8)	−.06 (35.0)	−.04 (49.2)	.00 (3.0)	−.04 (30.7)	.02 (15.9)
Other nonparental	.01 (5.7)	.00 (1.3)	.10 (48.9)	−.08 (26.5)	.04 (17.4)	.03 (12.4)
Parental	−.10 (17.8)	−.06 (13.2)	.06 (20.1)	.18 (67.0)	−.04 (9.2)	−.09 (17.9)
Pay for care	.09 (35.4)	.05 (12.2)	−.15 (29.8)	−.07 (14.6)	−.02 (6.2)	.09 (24.4)
Mother works	.10 (22.7)	.02 (4.2)	.06 (.7)	.22 (60.0)	−.01 (2.2)	.15 (28.8)

Source: Blau and Hagy 1998.

Notes: The simulations are computed by using the model estimates to calculate the predicted proportion of families who would use each type of child care, first assigning child age of zero, and again assigning child age of one. The differences in these proportions are shown in the table. The same approach is used for the other variables. See Blau and Hagy (1998) for further details.

creases by 30.2 percent from age five to six. These effects dwarf the effects of the economic variables, highlighting the limited scope for major impacts from policy interventions that affect the economic variables. The use of paid care rises with the age of the child up to age five.

Married mothers are much less likely than single mothers to use center and other nonparental care, and much more likely to use parental care. This is not surprising since two potential parental caregivers are available in a family with a married mother. Being married is also associated with lower use of paid arrangements. Black families are more likely to use center and other nonparental care than white families, and somewhat less likely to pay for care. More-educated mothers use more of all types of child care other than parental care, and are much more likely to use paid arrangements, than are less-educated mothers. The effects of child age, marital status, and education on the employment rate of mothers are all quite large as well.

OTHER RESULTS

One of the drawbacks of the results reported so far in this chapter is that the data do not contain a direct measure of child care quality, such as the ECERS. I analyzed group size, staff-child ratio, and staff training instead, but these are *inputs* to the production of quality, not direct measures of quality. As discussed in chapter 7, with the exception of recent training, these inputs do not appear to have strong effects on quality. Hence, the findings in this chapter that parents have relatively little willingness to pay for smaller group size, higher child-staff ratios, and better trained providers could reflect a correct perception on the part of parents that these inputs are not what really matter for producing high-quality child care. It would be very informative to estimate consumer demand for a direct measure of child care quality such as ECERS. But the available data with measures of quality include day care centers only.[10] Estimates of the demand for quality using centers only could be biased if center users are not representative of all families with young children. Nevertheless, because of the importance of the issue, it is worth examining the demand for quality using such data.

The data source I use is the Cost, Quality, and Outcomes Study (CQOS), which provides the data for much of the analysis in chapters 5, 6, and 7 as well. Parents of children in the rooms in which quality was assessed were asked to complete a short questionnaire. The response rate was relatively low, and 20 percent of the observed rooms had no data on parents and therefore are not used in the analysis. The dependent variable is the logarithm of the room's ECERS-ITERS score. The main variables of interest are the logarithm of the family's income other than the mother's earnings, and the logarithm of the mother's wage rate. In one specification, I use the

Table 4.8 / Regression Results for Demand for Quality Using Log(ECERS-ITERS) Score

Explanatory Variable	Coefficient Estimate (Standard Error)			
Intercept	1.36	(.07)*	1.25	(.10)*
Infant-toddler room	−.23	(.01)*	−.23	(.01)*
Log(nonwage income)	.0011	(.0022)	—	
Log(family income)	—		.023	(.009)*
Log(mother's wage rate)	.060	(.014)*	—	
Mother's age	−.0003	(.0013)	.0002	(.0010)
Mother is not married	.035	(.021)	.039	(.016)*
Other race-ethnicity	.047	(.023)*	.040	(.019)*
Black	−.064	(.024)*	−.060	(.020)*
Hispanic	.075	(.027)*	.064	(.023)*
Mother's education				
High school graduate	−.14	(.05)*	−.12	(.04)*
Some college	−.06	(.05)	−.04	(.04)
Community college degree	−.07	(.05)	−.05	(.04)
Bachelor's degree	−.06	(.05)	−.04	(.04)
Attended graduate school	−.03	(.06)	−.01	(.04)
Graduate degree	.03	(.06)	.05	(.04)
Sample size	1,691		2,332	
R^2	.20		.17	

Source: CQOS data. Unit of observation is a child-family.
*The hypothesis that the coefficient estimate equals zero can be rejected at the 5 percent level of significance.

logarithm of total family income because the response rate to the wage question was low. Using logarithms improves the statistical fit of the model. No measure of price is included, since price and quality are jointly determined by the choice of a center. Regression results are given in table 4.8.

The results show that family income other than the mother's earnings has a small positive association with child care quality. The results show an income elasticity of demand for quality of .0011: even a very large increase in family nonwage income would lead to a tiny increase in the level of quality demanded.[11] The mother's wage rate has a positive effect on quality, with an elasticity of .06: a 10 percent increase in the mother's wage rate would lead to a 0.6 percent increase in the level of quality demanded. These are relatively small effects. Bearing in mind the caveats associated with these estimates, we find that they are consistent with the findings from the NCCS in showing that the income elasticity of demand for quality is small, and wage effects are fairly small as well. In the second column, the effect of family income, which combines the wage and nonwage income effects, is about .023. This is also quite small.

SUMMARY AND CONCLUSIONS

The main findings in this chapter are that a decrease in the price of child care increases the quantity of child care demanded and the employment rate of mothers, but does not increase the quality of care demanded; an increase in the mother's wage rate increases the mother's employment and the demand for center care and paid care, but does not increase the quality of care demanded; and an increase in family income other than the mother's earnings increases the quality of care demanded, but by a very small amount.

Several alternative explanations are consistent with these findings. First, consumers may place little value on quality in child care as defined by developmental psychologists. In studies of parents' attitudes toward child care, quality is always cited as an important feature that parents care about. However, Sonenstein (1991) found that the best predictors of a mother's satisfaction with her child care arrangement were her rating of the convenience of the hours and the location and reliability of the arrangement. The mother's rating of the quality of the arrangement was not associated with her level of satisfaction.

Second, consumers may not have the information they need to distinguish between low-quality and high-quality child care arrangements. Evidence discussed in chapter 8 suggests that parents are not well informed about the quality of the child care they use: they systematically overrate quality (Cryer and Burchinal 1995).

Third, consumers may value quality but believe that group size, staff-child ratio, and provider training are not associated with child care quality. The literature discussed in chapter 7 raises considerable doubt that group size, staff-child ratios, and provider training are major determinants of quality. However, the evidence in table 8 from the CQOS shows that parents appear to be not very willing to pay for improvements in ECERS-ITERS, which is a direct measure of the developmental appropriateness of child care.

Finally, consumers may value quality but cannot find child care of the quality they desire at the market price. They may believe that group size, staff-child ratios, and training are productive inputs but are unable to find an arrangement with the combination of attributes they prefer. That is, the child care market may not be in equilibrium. Market disequilibrium exists if parents are willing to pay the market price for an arrangement with a given set of attributes and cannot find such an arrangement. However, the NCCS and PCS data show that arrangements with a wide range of attributes are present for each type of child care in every site in which these surveys were conducted. For example, an average of about six families per site across the one hundred sites in the NCCS use child care centers, yet the range of observed group size is almost always on the order of six to twenty-five *per site*. It is hard to argue on the basis of these data that supply constraints are a major factor in determining the observed outcomes. Parents may "prefer" high-quality arrangements, but if they are not willing to pay the market price for them, then this is evidence of parents' preferences, not evidence of a supply constraint.

These four explanations are not mutually exclusive and cannot be definitively rejected or supported based on the results of this study. However, evidence from other sources provides some support for the first two explanations, while the data used here cast some doubt on the third and fourth ones.

These results have important implications for how government child care policy affects the demand for child care quality. As discussed in chapter 8, the majority of child care subsidy funds in the United States can be used by families for any type of child care arrangement that is licensed or legally exempt from licensing. In other words, there are few restrictions on the quality of care that can be purchased with such subsidies. The evidence in this chapter implies that subsidies of this type will increase the quantity of child care used but will not lead to increased demand for high-quality care. If government child care subsidies are intended to increase the quality of child care in the United States, they must be substantially redesigned. In chapter 10, I propose a specific reform of child care subsidy policy that addresses this shortcoming of current policy.

Additional research is needed to resolve some of the uncertainty about the demand for child care and the supply of labor by mothers. I believe that my estimate of the price elasticity of employment of mothers of $-.20$ is reliable, but many other studies have produced substantially larger estimates. A careful and thorough sensitivity analysis could narrow the range of plausible estimates. Consumer demand for quality in child care is not well understood, and additional research could make useful contributions to our knowledge.

It is important to go beyond studying consumer demand for inputs to the production of quality in child care (group size, and so on). The demand function for quality itself, as measured by ECERS and related instruments, should be estimated. This will require data containing such measures of quality as well as the price and other key variables from a representative sample of families. Such data are becoming available in the ongoing National Institute of Child Health and Human Development's Study of Early Child Care.[12]

APPENDIX

Table 4.A1 / Means (and Standard Deviations) for the Explanatory Variables Used in Tables 4.3 Through 4.7

Variable	Means (Standard Deviation)
Price of child care (dollars per hour)	
Center care	1.57 (0.36)
Family day care	1.49 (0.31)
Other nonparental care	1.15 (2.44)
Mother's wage rate (dollars per hour)	9.25 (6.03)
Spouse's annual earnings ($10,000)	2.38 (1.83)
Age of the youngest child (years)	
One	0.20 (0.40)
Two	0.19 (0.39)
Three	0.14 (0.35)
Four	0.14 (0.34)
Five	0.07 (0.25)
Six	0.04 (0.19)
Number of children in the household by age	
Zero to two years	0.07 (0.27)
Three to five years	0.29 (0.50)
Six to seventeen years	0.69 (0.98)
Number of adults in the household other than parents	0.15 (0.54)
Mother is married	0.84 (0.36)
Mother's age	30.4 (5.54)
Mother's education (years)	13.3 (2.19)
Spouse's education (years)	13.6 (2.27)
Mother is black	0.10 (0.30)
Mother is Hispanic	0.09 (0.29)
Suburban residence	0.34 (0.47)
Rural residence	0.26 (0.44)
Region	
South	0.32 (0.47)
North Central	0.28 (0.45)
Northeast	0.20 (0.40)
Sample size	2,426

Source: Blau and Hagy 1998.
Notes: Omitted categories are zero for child age, urban residence, and West region.

Chapter 5

The Supply of Child Care

In this chapter, I analyze the determinants of the behavior of child care providers, including the relationship between cost and quality, the supply of quality, and the supply of child care labor. The first part of this empirical analysis is guided by the model developed in chapter 3 of child care providers who charge a fee for their services. This part of the analysis relies exclusively on data from day care centers. Other types of providers, such as family day care homes, baby-sitters, and some relatives, charge fees as well, but the data needed to analyze their behavior in the same depth as centers do not exist. Day care centers are different in important respects from these other types of providers, so it would be unwise to draw general conclusions from this analysis about the behavior of all providers who charge a fee. A large segment of the day care center market is served by nonprofit providers, and an important part of the analysis investigates how the behavior of for-profit and nonprofit centers differs. The main issue of interest is how day care centers choose the quality of care. To address this issue, I analyze the relationship between cost and the quality of care provided, between price and the quality of care, and the implications of these relationships for the quality of care chosen by centers.

The second part of the chapter analyzes the supply of paid labor to the child care market. This part of the analysis includes all sectors of the paid child care market: centers, family day care homes, baby-sitters, and relatives. The focus here is on understanding the relationship between the wage rate offered for child care labor, relative to wages in other occupations, and the number of women who choose to work in the child care sector, as well as the number of hours they work. This part of the analysis deals exclusively with the quantity of care and therefore complements the analysis of quality in the first part of the chapter. The goal of both parts of the analysis in this chapter is to provide a basis for policy analysis: If government child care subsidies reduce the cost of providing child care or raise the price received by providers, by how much will the quantity and quality of child care increase in response?

COST, PRICE, AND QUALITY IN DAY CARE CENTERS

Throughout this chapter, the term "quality" is used to denote the developmental appropriateness of child care, as measured by the Early Childhood Environment Rating Scale and its infant-toddler counterpart (ECERS and ITERS), described in chapter 2. A day care center chooses the quality of the service it provides by choosing how many teachers of different levels of skill to employ, the size of the groups in which care is provided, the amounts of other inputs such as materials, books, and so forth used in providing care, and an overall program philosophy or curriculum.

Cost and Quality

Two factors interact to determine the relationship between the cost of child care and the quality of care: the prices of teacher labor of different levels of skill, and the "technology" of producing quality.[1] The price of labor of a given level of skill is the compensation the provider must pay in order to obtain the services of a worker with the specified level of skill. Skill refers to the worker's ability to provide developmentally appropriate child care and can be measured by education, training, child care experience, tenure with the provider, job title, and other characteristics. For example, if a firm must pay compensation in salary and benefits of $20.00 per hour to induce a woman with a bachelor's degree in early childhood education and ten years of child care experience to work as a lead teacher, then the price of labor with this particular level of skill is $20.00 per hour. If it takes $10.00 per hour to induce a high school graduate with a child development associate (CDA) credential and ten years of child care experience to be a lead teacher, then the price of labor with this level of skill is $10.00 per hour.

Both absolute and relative prices of labor are important to a center's decision about the quality of care and the mix of skill levels it uses to produce a given level of quality. If the price of labor of all skill levels increases as a result of general wage inflation, then the cost of providing care of any quality will rise. If there is no compensating increase in the provider's revenue, then the provider will be forced to reduce the level of quality offered. On the other hand, if the price of the more-skilled type of labor in the example just given rises while the price of the less-skilled type decreases, the provider may or may not change the quality of care offered but will clearly have an incentive to substitute less-skilled labor for more-skilled labor even if quality remains unchanged. The amount of such substitution depends on the second factor cited earlier: the technology of producing quality. Suppose that in response to a change in the relative wage by skill level a provider leaves quality unchanged but decides to replace some high-skilled labor with some low-skilled labor. The amount of the less-skilled type of labor required to replace a unit of the highest-skilled labor type without reducing quality is a measure of the technology of producing quality.

The model of provider behavior developed in chapter 3 assumes that providers will want to produce child care of the desired quality at the lowest possible cost. If not, the provider would be sacrificing profits or quality or both by producing at unnecessarily high cost. If providers choose group size and the amounts of the different types of labor to minimize the cost of providing child care of the desired level of quality, given the labor prices and technology they face, the relationship between cost and quality can be characterized by a *cost function*. The dependent variable in the cost function is the total cost of producing a given quantity of child care of a given level of quality. The independent variables are the quantity and quality of care; the prices of labor of different skill levels; group size; other characteristics of the provider that might affect cost, such as nonprofit status and years in business; and characteristics of the children and families served. The cost function gives the relationship between cost and quality in child care. If you specify the quality and quantity of care that you would like to offer, and the labor prices and other independent variables, then the cost function shows you the total cost of providing the care. Later in the chapter, I specify and estimate a particular form of this function.

Price and Quality

The price per hour of care that a provider can charge depends on the quality of care offered. Child care markets are local, and the price function is market-specific: the relationship between price and quality need not be the same in each market. The example used in chapter 3 was linear $(P = \alpha + \beta Q)$ for purposes of exposition. However, economic theory does not imply that it must be linear, so the form of the price function must be determined empirically.

Choice of Quality

Given the cost function and the price function in its local market, a provider chooses the quality of care to maximize its utility, where the utility of the provider depends on profit or quality or both. I estimate the relative weight placed by providers on quality versus profit in their utility function, allowing it to differ for nonprofit and for-profit providers. As noted in chapter 3, this weight can range from zero (no weight placed on quality—a profit-maximizing provider) to one (no weight placed on profit—a quality-maximizing provider). With estimates of the parameters of the cost function, the price function, and the relative weight on quality, it is then possible to derive the *quality supply function:* the relationship between price and the level of quality offered by providers. This function characterizes how providers respond to changes in market conditions and can be used to analyze how the quality of care they provide would be affected by child care subsidies.

DATA

The Cost, Quality, and Outcomes Study (CQOS) data are used to estimate the cost function, price function, and relative weight on quality. Some aspects of this survey were described in chapters 2 and 4, so here I discuss only the new variables not yet described. The CQOS sample consists of about 400 centers evenly divided among four states (California, Colorado, Connecticut, and North Carolina), and between for-profits and nonprofits within each state. I use here the subsample of 266 centers that employed all three types of labor in the staff classification scheme described later.[2] The data were collected in 1993 and include directly observed measures of quality (ECERS-ITERS) in up to two randomly selected rooms per center; direct observations of group size and staff in the selected rooms; rosters of all rooms and staff in the center with extensive data on each room and staff member; thorough information on cost and fees; and data from questionnaires distributed to parents and staff in the observed rooms. (For further details on the CQOS, see Helburn 1995.)

Total cost is measured as the sum of annual wage, salary, and fringe benefit expenditure, staff education costs, subcontracting costs, food costs, other operating expenses, the estimated replacement value of in-kind donations (food, volunteer services, and supplies), overhead, insurance, and occupancy costs (rent or mortgage, utilities, repair and maintenance). For centers that use donated space, the annual rental value of the space is calculated and treated as an occupancy cost.[3] For centers that receive financial help with rent, the discount they receive on rent is added to their occupancy costs. Annual cost is divided by fifty-two to obtain the measure of weekly total cost that is used in the analysis.

The center director provided information on the total number of children enrolled in the center by age, average hours per child by age, and the number of rooms by age. As shown in table 5.1, average weekly cost per child is $89 overall, and slightly higher in nonprofit centers than in for-profit centers. Average total cost per unit of quality is lower in nonprofit centers, at $1,425, than in for-profit centers at $1,560, but average cost per child per unit of quality is virtually identical in for-profits and nonprofits, at $22.60. The interpretation of this figure is that increasing the ECERS-ITERS score by one unit (for example, from 4 to 5) would increase cost by $22.60 per child per week.

The center director provided a roster of all workers in the center, includ-

Table 5.1 / Sample Means (and Standard Deviations)

	All		For-Profit		Nonprofit	
Total weekly cost	5,920	(3700)	6,010	(3,079)	5,824	(4,264)
Enrollment	75	(47)	81	(49)	68	(44)
Weekly hours of care	2,887	(1,884)	3,022	(1,767)	2,745	(1,994)
Total weekly cost per child	89	(41)	88	(42)	91	(40)
Quality of care (ECERS-ITERS)	4.1	(0.9)	3.9	(0.9)	4.2	(0.9)
California	4.5	(0.9)	4.3	(0.8)	4.6	(0.9)
Colorado	4.1	(0.8)	4.0	(0.7)	4.3	(0.8)
Connecticut	4.2	(1.0)	4.3	(1.0)	4.0	(1.0)
North Carolina	3.5	(0.9)	3.0	(0.7)	4.0	(0.9)
Total weekly cost/ quality	1,494	(900)	1,560	(770)	1,425	(1,017)
Total weekly cost per child/quality	22.6	(10.8)	22.5	(9.9)	22.6	(11.6)
Average staff compensation per hour by education						
Twelve years or less	6.86	(2.02)	6.52	(1.68)	7.22	(2.29)
Thirteen to fifteen years	7.75	(2.80)	7.43	(3.11)	8.10	(2.38)
Sixteen years or more	9.71	(4.24)	8.90	(4.10)	10.55	(4.23)
Average group size	14.6	(6.5)	14.4	(6.9)	14.8	(6.1)
Annual family income ($1,000)	53	(24)	60	(24)	45	(23)
Proportion of children with married parents	.71	(.24)	.77	(.19)	65	(.28)
Proportion of children with college graduate parent	.45	(.26)	.51	(.25)	.39	(.26)
For-profit	.51	(.50)	1.00	(0)	0	(0)
Percentage of children who are white	71	(29)	79	(22)	63	(33)
Meets higher standards[a]	.06	(.25)	0	(0)	.13	(.34)
Over half of revenue from subsidies	.09	(.28)	.03	(.17)	.15	(.35)
Church-sponsored	.22	(.42)	0	(0)	.45	(.50)
Center age (years)	13.1	(12.5)	9.8	(8.3)	16.7	(15.1)
Proportion of infant-toddler rooms	.33	(.26)	.39	(.24)	.27	(.28)

Table 5.1 / *Continued*

	All		For-Profit		Nonprofit	
Proportion of preschooler						
rooms	.48	(.25)	.42	(.22)	.55	(.27)
State						
California	.22	(.42)	.21	(.41)	.24	(.43)
Colorado	.28	(.45)	.29	(.45)	.28	(.45)
Connecticut	.27	(.45)	.30	(.46)	.24	(.43)
North Carolina	.23	(.42)	.21	(.41)	.25	(.43)
Average hourly fee	2.10	(.83)	2.26	(.75)	1.94	(.87)
Number of centers	266		136		130	

Source: Calculations based on data from the Cost, Quality, and Outcomes Study.
ᵃThis group includes Head Start programs, centers where 20 percent or more of the enrollment constitutes special needs children, special preschool programs sponsored by the state or federal department of education, and other special programs in Connecticut and California.

ing data on the hourly wage or annual salary, hours of work per week, years of experience, tenure at the center, training, age, race, gender, the age group of children served, and the worker's job title. After considerable experimentation, I classified staff into three skill categories by years of formal education: no college attendance, some college, and college graduate. Table 5.1 shows average hourly compensation by staff type. Compensation consists of average hourly earnings plus estimated average fringe benefits per hour.[4] Nonprofit centers pay substantially higher wages than for-profits at all levels of education. Compensation rises with education at a faster rate in nonprofits than in for-profits, but even in the nonprofit sector the monetary returns to education are smaller than in other jobs held by women, as noted in chapter 2.

Group size is derived from a roster of all the rooms in the center that lists the number of children enrolled in each room and their age group. Also available are alternative measures based on the number of children present in each room on the day of the interview and on measures of group size recorded during the morning observation period for the two rooms. The results of the analysis using these alternative measures were similar to the results based on enrollment. Average enrolled group size is 14.4 in for-profit centers, and 14.8 in nonprofits.

Table 5.1 shows descriptive statistics on three family characteristics of the enrolled children that are included in the cost function model: family income, marital status, and the percentage of families in which at least one parent has graduated from college. These were collected in a survey instrument distributed to the parents of children in the observed rooms. Table 5.1 also describes the center characteristics included in the cost function: the state in which the center is located; whether the center is for-profit or nonprofit; whether the center receives public money tied to meeting higher than normal standards; whether the center receives more than half its revenue from public sources; whether the center is church-sponsored; the center's age; and the percentage of children enrolled in the center who are white.

RESULTS

Cost Function

The cost function is specified as log-linear: the logarithm of cost is a linear function of the explanatory variables. This specification resulted in the most sensible estimates. Table 5.2 presents the cost function parameters, estimated by ordinary least squares regression.

The main finding in table 5.2 is that quality is positively related to cost, with a coefficient estimate of .056 (significantly different from zero at the 5 percent level). The interpretation of this estimate is that a one-unit increase in quality (for example, a change in the ECERS score from 3 to 4, equal to about a one-standard-deviation increase) would raise cost by 5.6 percent. This is a small effect, and it suggests that with the current structure of teacher wages, it is not very costly to raise the quality of child care in centers. The coefficient estimate on the for-profit indicator variable is − .053, suggesting that for-profits have lower cost. But the hypothesis that this coefficient is zero cannot be rejected at the 5 percent level of significance, so there is no strong evidence that costs differ between for-profit and nonprofit centers. In a specification not shown here that included an interaction between profit status and quality, the coefficient on the interaction term was small and insignificantly different from zero. This indicates that the *marginal* cost of improving quality is also similar for nonprofits and for-profits.

Cost is positively related to the wages of all three teacher types, with the wage rate of the least educated workers showing the biggest impact. Labor is by far the biggest cost of operating a day care center, so it makes sense that paying higher wages would result in higher total cost for a given quality of care. Cost is on average similar in Colorado and California (the omitted category), higher in Connecticut, and lower in North Carolina. Cost is higher for older centers, centers that voluntarily meet higher-than-required standards, centers that serve a higher proportion of infants and toddlers, and centers serving children of well-educated parents. Cost is lower for church-affiliated centers.

Price Function

Experimentation with the price function indicated that the best-fitting functional form has the logarithm of price as the dependent variable, and the

Table 5.2 / Log Weekly Cost Function Coefficient Estimates (Standard Error)

Quality (Q)	.056	(.023)*
For-profit	−.053	(.055)
Teacher wage, by education level		
Twelve years or less	.027	(.014)
Thirteen to fifteen years	.019	(.009)
Sixteen years or more	.010	(.005)*
Annual hours of care (1,000) (O)	.0085	(.0007)*
O^2 (10,000)	−.144	(.020)*
Group size (G)	.0009	(.0094)
G^2 (100)	−.028	(.044)
O × G	−.28	(.22)
Location[a]		
Colorado	.00	(.07)
Connecticut	.11	(.06)
North Carolina	−.19	(.07)*
Percentage of children who are white	.0005	(.0008)
Over 50 percent of revenue from subsidies	.018	(.084)
Years in operation	.0026	(.0017)
Church-affiliated	−.17	(.06)*
Meets higher standards	.29	(.10)*
Proportion of children with at least one college graduate parent	.22	(.10)*
Parent income	−.0006	(.0012)
Proportion of children with married parents	.039	(.111)
Proportion of infant-toddler rooms	.29	(.11)*
Proportion of preschooler rooms	−.12	(.11)
Intercept	6.72	(.21)*
R^2 (sample size)	.77	(266)

Source: Calculations based on data from the Cost, Quality, and Outcomes Study.
[a]The omitted location category is California.
*The hypothesis that the coefficient estimate equals zero can be rejected at the 5 percent level of significance.

logarithm of quality as the main explanatory variable of interest. The only other explanatory variable included is the proportion of infants and toddlers among the center's clientele. I experimented with alternative market definitions, including zip code, town, and state. Regression estimates of the quality coefficients from state-specific estimates of the price function are presented in table 5.3. A statistical test indicated that the price functions are significantly different across states, but that there are no significant differences within states. This does not mean that each state is a single child care market, but rather that the local markets within states are similar to each other in terms of the price-quality relationship.

The results indicate that the market rewards higher-quality care with a significantly higher price in three of the four states, with elasticities of .40

Table 5.3 / Log Hourly Price Function Coefficient Estimates (Standard Error)

	California		Colorado		Connecticut		North Carolina	
Intercept	.15	(.24)	.07	(.16)	.63	(.15)*	.12	(.12)
Proportion of infants and toddlers	.09	(.14)	.53	(.10)*	.31	(.09)*	.14	(.10)
Log quality	.40	(.16)*	.32	(.11)*	.22	(.10)*	.13	(.08)
R^2 (sample size)	.06	(97)	.24	(98)	.13	(99)	.03	(94)

Source: Calculations based on data from the Cost, Quality, and Outcomes Study.
*The hypothesis that the coefficient estimate equals zero can be rejected at the 5 percent level of significance.

in California, .32 in Colorado, .22 in Connecticut, and .13 in North Carolina. An elasticity of .40 means that a 10 percent increase in the quality of care is associated with a 4 percent higher price. The price-quality relationship is upward-sloping in all states, as depicted in figure 3.3. Price is higher in Colorado and Connecticut for providers that care for larger proportions of the youngest children. These results suggest that consumers in California and Colorado are willing to pay more for an improvement in quality than consumers in Connecticut and North Carolina. Why this should be so is not obvious—these results document the relationship but do not explain it. In a more detailed exploration of the price-quality relationship, chapter 6 examines alternative explanations for these differences.

The Supply of Quality

The final step in this part of the analysis is to estimate the relative weight on quality in the preferences of for-profit and nonprofit day care centers. The statistical method I used to do this is somewhat complicated, so I do not provide the details here (see Blau and Mocan 2000, for the details).

The intuition behind the method is illustrated in figure 5.1. The cost function estimates in table 5.2 are used to derive the *marginal cost* function facing day care centers. This function shows the additional cost incurred as a result of increasing the quality of care. The price equation estimates in table 5.3 are used to derive the *marginal revenue* function facing day care centers. This shows the additional revenue gained by increasing the quality of care. The marginal cost and marginal revenue functions are different for each provider, depending on the state in which the provider is located and its other characteristics that enter the cost and revenue functions. The average marginal cost and marginal revenue functions facing the for-profit and nonprofit firms in the CQOS sample are shown in the upper and lower parts of the figure, respectively. Basic economic principles imply that a profit-maximizing provider would choose to provide the level of quality at which marginal revenue equals marginal cost, labeled Q* in the figure. Pro-

Figure 5.1 / Estimated Average Marginal Cost and Marginal Revenue

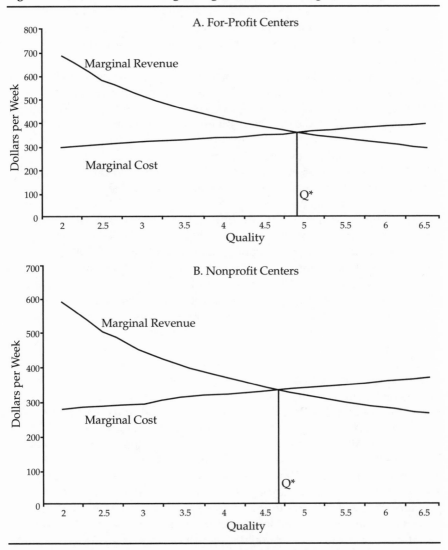

Source: Calculations based on data from the Cost, Quality, and Outcomes Study.

viding quality lower than Q* means forgoing some potential profit, and providing quality in excess of Q* means sacrificing some profit.

The basic idea of the approach to estimating the relative weight on quality is to compare each center's actual level of quality to its profit-maximizing level of quality, Q*, in order to infer its preferences. A center that chooses quality greater than Q* is sacrificing some profit in order to raise quality and therefore must care about quality for its own sake. The magnitude of the gap between actual Q and Q* is used to infer the relative weight on quality in the provider's utility function. Averaging over providers gives the estimate of the relative weight. If most providers choose Q close to Q*, then we will infer that on average most providers are profit-maximizers.

The estimation results indicate that the relative weight on quality is approximately zero for both for-profit and nonprofit centers. This is not a surprising finding for the for-profit centers: they are in business to make a profit and presumably care about quality only insofar as it affects their profit. As indicated in table 5.1, average quality in the for-profit sector is 3.9, while the profit-maximizing quality in figure 5.1 for for-profits is close to 5. This indicates that for-profits could increase their profit by *increasing* quality, so there is no evidence from the analysis that they put any weight at all on quality for its own sake.

The finding that nonprofits also put no weight on quality is surprising, but it is very robust: I estimated many different versions of the model, and this result always appeared. Average nonprofit quality, according to table 5.1, is 4.2, and the profit-maximizing level of quality for nonprofits in figure 5.1 is about 4.5, so the evidence provides no indication that nonprofits are producing quality in excess of the profit-maximizing level.

Having estimated the cost function, the price function, and the relative weight on quality, we can now calculate the supply function of quality, using the following procedure (for details, see Blau and Mocan 2000). As noted earlier, the price function used here has the form $Log(P) = \alpha + \beta log(Q)$. First, all centers are assigned the same arbitrary value of α. Each center's optimal choice of quality to maximize its profit is computed under the assumption that the center faces this arbitrary value of α. The resulting level of quality is averaged over centers. The process is repeated several times for different values of α. This can be thought of as measuring how a center would change the level of quality it offers if there were a change in the intercept of the price-quality relationship in its market. It can also be interpreted as measuring the effect of a subsidy per hour of care provided that can be used for care of any quality. This somewhat indirect procedure is required to estimate the effect of price on the supply of quality because we have to account for the fact that a center's choice of quality affects the price it can charge.

The simulated quality supply function is shown in the upper panel of table 5.4 separately for for-profits and nonprofits. The first column shows the value of P that corresponds to the underlying arbitrary value of α used in the simulation when the price function is evaluated at an arbitrary level of Q (in this case, the sample mean of Q). The values of α were chosen to yield values of P varying between $1.00 and $3.00 per hour. The supply functions show that a higher price induces centers to provide higher-quality care. A summary indicator of the magnitude of the quality increase in

Table 5.4 / The Supply Function of Quality

A. Price Simulations		
Price	For-Profit	Nonprofit
$1.00	$2.62	$2.96
1.22	3.02	3.19
1.44	3.49	3.61
1.67	3.98	3.84
1.89	4.42	4.27
2.11	4.81	4.64
2.33	5.08	4.88
2.56	5.29	5.09
2.78	5.48	5.41
3.00	5.65	5.54
Elasticity	0.66	0.48

B. Wage Simulations		
Wage	For-Profit	Nonprofit
$5.00	$5.65	$5.70
7.00	5.41	5.46
9.00	5.14	5.04
11.00	4.83	4.67
13.00	4.45	4.43
15.00	4.04	4.08
17.00	3.62	3.71
19.00	3.31	3.31
21.00	2.98	3.03
23.00	2.69	2.74
Elasticity	-0.80	-0.77

Source: Cost, Quality, and Outcomes Study.
Notes: The ECERS-ITERS quality scale has a minimum value of 1 and a maximum value of 7. These bounds were imposed when solving for the optimal level of quality. The wage simulations vary the wages of all three teacher types jointly. The wage rates shown in the table are for the lowest education group: high school graduate or less. The wages of college attendees in the simulations are two dollars more than for the lowest group, and the wage rate for college graduates is four dollars more. The elasticities are the average arc elasticities from one simulated value to the next, averaged over the simulations.

response to an increase in price is the price elasticity of supply: the percentage increase in quality caused by a 1 percent increase in price. As shown in the last row of the upper panel of the table, the average price elasticity is .66 among for-profits, and .48 among nonprofits. These figures indicate that an increase in the intercept of the price function that results in a 10 percent increase in price would cause for-profit and nonprofit providers to raise quality by 6.6 percent and 4.8 percent, respectively. These moderately large elasticities result from the fact that cost is estimated to increase only modestly with increases in quality, while the market price can be increased fairly substantially as quality increases.

From a policy perspective, the simulation results can be interpreted as the effects that would result from increased demand for child care generated by child care subsidies to consumers. Consumer subsidies such as the Dependent Care Tax Credit (DCTC) and the Child Care and Development Fund (CCDF) (described in chapter 8) are not targeted specifically toward high-quality child care. Nevertheless, they cause an increase in the demand for child care, which causes the intercept of the price-quality function to rise: child care of all quality levels becomes relatively more scarce as a result of increased demand. According to the results in table 5.4, this would cause an increase in the supply of higher-quality child care.[5] Thus, we would predict that the major expansion of child care subsidies as part of the welfare reform of 1996 would lead to an improvement in the quality of care. However, one major caveat to this conclusion is that the analysis here applies only to centers, while most child care subsidies can be used for home-based arrangements as well. To the extent that consumers prefer home-based arrangements, the impact of subsidies on quality in centers would be dampened. And unfortunately, we have no data with which to analyze quality supply in home-based child care arrangements. The results from this analysis are used in chapter 8 to infer the effects of current child care policy on the quality of child care, and in chapter 10 to guide the formulation of a new policy proposal.

Since the major cost of child care is labor, another policy of interest is a wage subsidy for child care labor. The lower panel of table 5.4 shows the results of quality supply simulations in which wage rates of the three types of child care labor are set at alternative values. Quality supply appears to be fairly sensitive to the wage rate, with average elasticities of $-.77$ to $-.80$. Thus, wage subsidies that reduce the cost to centers of hiring teachers could be another method of inducing an increase in the supply of quality in child care.

THE SUPPLY OF CHILD CARE LABOR

In this section, I address the other main issue on the supply side of the market, the determinants of the *quantity* of child care supplied. The analysis here uses the supply of child care labor as a proxy for the supply of child care, because data on the supply of child care are unavailable. Child care is a very labor-intensive activity, and the technology of providing child care is unlikely to have changed much over time, so trends in the supply of child care labor should be a good proxy for trends in the supply of child care. Thus, while we cannot determine with any certainty how much child care is supplied in a given year based on the supply of child care labor in that year, we can be reasonably confident that trends in child care labor supply will closely track trends in child care supply.[6]

The analysis is based on the following simple conceptual framework. I assume that during a given period of time a woman can engage in one of the following three activities: working for pay in the "child care sector"; working for pay in another sector of the labor force ("other sector"); and not working for pay (the "home sector"). She chooses the option that gives her the highest level of satisfaction, and in the first two sectors she also chooses how many hours to spend working at the activity per time period, with the remaining time spent in non-employment activities (housework, caring for her own children, leisure, and so on). In the home sector all her time is spent in non-employment activities. The satisfaction she derives from her activities in a particular sector depends on how much income she earns per hour in the sector, and on how much direct satisfaction she gets from working in the sector. The first factor can be quantified by the hourly wage rates available to her in the two working sectors, given her skills and abilities.[7] The second factor cannot be directly measured, so observable factors that might be associated with satisfaction are included in the analysis. There are no doubt other unobservable determinants of the direct satisfaction (or dissatisfaction) from engaging in each activity, and these by definition are captured by the statistical disturbances in the econometric model.

The statistical model based on this framework is a multinomial logit model of women's choices among the three sectors and a regression model of hours of work per week for those employed in child care. The key explanatory variables of interest in both models are wage rates. The coefficient estimate on the child care wage rate can be used to measure the supply function of child care labor: the amount by which the quantity of child care labor supplied increases as a result of an increase in the child care wage relative to the wage in other employment.

There are two obstacles to estimation of these models. First, we observe the wage rate in the sector a woman actually chose, but we do not observe the wage rate a woman could have earned in another sector. To estimate the choice-of-activity model, we need to know wages rates in both of the employment sectors for all women, including women who chose not to be employed in either sector. That is, we need to know what each woman could have earned in each sector in order to infer how sensitive their decisions are to changes in wages. A standard approach to this problem in labor economics would be to specify and estimate equations for the wage rate in each sector and to use these equations to predict the wage rate in each sector for each woman, regardless of the sector she actually chose.

The second problem applies to the wage equations and the child care hours equation. The women who chose to become child care workers are most likely not randomly selected from the population of all women but rather have unobserved characteristics that influenced their choice. If these same unobserved characteristics also affect the wage rate that a woman could earn as a child care worker and her choice of hours of work in child care, then the sample available to estimate the child care hours and wage equations is self-selected, and the resulting parameter estimates will be biased. Here I use a common solution to this problem: a statistical "selectivity correction" that purges the selectivity bias. (For the origin of this approach, see Heckman 1979, and for an application in the context of child care supply, see Blau 1992, 1993.)

The data used to estimate the model are from the Current Population Survey (CPS) for the years 1977 to 1998. These data were used in chapter 2 to document trends in the child care labor market. Here I use them to estimate the models described earlier for the choice of sector, wages, and hours worked by child care workers. As noted already, in order to understand how the supply of child care responds to economic incentives, it is essential to measure the total supply of child care, not just the supply of a particular form, such as day care centers. The CPS provides data on the occupational choices, wages, hours worked, and other characteristics of a random sample of individuals. The detailed occupational codes provided in the CPS make it possible to identify child care workers. It is also very useful to have data that are comparable over a long time period and thus allow us to detect changes in supply behavior over time.

Selected results from the model are presented in table 5.5. The wage rate enters in logarithmic form because this provided the best fit to the data. The estimated coefficient on the log of the child care wage in the choice of activity model, .75, is significantly different from zero at the 5 percent level. The implied elasticity is .73: a 10 percent increase in the child care wage rate, holding constant the wage rate in the other sector, would increase the number of women who choose to be child care workers by 7.3 percent. The estimated coefficient on the log of the child care wage in the log hours model is .42, also significantly different from zero, and this is a direct estimate of the elasticity of supply of hours worked in the child care sector with respect to the child care wage. The total elasticity of supply of child care labor is the sum of the two elasticities; this model yields an estimate of 1.15.[8] Thus, a 10 percent increase in the child care wage rate, holding constant the wage rate in alternative occupations, would increase the total number of child care hours worked by 11.5 percent, accounting for both new entrants to the sector and increased hours supplied by workers already in the child care sector.

Is a supply elasticity of 1.15 large or small? Child care demand has increased substantially, and this would be expected to drive up the wages of child care workers. To gauge the implications of the estimated supply elasticity, I use it to compute the amount by which we would expect child care wages to rise as a result of the increased demand for child care. This can

Table 5.5 / Selected Estimates of the Supply of Child Care Labor

	Choice of Sector Model	Log(Weekly Hours) Model	Total Elasticity
Coefficient estimate on log(child care wage)	.75 (.13)*	.42 (.13)*	—
Implied elasticity	.73	.42	1.15

Source: Current Population Survey, 1977 to 1998.
Notes: The other explanatory variables included in the models are race, age, education, urban location, family size, marital status, number of children, and interactions among state dummies and dummies for four time periods: 1977 to 1981, 1982 to 1987, 1988 to 1993, and 1994 to 1997. The choice of sector model is estimated by multinomial logit, with predicted wages generated from selectivity-corrected wage equations. The log(weekly hours) model is estimated by instrumental variables, treating the log wage as endogenous, with a correction for self-selection into the child care sector. The identifying variables in the first-stage log wage equation and in the selectivity correction equation are interactions among state dummies and a more finely disaggregated set of time period dummies. Additional results from these models are available from the author. Standard errors are in parentheses.
*The hypothesis that the coefficient estimate equals zero can be rejected at the 5 percent level of significance.

then be compared to the actual increase in child care wages to determine whether the supply elasticity accounts for the increased wages, or whether other factors must have changed as well.

This approach is illustrated in figure 5.2. Demand for child care labor increased, represented in the figure by a shift in the demand curve to the right from D_1 to D_2. We predict that this would cause the child care wage rate to increase from W_1 to W_3 if supply was unchanged. If the actual wage change was of this magnitude, then we infer that the supply elasticity is large in a sense: we can "explain" the entire wage increase by the slope of the supply curve, as measured by the elasticity, without resorting to other explanations. If the observed wage increase is smaller than the predicted increase—for example, only to W_2 in the figure—then we infer that something else must have changed. This is illustrated in the figure by a shift in the supply curve of child care labor to the right from S_1 to S_2. Such a shift might occur if, for example, a large influx of immigrants sought employment in the child care sector.

Child care wages increased by about 8 percent in real terms from 1983 to 1998.[9] As a rough proxy for growth in the demand for child care, I use growth in the labor force participation rate of mothers of preschool-age children, which increased by 24 percent (from 58 percent to 70 percent) from 1983 to 1998. An estimate of the elasticity of demand for child care labor is also needed. The price elasticity of demand for paid child care of −.34 reported in chapter 4, together with a labor cost share of .70 in day care centers (Helburn 1995), implies an elasticity of demand for child care labor of −.238 = −.34 × .70.[10] Given the supply elasticity of 1.15, we predict

Figure 5.2 / The Market for Child Care Labor

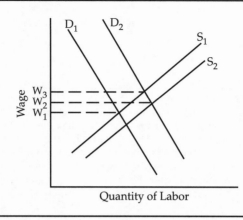

Quantity of Labor

Source: Author's configuration.

that a 24 percent increase in the demand for child care would have caused the child care wage rate to rise by 17 percent.[11] The actual increase in the average child care wage rate was only 8 percent, so the model overpredicts the wage increase by about a factor of two. Thus, in a sense, a supply elasticity of 1.15 is not very large: together with the demand elasticity of −.238, it implies that child care wages ought to increase substantially in response to an increase in demand for child care; specifically, by 17 percent (72 percent of the 24 percent increase in demand).

The actual wage increase (8 percent) was only one-third the size of the 24 percent demand increase, so some other factors that affect child care labor supply must account for why the child care wage rate increased by as little as it did; the supply elasticity alone cannot explain it. I can only speculate about what these factors are. One possibility is that the supply of child care workers increased (the supply curve shifted to the right) as a result of an increase in the immigration of low-skilled women for whom child care is a relatively attractive employment option. But I have no evidence to support this speculation. Another possibility is that day care centers use less labor per child than home-based arrangements, so the increase over time in the share of child care provided in centers could help explain why child care wages have not grown as much as expected in response to the enormous increase in the labor force participation of mothers. This suggests that my earlier analysis, which does not distinguish between the center and home-based sectors, may be overly simple.

CONCLUSIONS

The basic message of the results in this chapter is that the quantity and quality of child care supplied are quite responsive to the price of child care. As demand for child care increases owing to the increased labor force participation of mothers of young children, the market responds with an increase in the quantity of care supplied. The supply elasticity of child care labor over the last two decades is 1.15. Thus, increased demand for child care results in an increase in the quantity supplied with only moderately higher child care prices and wages. As price rises, day care centers increase the quality of the care they provide. The price elasticity of quality supply in day care centers is estimated to be .66 in the for-profit sector and .48 in the nonprofit sector. Increased demand for child care induces centers to improve the quality of the care they offer because they can increase profit by doing so.

These findings suggest that the child care market "works" in the sense that providers are able to expand both the quantity and quality of child care in response to increased demand. The findings do not necessarily indicate that the "socially optimal" level of quality is provided in the market. To the extent that parents are willing to pay a higher price for higher-quality care, the market is able to respond by increasing quality. Whether consumers are willing to pay enough to cover the cost of the socially optimal level of quality is unclear, because we do not know what the socially optimal level of quality is. Nevertheless, the results presented here have important implications for child care policy, discussed in chapters 8 and 10.

It is also important to note that this is the first analysis of the supply of quality of child care and as such should be regarded as suggestive but not definitive. Much more analysis is needed to determine whether these results are robust. And as yet we have no information at all about the supply of quality in the informal sector of the market, a major gap in our knowledge. New research on the supply of child care in both the formal and informal sectors would be useful. Subsidies to consumers may bid up the price of child care, and it is important to be able to quantify such effects. It would also be useful to examine the quality supply decisions of providers to determine how responsive the supply of high-quality care might be to supply-side subsidies.

Chapter 6

Equilibrium Price and Quality in the Child Care Market

This chapter analyzes the relationship between price and quality in the child care market, based on the model of market equilibrium developed in chapter 3. That model predicts that if consumers are willing to pay a higher price for higher-quality child care, and if higher-quality child care costs more to provide than lower-quality care, then there will be a positive relationship between price and quality in equilibrium. If either condition fails to hold, then we should observe no systematic relationship between price and quality. The strength of the price-quality relationship will depend on the distribution of consumers according to their willingness to pay for higher-quality versus lower-quality child care, and on how much more it costs to provide higher-quality than lower-quality care. These factors may differ across child care markets, so there is no presumption that the strength of the price-quality relationship will be the same in all markets.

The three questions addressed in this chapter are: Is there on average a positive relationship between price and quality in child care? If so, how strong is the relationship? And how does the relationship between price and quality vary across markets?

The answers to these questions are important because they help us make inferences about consumer preferences for quality and the likely effects of child care subsidies on the quality of care. Evidence presented in chapter 5 showed that higher-quality child care costs more to produce than lower-quality care. Thus, the first condition for the existence of a positive price-quality relationship is satisfied. The other condition is that consumers on average are willing to pay a higher price for higher-quality child care. If this condition holds, then we should find a positive price-quality relationship. If it fails to hold, then we should not observe a positive price-quality relationship: despite the higher cost of higher-quality care, if consumers are unwilling to pay a premium for higher-quality care, such care will not command a price premium in the market. Nonprofit providers may produce high-quality care for altruistic reasons, but they will not be able to charge a higher-than-average price for it. Failure to find a positive price-quality relationship indicates that if government child care subsidies are to help increase the level of quality in the market, they will have to be "tilted" toward higher-quality care.

The model developed in chapter 3 makes predictions about equilibrium outcomes, but it is difficult to determine whether a market is in equilibrium at any given moment. Failure to find a positive relationship between price and quality in a market could be due to the absence of such a relationship in equilibrium, or to the failure of the market to be in equilibrium when we observe it. A market that is out of equilibrium is unstable and will move toward equilibrium. Market participants can improve their well-being as the market moves toward equilibrium, so they have an incentive to take actions that will move the market toward equilibrium. For example, if consumers cannot find child care of the quality they prefer at the going market price, they have an incentive to offer a higher price.

We do not have a rigorous and widely accepted theory of the exact process by which a market that is out of equilibrium moves toward equilibrium. But most economists believe that markets that are out of equilibrium will move toward equilibrium. I will interpret the results of the empirical analysis in terms of equilibrium. I have no more compelling basis for doing this in the context of the child care market than in any other empirical economic analysis. Other interpretations of the results are possible, but they would inevitably be based on ad hoc stories dreamed up to explain the particular results I find.

There are two challenges to carrying out an empirical analysis of market price and quality: defining quality and defining the market. Consistent with the approach I take throughout the book, I use the developmental psychology definition of quality. Specifically, I use scores of day care centers from the Early Childhood Environment Rating Scale and its infant-toddler counterpart. If most parents think of child care quality as something quite different from the concept measured by ECERS, then we would not expect to see a positive relationship between price and ECERS in the market.

I believe that society should care about ECERS-type measures of quality, regardless of whether most parents actually do care about such measures, and this belief plays an important role in my policy proposal in chapter 10. It is interesting and important to learn which features of child care parents are willing to pay for, an issue I explore later in the chapter. But in my view the most important aspect of child care is its quality as measured by developmental appropriateness, so most of my analysis is focused on the price-quality relationship. The available data sets that measure both quality and price cover only day care centers. I would like to analyze the relationship between price and quality in other settings, but the data needed for such an analysis are not available.[1] As a second-best option, I analyze the relationship between price and *inputs* to the production of quality for a sample of centers and family day care homes. This is second best because if the inputs that we can measure are not highly related to quality, then drawing inferences about the price-quality relationship from the price-input relationship would be misleading.[2] The analysis of the relationship between inputs and quality in chapter 7 shows that the relationship is in fact quite weak for most of the easily measurable inputs.

Defining the market empirically is inherently arbitrary, since there is no reliable method of determining which consumers have access to which providers. I use definitions of the market based on geographic measures that are available in each data set, and I test the sensitivity of the findings to alternative definitions of the market.

RESULTS

The Cost, Quality, and Outcomes Study

The Cost, Quality, and Outcomes Study (CQOS) data provide detailed information, including price and quality, on four hundred day care centers in specified regions of California, Colorado, Connecticut, and North Carolina in 1993. The data provide the zip code in which each center is located, making it possible to define markets as consisting of zip code areas, clusters of zip code areas, towns, counties, or states. It seems likely that child care markets are smaller than a state and larger than a zip code, but exactly where to draw the line is unclear, so I present results for alternative definitions of the market. One problem with using a zip code as the definition of the market is that there are not enough centers in the data per zip code to estimate separate price-quality relationships for each market. In this case I constrain the slope parameter to be the same within towns, counties, or states and allow the intercepts to differ across markets.[3]

I begin by presenting scatter plots of price against quality in each of the four states, shown in figure 6.1. Price is measured by the average hourly fee charged by the center for full-time child care, and quality is the average ECERS-ITERS score of the rooms observed in the center. The quality score can vary from 1 through 7. The graphs suggest that there may be a positive relationship between price and quality in California, but any such relationship is barely discernible in the other states. A scatter plot is not a substitute for a careful statistical analysis, but it does draw attention to outliers that could have an unreasonably large impact on the statistical results. There appear to be some outliers with unusually high prices in all of the states except North Carolina, so it will be important to determine whether the results are unduly influenced by these cases.

If the appropriate market definition is smaller than a state, then failure to find a positive price-quality relationship could be a result of inappropriately pooling the data within states. Figure 6.2 plots the data by city in Connecticut, Colorado, and North Carolina. The California data are all from the Los Angeles metropolitan area, and there did not seem to be any obvious way of splitting that area into distinct markets. The city plots for the other states are somewhat arbitrary because they do not include suburbs and other towns that are fairly close to each city. In Connecticut the Hartford data suggest a mild positive relationship between price and quality, but except for the outliers, the New Haven and Waterbury plots do not show any price-quality relationship. There is little suggestion of a positive relationship in any of the Colorado and North Carolina cities, with the possible exception of Denver. However, there are two outliers in the Denver data that could affect the results.

Table 6.1 presents regression results in which quality and price are both measured in logarithms. This specification fit the data better than a specification in levels. The coefficient on log quality in a log price regression can be interpreted as the elasticity of price with respect to quality: the percentage change in price associated with a 1 percent change in quality, moving along the equilibrium price-quality locus (as depicted in figure 3.3). The first row shows results pooled across all sites within a state, with only one control variable: the proportion of infants and toddlers among the center's clientele. This variable is included to adjust for the fact that centers tend to charge more for the care of infants and toddlers. There is a positive relationship between price and quality across states and within each state. The hypothesis of a zero elasticity can be rejected at the 5 percent level of significance, except in North Carolina. The estimated elasticity is .40 in California, .32 in Colorado, .22 in Connecticut, and .13 in North Carolina.[4]

The next two rows show results in which the intercept of the price-quality relationship is allowed to vary by town or zip code. This causes a substantial reduction in the estimated price-quality elasticity in California and Colorado, while the elasticities in Connecticut and North Carolina change by smaller amounts. Controlling for zip code effects, we reject the hypothesis of a zero effect of quality on price only in Connecticut. Zip code effects may "overcontrol" for differences across markets, since it seems likely that a given market includes more than one zip code. Towns may be a more plausible market definition, but as noted earlier, defining towns is problematic in the Los Angeles metropolitan area. The definition of towns used here is based on the U.S. Postal Service correspondence between towns and zip codes, which may not accurately represent child care markets. The results with controls for town in row 3 show price-quality elasticity estimates of .16 to .25, with the hypothesis of a zero effect rejected only for Colorado. The generally smaller price-quality relationship at the town and zip code levels suggests that the relatively strong relationship found at the state level may be spurious. Price and quality are both higher in some towns than in others within a state, but the results suggest that the relationship is not causal. For example, prices for all goods and services may be

Figure 6.1 / Price and Quality by State in the CQOS Data

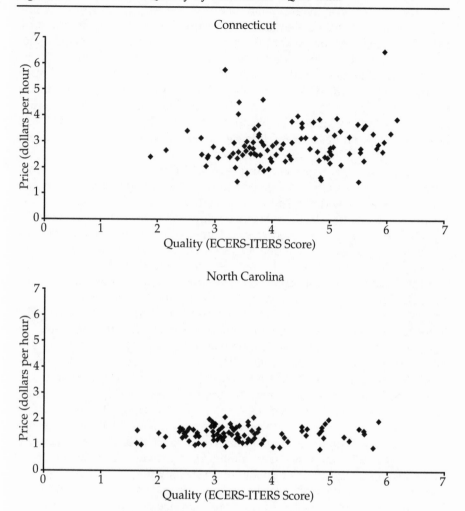

higher in larger cities, and larger cities may contain more consumers with strong preferences for high-quality care or more nonprofit providers.

Center characteristics other than quality could affect the price a center can charge. For example, if parents believe that older centers provide better and more stable child care services than newer centers, they might be willing to pay more for child care of a given quality in an older center than in a newer center. The results shown in row 4 of table 6.1 are from a specification that includes a set of center characteristics in the regression to control for other factors that might affect price. The characteristics are listed in the note to table 6.1. These factors are in some cases correlated with quality,

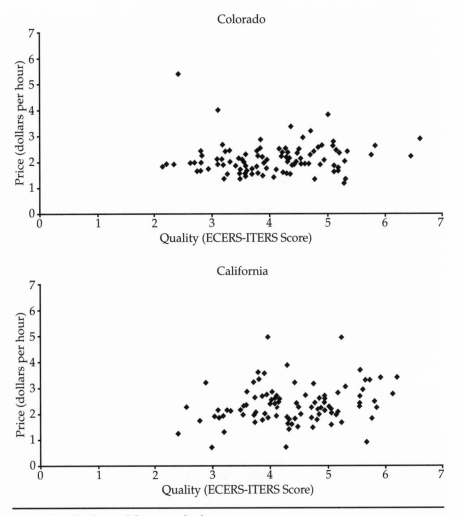

Source: Cost, Quality, and Outcomes Study.

and as a result controlling for them affects the price-quality elasticity. The elasticity becomes larger and significantly different from zero in California and North Carolina, and smaller and insignificantly different from zero in Colorado and Connecticut. The elasticities in row 4 are in the .08 to .18 range, except for California, which has an estimate of .51.

Rows 5 through 18 of the table report results from separate regression models by city or county, in which both the intercept and the elasticity are allowed to vary by location. The sample sizes are quite small in some cases, so these results may not be robust. The price-quality elasticity of .45 within Denver and its suburbs is quite large. Removing outliers in the Denver

Figure 6.2 / Price and Quality by City or County in the CQOS Data

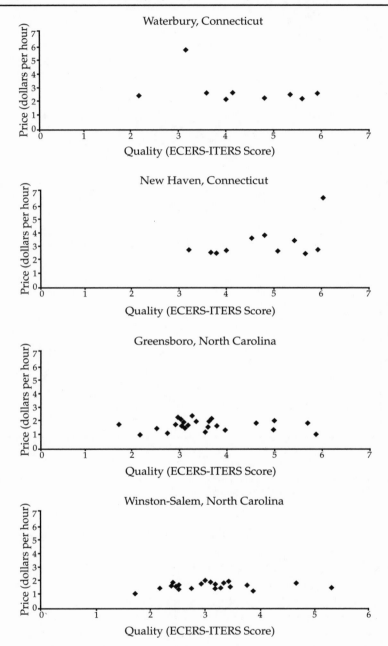

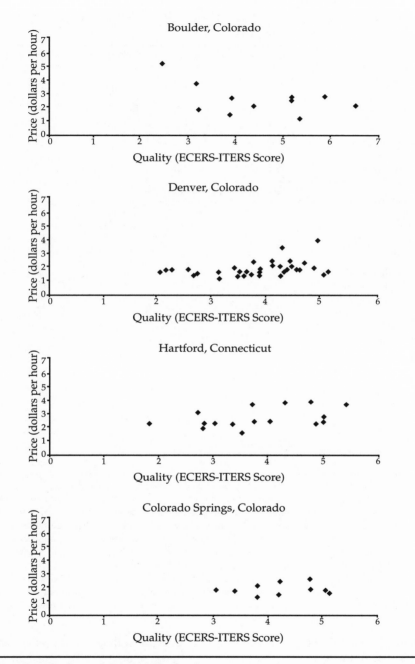

Source: Cost, Quality, and Outcomes Study.

Table 6.1 / Elasticity of Price with Respect to Quality: Cost, Quality, and Outcomes Study Data

	California	Colorado	Connecticut	North Carolina
No geographic controls	.40 (.16)*	.32 (.11)*	.22 (.10)*	.13 (.08)
Zip codes	.03 (.24)	.16 (.19)	.26 (.13)*	.09 (.11)
Towns	.16 (.19)	.25 (.11)*	.19 (.12)	.16 (.09)
No geographic controls; includes other regressors	.51 (.18)*	.08 (.14)	.17 (.10)	.18 (.09)*
City- or County-Specific Models				
Hartford	—	—	.20 (.20)	—
New Haven	—	—	.48 (.31)	—
New Haven; no outliers	—	—	.09 (.23)	—
Forsyth County	—	—	—	.16 (.10)
Guilford County	—	—	—	−.01 (.18)
Alamance County	—	—	—	.40 (.15)*
Davidson County	—	—	—	.32 (.21)
Denver	—	.45 (.12)*	—	—
Denver; no outliers	—	.41 (.11)*	—	—
Denver; with other regressors	—	.31 (.17)	—	—
Denver; with other regressors and no outliers	—	.24 (.16)	—	—
Boulder	—	−.28 (.40)	—	—
Boulder; no outliers	—	.14 (.38)	—	—
Colorado Springs	—	.18 (.15)	—	—

Notes: The dependent variable is the logarithm of the average hourly fee. The figures reported in the table are the coefficient (and standard error) on the logarithm of the average ECERS-ITERS score. All models include as an additional regressor the percentage of children under age three. Additional regressors in the models in rows 4 and 14 through 15 are dummies for part-day, extended day, Head Start, public school–sponsored, before- and after-school care, summer camp program offered, evening care, weekend care, sick care, twenty-four-hour care, bilingual staff, for-profit, meets higher standards voluntarily, receives over 50 percent of revenue from public subsidies, on-site, church-sponsored, Waldorf program, and national chain; and percentage of children subsidized, age of the center, and full-time equivalent enrollment.
*The hypothesis that the coefficient is equal to zero is rejected at the 5 percent level.

sample has little effect on the estimate, but controlling for center characteristics reduces it to .31 (.24 with outliers removed). The elasticity is smaller and not significantly different from zero in Boulder and Colorado Springs. An apparently strong price-quality relationship in New Haven turns out to be due to the influence of the single outlier illustrated in figure

6.2; removing the outlier eliminates the relationship. Positive relationships appear in three of the four North Carolina counties, although only in Alamance County can the hypothesis of a zero effect be rejected. The estimates for Alamance and Davidson Counties are .40 and .32, respectively.

Overall, these results suggest that the price-quality relationship is relatively weak and highly variable across locations. A positive price-quality relationship appears in three of four states when the data are analyzed at the state level, but vanishes in many cases when towns, counties, and zip codes are the unit of analysis. A few local markets show a strong price-quality relationship, but most do not. Recall that the market price-quality relationship is determined by the cost-quality relationship and by consumer willingness to pay for quality. The cost-quality relationship is likely to be similar across markets since it depends on the "technology" of producing quality, which is not market-specific. This suggests that consumer willingness to pay for higher quality is itself weak on average—consistent with the findings reported in chapter 4—and highly variable across markets.

The National Child Care Staffing Study

The NCCSS collected data on day care centers in Atlanta, Boston, Detroit, Phoenix, and Seattle in 1989. Price is measured in this case by the full-time *weekly* fee, since the information needed to convert fees to an hourly basis was not collected in the NCCSS. Figure 6.3 plots the data by city. There is little suggestion of a positive price-quality relationship in Atlanta, Boston, and Phoenix. A mild positive relationship may exist in Detroit and Seattle. Outliers appear in the samples in four of the five cities, including in this case some implausibly low prices. The only geographic identifier available in the public-use version of the NCCSS is the city, so no finer level of disaggregation can be investigated.

Table 6.2 reports regression results, again using the logarithms of price and quality. This facilitates comparison with the CQOS results, since elasticities, which are ratios of percentage changes, are invariant to units of measurement. Moderate price-quality relationships appear in Detroit, Phoenix, and Seattle, with the first two significantly different from zero. The elasticities are in the .23 to .30 range for those three cities. Controlling for other center characteristics that might affect price reduces the elasticity estimate in Detroit to .08, but increases it in Phoenix and Seattle to .36 to .37. Removing outliers reduces the effect by about one-third in Phoenix and increases it by over one-third in Seattle, and in the latter case the hypothesis of a zero effect can now be rejected. Adding the control variables in the sample that excludes outliers leads to an estimate of .62 in Seattle, with a small standard error. This is the largest effect estimated for any location in either data set. The effect for Phoenix is .33 and is significantly different

Figure 6.3 / Price per Week and Quality by City in the NCCSS Data

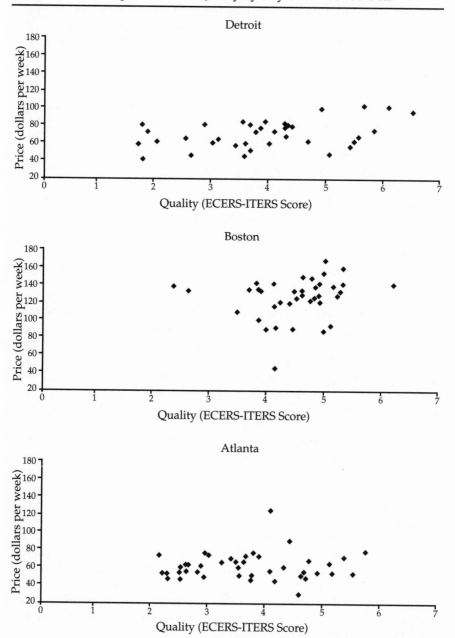

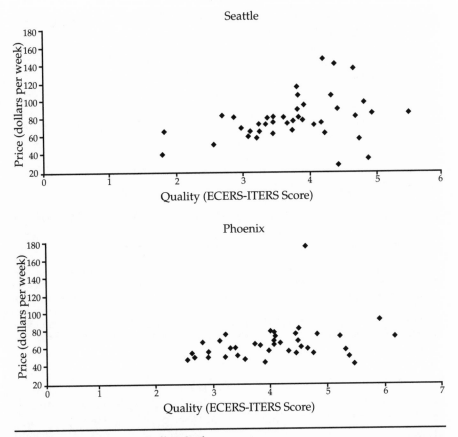

Source: National Child Care Staffing Study.

from zero. The effects are much smaller and statistically insignificant in the other cities.

The evidence from the NCCSS is thus broadly consistent with the evidence from the CQOS data. The price-quality relationship is weak and not very robust on average, but is consistently positive and fairly strong in some markets.

The Profile of Child Care Settings

The Profile of Child Care Settings (PCS) collected data from a large sample of day care centers and licensed family day care homes in 1989 and 1990. The data were collected by a telephone survey, so it was not possible to measure quality with an observational instrument such as ECERS. Instead, there are measures of *inputs* to the production of quality, such as group size, staff-child ratios, staff education and training, and other indirect indi-

Table 6.2 / Elasticity of Price with Respect to Quality: National Child Care Staffing Study Data

	Atlanta	Boston	Detroit	Phoenix	Seattle
No other explanatory variables	.04 (.13)	.15 (.19)	.23 (.09)*	.30 (.15)*	.29 (.19)
Includes other explanatory variables	−.05 (.14)	.04 (.28)	.08 (.14)	.37 (.18)*	.36 (.24)
No other explanatory variables; omits outliers	.08 (.09)	.10 (.14)	.23 (.09)*	.24 (.11)*	.51 (.13)*
Includes other explanatory variables; omits outliers	.11 (.12)	−.03 (.17)	.08 (.14)	.33 (.11)*	.62 (.14)*
Sample size	44	38	37	40	42

Source: National Child Care Staffing Study.
Notes: The dependent variable is the logarithm of the average weekly fee for full-time care. The figures reported in the table are the coefficient on the logarithm of the average ECERS-ITERS score. Additional regressors included in the models in rows 2 and 4 are dummies for location and neighborhood income type (low-density versus high-density, interacted with low-, middle-, and high-income neighborhood), years of operation, enrollment, tenure of the director, percentage of income for subsidies, and dummies for for-profit, Head Start, and church-sponsored.
*The hypothesis that the coefficient is equal to zero is rejected at the 5 percent level.

cators of quality such as accreditation. There are also many measures of center characteristics that parents might care about but that are not directly related to quality. These include distance from public transportation, operating schedule, and demographic characteristics of the provider. Results from the PCS provide a useful complement to the price-quality analysis by showing a broad picture of the factors associated with price, though they are not a substitute for direct study of the price-quality relationship.

The PCS sample was drawn from one hundred primary sampling units (PSUs), which are counties or county groups, in thirty-six states. This limits the possible choices for the definition of the market to county and states. The analysis strongly rejects a market definition based on states: including county intercept dummies improved the fit of the model substantially compared to state intercept dummies or no geographic controls. Table 6.3 shows the results of a regression for day care centers of the logarithm of the average hourly fee charged by the center on a large number of characteristics. In addition to the characteristics shown in the table, dummy variables for each county were included in the regression models.

The results indicate that centers with larger groups charge a lower price. The effect is not significantly different from zero and it is quantitatively small: an increase in group size of ten would cause the price to fall by 2.5 percent. Hence, the relationship is of the "right" sign (higher group size

Table 6.3 / Determinants of Log Price in Day Care Centers: Profile of Child Care Settings

Explanatory Variable	Coefficient Estimate (Standard Error)	
Group size	−.0025	(.0015)
Staff-child ratio	−.13	(.10)
Proportion of teachers with		
Graduate degree	.19	(.07)*
Bachelor's degreee	.18	(.06)*
Associate's degree	.08	(.07)
Child development associate credential	.13	(.07)
Some college, no degree	.06	(.06)
Characteristics of randomly selected teacher		
Years of job tenure	.0017	(.0035)
Years of child care work experience	−.0022	(.0029)
Training		
Community college	.035	(.025)
Resource and referral agency	.040	(.025)
Government agency	−.075	(.029)*
On-site	−.039	(.026)
Other	.050	(.025)*
Offers before-school care	−.10	(.03)*
Offers after-school care	.12	(.04)*
Number of weeks open per year	−.010	(.003)*
Licensed	.02	(.06)
Enrollment (100)	.08	(.03)*
Accepts non-English-speaking children	.02	(.03)
Listed with a resource and referral agency	.046	(.028)
Has a waiting list	−.026	(.026)
Proportion of children aged		
Zero	−.16	(.26)
One	.26	(.21)
Two	.37	(.13)*
Three	.36	(.12)*
Four	.19	(.10)
Five	.28	(.13)*
Proportion of children		
Black	−.27	(.05)*
Hispanic	−.58	(.10)*
Asian	−.16	(.15)
Other	−.14	(.17)
Proportion of families on welfare	−.07	(.08)
Accepts children with government subsidy	−.036	(.032)
Accredited by the National Academy of Early Childhood Programs	.004	(.032)
Do parents regularly drop in?	−.02	(.03)

(Table continues on p. 118.)

Table 6.3 / *Continued*

Explanatory Variable	Coefficient Estimate (Standard Error)	
Administers over-the-counter medication	.08	(.03)*
Administers prescription medication	−.001	(.042)
Located seven blocks to one mile from public transportation	−.01	(.05)
Located more than one mile from public transportation	.01	(.03)
Main program goal[a]		
Provide care so parents can work	−.20	(.06)*
Prepare children for school	.02	(.04)
Provide compensatory education for disadvantaged children	−.22	(.19)
Promote child development	.035	(.031)
Teach appreciation for culture	−.02	(.13)
Provide religious instruction	−.002	(.063)
Center auspice		
Nonprofit	−.13	(.03)*
For-profit independent	.11	(.03)*
For-profit national chain	−.06	(.06)
For-profit local chain	.05	(.07)
Provides physical, dental, hearing, speech, vision, psychological, cognitive, or social testing	−.031	(.026)
Years of operation	.0017	(.0011)
Allows sick children to attend	−.01	(.03)
Adjusted R^2 (sample size)	.33	(1,443)

Notes: Dependent variable is the logarithm of the average hourly fee. Ninety-nine site dummies and fifteen dummies for missing data were also included. Standard errors are in parentheses.

*The hypothesis that the coefficient is equal to zero is rejected at the 5 percent level.
[a]Omitted category is, "Provide a warm and loving environment."

causes lower quality and therefore lower price), but negligible in magnitude. The results show a negative effect on price of more staff per group. This effect is of the "wrong" sign, not significantly different from zero, and is also small in magnitude. An increase in the staff-child ratio of 0.1 (for example, from one teacher for every twenty children to two teachers for every twenty children) would result in a price decrease of 1.4 percent, a small effect for a relatively large increase in the ratio. Thus, the evidence shows that two of the inputs that are widely believed to affect quality, group size and staff-child ratio, have very little association with price. This finding could indicate that these inputs in fact do not affect quality much, or that quality itself is not highly valued by consumers. We already have evidence to support the latter hypothesis, and the next chapter provides evidence in support of the former hypothesis.

Centers with higher proportions of well-educated teachers charge higher prices. Switching from no teachers with a bachelor's degree to all teachers with a bachelor's degree would cause price to increase by 18 percent. The magnitude is similar for teachers with a graduate degree and is about one-third smaller for teachers with a child development associate credential. These effects are significantly different from zero, and I would characterize them as modest but not negligible in magnitude. Teacher education is another input that is widely touted as a determinant of child care quality, and here the evidence is more supportive: by employing better-educated teachers, centers are able to charge a higher price.

Being listed with a resource and referral (R&R) agency is associated with about a 5 percent price premium, which could indicate that R&R listing is a signal of quality. Nonprofit status is negatively associated with price, despite the fact that nonprofits generally provide higher-quality care. Among for-profits, independents charge higher prices. Other possible indicators of quality, such as teacher training, accreditation, years of teacher experience, and years of teacher tenure with the center, have very small associations with price that are generally not significantly different from zero.

Some characteristics that are unlikely to be related to quality but are nevertheless associated with price include offering before-school care (negative effect on price), after-school care (positive), the proportion of children age two years and older (positive), the proportion of black and Hispanic children (negative), willingness to administer over-the-counter medication to children (positive), and having as a primary goal facilitating parental employment (negative), relative to providing a warm environment, the omitted category. The largest and most striking effects are for race and ethnicity. The large negative price effect for centers serving large proportions of black and Hispanic children could result from the fact that such centers are located in low-income neighborhoods in which many parents can pay little for child care and either therefore choose low-price care or are provided low-price care by altruistic nonprofits. Thus, the proportions of children who are black and Hispanic may proxy for low-income neighborhoods within a county, a hypothesis that cannot be tested with the PCS data since county is the lowest level of geographic identifier available.

The results presented in table 6.3 restrict the effects of the explanatory variables to be the same across markets, allowing only the intercepts to differ. In fifteen of the thirty-six states in the sample, there are enough observations to estimate models in which the effects of the explanatory variables are allowed to differ across states along with the intercepts. There are not enough observations in any county to allow separate models by county. I eliminated many of the regressors that seemed not to matter in table 6.3 in order to focus on those that appeared most important. A selection of results from these state-specific models is presented in table 6.4.

The results confirm the finding in table 6.3 that group size and staff-

Table 6.4 / State-Specific Results for Determinants of Log Price in Day Care Centers: Profile of Child Care Settings

State	Group Size	Staff-Child Ratio	Proportion of Black Children	Proportion of Hispanic Children	Proportion on Welfare	Proportion of College Graduates Among Teachers	Nonprofit	Independent For-Profit	Adjusted R²	Sample Size
California	−.010*	−.29	−.31	−.30	−.59	−.02	−.26*	.38*	.24	160
Florida	−.023	.10	−.89*	−.81*	−.83	.05	−.08	.06	.35	54
Georgia	−.009	.65	−.10	−.44	−.39	.43	−.22	−.12	.22	47
Illinois	−.002	−.60	.27	−1.62	−1.03	.18	.13	−.12	.11	72
Massachusetts	.036*	−1.00	−1.25	−1.62	.29	−.01	−.40*	.42*	.27	76
Michigan	.005	−.49	−.28	1.19	.44	.38	.06	.06	−.10	66
Minnesota	−.007	−.07	.11	−1.95	−.75*	.26	−.11	−.13	.39	55
Nebraska	−.007	.71	−1.06	.18	−.39	−.18	−.14	.02	−.00	56
New York	−.003	.54	−.71	−.50	.32	.20	−.54	.57*	.54	44
North Carolina	−.003	.06	−.29	−.37	.50*	.20	.21	−.16	.26	90
Oklahoma	.002	−.58	−.24	−.29	−.05	.00	−.10	.30	.12	75
Pennsylvania	−.008	.31	−.41	1.27	−.16	.12	−.20	−.09	.14	50
South Carolina	−.001	.36	−.16	−1.00	−.35	−.12	−.27	.29	−.23	51
Texas	.002	.04	−.19	−.69*	−.83	.64*	−.16	.08	.43	82
Virginia	.008	−.14	.07	−1.44*	.56	.06	−.20	.22	.17	48

Source: Calculations based on data from the Profile of Child Care Settings.

Notes: Dependent variable is the logarithm of the average hourly fee. Other regressors included in the models were county dummies, before-school care, after-school care, enrollment, listed with R&R agency, percentage of children age two to five, percentage of teachers with a CDA, the training variables listed in table 6.3, and the number of weeks open per year.

*The hypothesis that the coefficient is equal to zero is rejected at the 5 percent level.

child ratio are not closely associated with price. Larger groups are associated with lower price in ten of the fifteen states, but the effect is significantly different from zero only in California, and moderately large only in Florida. College-educated teachers are associated with a higher price in eleven of the fifteen states, but the effect is large and significantly different from zero only in Texas. The proportion of black and Hispanic children has negative effects on price in twelve of the fifteen states, with large and/or statistically significant effects in most cases. Given the relatively small samples in some of the states, these results should be interpreted cautiously. They suggest that child care markets differ across states in quantitative terms but are similar qualitatively.

Table 6.5 presents regression results for licensed family day care homes, with county dummies included and slope coefficients restricted to be the same across all counties.[5] The dependent variable is the logarithm of the average hourly fee. Group size and staff-child ratio have small effects on price, not significantly different from zero. The only effect of education is an 8.7 percent higher price for a provider with a bachelor's degree. Training effects on price are small and insignificantly different from zero. Listing with a resource and referral agency is associated with a 7.7 percent higher price. In contrast to centers, prices are significantly lower for younger children relative to the omitted category of school-age children. Providers who report that their main goal is to facilitate parental employment command a price that is 10 percent lower than providers whose main aim is to provide a warm and loving environment (the omitted category). Having religious instruction as the main goal reduces the fee by 14 percent, while teaching appreciation for culture raises the price by 30 percent compared to a main goal of providing a warm and loving environment. Serving black children in a family day care home has no significant impact on price, but serving Hispanic children reduces price substantially. However, if the provider herself is black, the fee is 19 percent lower than if she is white, other things being equal, while Hispanic providers command about the same price as white providers.

The results for family day care homes are broadly consistent with the results for centers. Group size, staff-child ratio, and teacher training are not associated with price, while teacher education is positively associated with price. Providers listed with a resource and referral agency charge a higher price in both the center and home market, and providers mainly concerned with facilitating the employment of parents charge a lower price in both segments of the market. The consistency of the evidence across centers and family day care homes suggests that the same forces are at work: technology and consumer preferences.

Table 6.5 / Determinants of Log Price in Family Day Care Homes: Profile of Child Care Settings

Explanatory Variable	Coefficient Estimate (Standard Error)	
Group size	.0027	(.0057)
Staff-child ratio	.0057	(.0058)
Highest degree of provider (omitted category is high school)		
Graduate degree	.023	(.135)
Bachelor's degree	.087	(.046)
Associate's degree	.052	(.049)
Child development associate credential	.009	(.059)
Vocational or technical school after high school	−.024	(.068)
Some college, no degree	.021	(.032)
Provider training		
Government agency	−.058	(.059)
Other	.038	(.029)
Number of weeks open per year	−.0032	(.0021)
Listed with a resource and referral agency	.077	(.038)*
Proportion of children age		
Less than one	.11	(.09)
One	−.04	(.08)
Two	−.10	(.08)
Three	−.16	(.09)
Four	−.34	(.10)*
Five	−.16	(.11)
Proportion of children		
Black	.11	(.11)
Hispanic	−.23	(.12)*
Asian	−.04	(.17)
Other	.23	(.23)
Proportion of families on welfare	.026	(.038)
Located seven blocks to one mile from public transportation	.047	(.042)
Located more than one mile from public transportation	−.053	(.034)
Main program goal[a]		
Provide care so parents can work	−.10	(.06)
Prepare children for school	−.05	(.05)
Provide compensatory education for disadvantaged children	−.13	(.13)
Promote child development	.02	(.05)
Teach appreciation for culture	.30	(.13)*
Provide religious instruction	−.14	(.07)*
Years of operation	−.0030	(.0024)
Allows sick children to attend	.065	(.028)*
Member of a family providers organization	−.003	(.031)

Table 6.5 / Continued

Explanatory Variable	Coefficient Estimate (Standard Error)	
Has liability insurance	.018	(.029)
Sponsored by a group that organizes family day care	−.035	(.033)
Provider's own children are at home during business hours	.054	(.033)
Participates in the Child Care Food Program	−.015	(.034)
Provider is divorced, separated, or widowed	−.04	(.04)
Provider is never-married	−.04	(.07)
Closed in the summer	.02	(.03)
Open weekends	.16	(.07)*
Open extended hours	.02	(.05)
Hours of operation	−.0065	(.0016)*
Provider's age	.0007	(.0017)
Provider's race		
Black	−.19	(.10)*
Hispanic	.02	(.07)
Asian	.19	(.15)
Other	−.15	(.09)
Adjusted R^2 (sample size)	.57	(524)

Source: Calculations based on data from the Profile of Child Care Settings.
Notes: Dependent variable is the logarithm of the average hourly fee. Ninety-nine site dummies and fifteen dummies for missing data were also included. Standard errors are in parentheses.
*The hypothesis that the coefficient is equal to zero is rejected at the 5 percent level.
ᵃOmitted category is, "Provide a warm and loving environment."

CONCLUSION

Does the price of child care increase with the quality of the service, when quality is measured by the developmental appropriateness of the care? The answer is that it depends on where you live. In the majority of locations in which this question can be addressed, the association between price and quality is positive, but small and insignificantly different from zero. In several locations, however, the effect is moderately large and significantly different from zero. In other cases there appears to be a sizable positive effect, but the effect is not robust to controls for other center characteristics, location, and outliers. There is no clear pattern to these effects. The price-quality relationship is quite idiosyncratic. This has important implications for the design of child care policy, as discussed in chapters 8 and 10. Overall, the association between price and quality in day care centers is small.

The association between price and inputs to the production of quality is quite small as well, with the exception of teacher education. However, price is associated with provider characteristics other than quality, including the age, race, and ethnicity of children, the race of the provider, size of the center, and hours of operation. This suggests that consumers care about features of child care other than quality. The association between price and race and ethnicity of children served is particularly striking. This finding suggests that altruistic nonprofits charge relatively low prices in low-income neighborhoods, beyond the generally lower prices they charge overall.

Chapter 7

The Determinants and Effects of Child Care Quality

What determines the quality of child care? Does the quality of child care affect the development and behavior of young children? These are the issues addressed in this chapter. They are important because any policy proposed as a solution to the child care problem must take a stand on whether improving the quality of care is the primary goal of the policy. To have a sound basis for choosing such a goal, it is important to be clear about what we mean by child care quality, how quality is produced, and how quality affects children.

Developmental psychologists have created a large literature on issues of child care quality, and most of the discussion in this chapter is of studies from this literature, which I review as an outsider—I am not trained as a developmental psychologist. I believe that the perspective of an economist on this literature is useful, however, because there are many topics in economics that raise issues of methodology and interpretation very similar to those encountered in the child care quality literature. Examples include the effect of school resources on student academic achievement and the effect of education on earnings.

The chapter begins with a definition of quality and a conceptual framework for thinking about the issues. This is followed by an overview of the methods and findings of the literature and the general issues raised by the methods. The next section discusses several noteworthy studies in more detail. The last section summarizes what we have learned from the developmental psychology literature. Toward the end of the chapter, I discuss my own research on these issues.

A DEFINITION AND A CONCEPTUAL FRAMEWORK

Authoritative reviews of the literature on child care quality by Hayes, Palmer, and Zaslow (1990), Lamb (1998), and Love, Schochet, and Meckstroth (1996) present similar ideas on how to think about quality. They note that there are two distinct concepts of quality in the literature. The first type is variously referred to as "process" quality, "global" quality, and "dynamic features of care," while the second is called "structural" quality or "static features of care." Process quality characterizes the interactions between children and their caregivers, their environment, and other children. A child care arrangement is considered high-quality, according to this concept, when

> caregivers encourage children to be actively engaged in a variety of activities; have frequent, positive interactions with children that include smiling, touching, holding, and speaking at children's eye level; promptly respond to children's questions or requests; and encourage children to talk about their experience, feelings, and ideas. Caregivers in high-quality settings also listen attentively, ask open-ended questions, and extend children's actions and verbalizations with more complex ideas or materials, interact with children individually and in small groups instead of exclusively with the group as a whole, use positive guidance techniques, and encourage appropriate independence. (Love et al. 1996, 5)

Structural quality refers to characteristics of the child care environment such as the child-staff ratio, group size, teacher education and training, safety, staff turnover, and program administration. A child care arrangement is considered to be of high-quality, according to the structural definition, when it meets standards specified by professional organizations such as the National Association for the Education of Young Children (NAEYC). The NAEYC and other standards specify maximum child-staff ratios and group sizes by age of the children in care; curriculum content; minimum staff qualifications for alternative levels of responsibility; health and safety standards; and standards for other program characteristics. (For details of the NAEYC and other standards, see Hayes et al. 1990.)

These reviews argue that process quality is more closely related to child development than structural quality. This is not surprising, because the concept and measures of process quality were developed through research and practice with the express intention of discovering which features of child care environments are most conducive to child development. In contrast, structural features of child care "appear to support and facilitate more optimal interactions" (Hayes et al. 1990, 84); "factors indexed by the structural measures potentiate high-quality interaction and care but do not guarantee it" (Lamb 1998, 13); and "structural features of quality provide the foundation for higher-quality classroom dynamics" (Love et al. 1996, 3). The notion that process quality is the most direct determinant of child outcomes and that structural features facilitate, potentiate, and provide the foundation for process quality is intuitively reasonable. For example, caring for children in a smaller group is unlikely to lead to better child development unless a smaller group makes it easier for caregivers to provide developmentally appropriate care. A useful way to conceptualize the processes relating structural features of child care, process quality, and child

Figure 7.1 / The Relationships Between Structural and Process Quality of Child Care and Child Outcomes

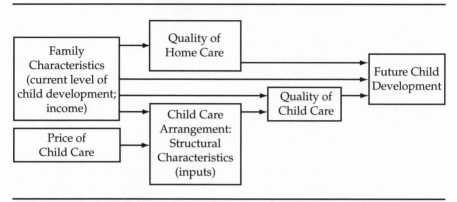

Source: Author's configuration.

outcomes is illustrated in figure 7.1 (For a similar conceptual framework, see Vandell and Wolfe 2000).

An arrow indicates a causal effect hypothesized in the model. The developmental psychology literature suggests that the structural features of child care arrangements affect the quality of child care, as measured by process quality, which in turn affects child development. Hence the arrow from the structural characteristics box to the child care quality box, and from the child care quality box to the child development box. For the remainder of the chapter, I refer to structural features of child care arrangements as "inputs" to the production of quality and reserve the term "quality" to refer exclusively to process quality. One of the issues discussed here is the nature of the "production process" for quality: What is the quantitative impact of each child care "input" on child care quality, holding all other inputs and determinants constant? Another key issue is determining what research reveals about the quantitative effect of child care quality on child development.

A third important research issue is the effect of inputs on child development, an effect that does not directly reveal either the effects of inputs on quality or the effect of quality on development. Thus, while not as informative as the direct effects, this approach is useful nevertheless. For example, suppose we find that child care quality has no impact on child development, and inputs have no effect on child care quality, but inputs are found to have effects on development. This might indicate that our measures of quality are flawed, or that the inputs operate through some other unobserved mechanism. Since the ultimate concern is child development, we might be encouraged by such a finding to attempt to improve the inputs in order to enhance child development, even without a clear understanding of the exact channels through which the inputs affect child development.

The model illustrated in figure 7.1 explicitly incorporates family characteristics. The family environment is no doubt at least as important for child development as the quality of the child care arrangement. Thus, parent and child characteristics (such as age, education, race, attitudes, income) are modeled as influencing the quality of care the child receives at home, and care at home, in turn, has a direct impact on child development. Furthermore, child development is clearly a dynamic process: a child's level of development influences the quality of care the child receives at home and the type of child care arrangement chosen by the family, and it directly affects the child's future development. For example, a child who is perceived by parents as not developing well may be placed in a high-quality child care arrangement to compensate. Family and child characteristics, along with the price of child care (and government subsidy, regulation, and information policies), also influence the nature of the child care arrangement: parents choose that arrangement, and it seems likely that family characteristics that affect the quality of home care will affect the type of child care arrangement selected. Family and child characteristics may also *interact* with child care inputs in determining the quality of the child care arrangement. (For instance, it is harder to provide high-quality care for a temperamental child.) Finally, family characteristics may have direct effects on child development through genetic and environmental influences on the child.

An important consequence of the ubiquitous role of family characteristics in this framework is that their influence must be accounted for if empirical estimates of the effects of child care inputs and quality are to be credible. This has been recognized in the developmental psychology literature but not often dealt with in a convincing way. Insights from the economics literature, in which analogous issues arise in many contexts, can fruitfully be applied to help understand the problems of interpretation that arise as a result of omitting possibly important family characteristics from the analysis.

The discussion suggests that estimates of the following empirical models are of interest. First, we would like to estimate the impact of child care quality on subsequent child development, controlling for home inputs, family and child characteristics, and the baseline level of development. Second, we would like to estimate the impact of child care inputs on child care quality, controlling for family and child characteristics and the baseline level of development. Third, we would like to estimate the net effects of child care inputs on child development, controlling for home inputs, family and child characteristics, and the baseline level of development. The first two models are "structural" in that all of the factors hypothesized in the conceptual framework as having a *direct* effect on the outcome of interest are included in the model. The third model is a "reduced form" because it does not reveal the effect of child care quality on child development or the effects of inputs on quality, but only the net effects of the inputs on child development.

Five conditions must be satisfied to obtain unbiased and precise statistical estimates of the parameters of these models that can be used to address the key questions of interest. First, the relevant variables must be measured with as little error as possible and included in the analysis.[1] The practical questions are whether any important factors that have been omitted (and are therefore captured in the statistical disturbances of the models) are likely to be correlated with included variables, and whether any important factors are measured with substantial error. If so, then we have reason to be concerned that estimates of the effects of variables that are included are biased. Second, the sample on which the analysis is based should be randomly drawn from the population of interest and should be representative of that population. Third, the sample size should be large enough so that the effects of interest can be measured with enough precision to ensure that they are not just an artifact of sampling variation. Fourth, parameter estimates, standard errors of the estimates, and descriptive statistics on the variables used in the analysis must be listed in the write-up of the study. This may seem like a trivial point, but without such statistics we cannot use the estimates to answer questions about the magnitudes of the impacts of interest. It is not very useful to know that variable A has an impact on variable B if we are not informed of the magnitude of the impact, the precision with which it is estimated, and (for example) the mean and standard deviation of both variables so that effects can be compared across studies.

The final condition is specific to the nature of the main outcome of interest, child development. Development is an inherently dynamic process and should be modeled accordingly. A positive correlation between child care quality and child development measured at the same date could be a consequence of placing children who have already developed well in high-quality child care. In this case, the positive association could be spurious: quality does not "cause" development. To guard against this possibility, it is important to have a baseline measure of child development prior to exposure of the child to the child care arrangement. This condition applies to infants as well—for example, a child's birthweight (an important measure of development) may influence the child care arrangement chosen by the family.

AN OVERVIEW OF METHODS AND FINDINGS IN THE CHILD CARE QUALITY LITERATURE

Reviews of the literature by Love, Schochet, and Meckstroth (1996), Doherty-Derkowski (1995), Dunn (1993a), Lamb (1998), and Hayes, Palmer, and

Zaslow (1990) identify more than forty studies of the effects of child care quality or child care inputs on child development or child behavior. Fewer than one-third of these studies meet most of the five conditions just discussed. A number of the studies fail on the first and most basic condition: including the relevant variables in the analysis. Some of these studies group child care arrangements into clusters based on the values of several of the inputs or quality and analyze the association between clusters and child outcomes (for example, Broberg et al., 1997; Field 1980; Howes and Rubenstein 1985; Howes and Olenick 1986; Kontos 1991; Peterson and Peterson 1986; Goelman and Pence 1988; Vandell and Powers 1983; Studer 1992; Marcon 1999). Some of these studies simply compare developmental outcomes of children according to whether their child care arrangement is classified as low-quality or high-quality based on the inputs. This approach does not provide estimates of the impact of varying each input separately, and such estimates are what we need for *policy* analysis. It might be useful for parents to know that child care arrangements with both small group size and well-trained staff are better for child development than arrangements with large groups and untrained staff. But for policy purposes we need to know the effect on development of group size holding training constant, and the effect of training holding group size constant. This is the only way to determine how policy can be used to provide the highest payoff in terms of child outcomes per dollar spent.[2]

Some studies of the effects of inputs on child development do include direct measures of the inputs instead of indicators for high versus low values of the inputs. Around half find that either smaller groups, more staff per group, or better-trained teachers have positive effects on child development and behavior that are significantly different from zero. The others find either no statistically significant effects of any of the inputs or statistically significant effects of the "wrong" sign. Some of these studies present simple correlations between inputs and child outcomes without controls for *any* other variables, including other inputs. Most of these studies use small convenience samples that have not been randomly selected, few or no measures of family and child characteristics, no measure of child development prior to exposure to the child care arrangement being studied, and no control for self-selection of children into child care arrangements. Most of the studies include at most one or two measures of the home environment, such as the mother's education and family income, and do not consider the possibility that families select child care arrangements on the basis of unobserved aspects of the home environment. In view of these problems, it is hard to use results from these studies to draw any conclusions about the effects of the inputs on child outcomes.[3] Similar comments apply to studies of the effect of child care quality on child development.[4]

The effects of the inputs on child care quality have also been analyzed extensively.[5] Many of these studies also suffer from small, nonrepresentative samples and lack of control for child and family characteristics. Their results are inconclusive: some find beneficial effects of small groups, low child-staff ratio, and teacher training; others find no effect; and still others find negative effects.

SPECIFIC STUDIES

In this section, I discuss in greater depth several studies that may be informative because of their methods and data.

The National Day Care Study

The National Day Care Study (NDCS; Ruopp et al. 1979) closely monitored a sample of sixty-four day care centers and approximately sixteen hundred of the children they served for about nine months. The children were given baseline developmental assessments and were assessed again at the end of the nine-month period, during which time classroom activities and inputs were monitored. The study design included two experiments in which some children were randomly assigned to classrooms with different staff-child ratios and teachers with different levels of training. The study found that preschool-age children (three to five) in classrooms with smaller groups and teachers with training in early childhood education made greater gains on tests of language receptivity and general knowledge and showed more cooperative behavior than other children. Staff-child ratio was not associated with child development for preschoolers, but it was for toddlers (age one to two). Doubling group size from twelve children to twenty-four was estimated to reduce the proportion of time spent by children in cooperative and reflective or innovative activities by about one percentage point each, and to reduce fall-to-spring gains on the Peabody Picture Vocabulary Test (PPVT) (a cognitive ability test) by 1.7 points, a 23 percent effect.

These results have been widely cited; moreover, the NDCS report is a model of clarity and thorough discussion. Nevertheless, this study does have some of the problems cited earlier. The day care centers included in the study were not randomly selected but chosen to be representative of centers that serve predominantly low-income children in urban settings. The analysis included more than the usual one or two measures of the home environment but did not deal with the possibility of selection of children into child care arrangements on the basis of unobserved family or child characteristics. The analysis of child development was conducted using centers rather than children as the unit of analysis, and the sensitivity of the results to unobserved center characteristics was not examined. The NDCS report (Ruopp et al. 1979, 79) is noteworthy for discussing these issues carefully:

If an unmanipulated center characteristic, such as group size, proved to be associated with several quality measures (as in fact it did), that association might be due to a causal relationship between group size and quality, but it might also be due to unmeasured center characteristics that were associated with both group size and the particular quality measures in question.

The bottom line is that the experimental evidence from the NDCS on the beneficial effect of higher staff-child ratio on the development of toddlers and of teacher training on preschooler development is credible, while the non-experimental evidence on group size is not as convincing, as acknowledged by the investigators.

The Florida Child Care Quality Improvement Study

In 1992 the legal minimum staff-child ratio for day care centers in Florida was raised from one teacher for six children to one for four, for children age zero; from one for eight to one for six, for age one; and from one for twelve to one for eleven, for age two. The new regulations also increased the amount of training that new staff members are required to complete within one year of hiring, from twenty to thirty hours.[6]

To evaluate the effects of the regulatory changes, the Florida Child Care Quality Improvement Study (Howes et al. 1998) drew a stratified random sample of 150 day care centers in four Florida counties in February-June 1992, before the new regulations went into effect.[7] The center director was interviewed, and three classrooms in each center were observed. The teachers in the selected rooms were interviewed, and two randomly selected children in each classroom were given developmental assessments. The centers were revisited in February-May 1994 and February-June 1996, and the same process repeated.[8]

The study found that observed staff-child ratios increased on average from 1992 to 1994, from 1:4.84 to 1:3.87 (a 20 percent increase) for infants, 1:6.64 to 1:5.88 (13 percent increase) for toddlers, and 1:10.07 to 1:9.95 (1 percent increase) for preschoolers. Before the new regulations went into effect, 29 percent of infant classrooms, 17 percent of toddler classrooms, and 5 percent of preschool classrooms would have been in violation of them. By 1994 the percentage of classrooms actually out of compliance with the new regulations was 9 percent in infant rooms, 6 percent in toddler rooms, and 2 percent in preschool rooms. By 1996 the percentage of classrooms out of compliance had increased to 19 percent for infants and 11 percent for toddlers, and remained at 2 percent for preschoolers. The study found small improvements in teacher sensitivity and harshness that were not significantly different from zero, and a statistically significant 12 percent decrease in teacher detachment from 1992 to 1994. By 1996 detachment had increased and was not significantly different from the original 1992 level. There were also improvements of similar orders of magnitude in the responsive involvement of teachers with children.

Classroom quality as measured by the Early Childhood Environment Rating Scale and the Infant-Toddler Environment Rating Scale increased by 12 percent from 1992 to 1994 and fell by 2 percent from 1994 to 1996, but none of the changes were significantly different from zero. The study found that the complexity of peer and object play increased by 4.2 percent from 1992 to 1994, and by another 6 to 12 percent by 1996, both statistically significant increases. Behavior problems and cognitive development as measured by language improved slightly by statistically insignificant amounts, and attachment security improved by 19 percent from 1992 to 1994 and by 21 percent from 1994 to 1996, both statistically significant increases.

There are two problems with the design of the Florida study that make it difficult to be confident that its findings represent causal effects of the changes in regulations. First, there is no comparison or control group. Other things that changed between 1992 and 1996 could have caused the observed changes in quality and child outcomes. There is no sound basis in the study design for attributing the observed changes in quality and child outcomes to the changes in regulations rather than to other unobserved changes that occurred during the same period of time. In the absence of a randomized trial, it is of course difficult to control for the possibility of spurious correlation due to changes in other unobserved factors. But a carefully selected comparison group could have helped control for some potentially confounding unobserved factors. For example, a sample of centers drawn from another state that did not change its regulations but that had economic and social conditions similar to those in Florida from 1992 to 1996 would have provided a means of at least attempting to control for unobserved changes in the economic or social environment that might have influenced quality and child outcomes. A sample of family day care homes in Florida might have served a similar purpose, since regulations governing such homes did not change.

A second problem with the Florida study is that different children were observed and assessed at each wave, even though many of the same classrooms and centers were observed. During a two-year period, infants and toddlers become preschoolers and move to other classrooms, switch centers, or leave day care altogether. This explains why the same children were not observed at each wave. But this makes it impossible to determine whether the observed gains in child outcomes were caused by changes in the quality of child care due to the tighter regulations or by changes in the clientele served. For example, parents who care strongly about quality might have been reluctant to place a child in a day care center before the regulatory change. Following the improvement in standards, a family who would have avoided center care might now use it, and such a family might have children with better development outcomes than those who would have attended a center in the absence of regulatory change. To the extent that changes in clientele are responsible for the observed improvements in child outcomes, we cannot be confident that changing regulations would improve outcomes for a *given* group of children.

The Study of Early Child Care

A third interesting study is the NICHD Study of Early Child Care. The SECC has followed a sample of more than thirteen hundred children from their birth in 1991 through the present, closely monitoring their home and child care environments and their development. The study used hospital birth records in ten sites in the United States in 1991 to select a sample of healthy births to English-speaking mothers over age eighteen who planned to remain in the site during the next year. Families were visited periodically for assessments of the home environment, and children who were in a nonmaternal child care arrangement were visited in that arrangement. The quality of the arrangement was measured using a variety of assessment instruments, and data on child care inputs were recorded by direct observation. A novel feature of the study was the inclusion and assessment of all types of nonmaternal child care arrangements, not just centers and family day care homes. Child development was assessed at regular intervals, and extensive psychosocial data on the mother and data on the home environment were collected as well. As children changed child care arrangements, the new arrangements were visited and observed.

The effects of child care quality on the cognitive and social development of children and on child behavior up to age three have been analyzed in the SECC by the NICHD Early Child Care Research Network (ECCRN) (1998a, 1998b, 2000b, 2000c). The first analysis of cognitive development and school readiness (NICHD ECCRN 1998a) examined only correlations, with no control variables. The analysis was limited to a comparison of outcomes between children who had been in continuous full-time nonmaternal care since four months of age and those who had never been in full-time care through thirty-six months.

No substantive conclusions about the effect of child care quality on cognitive development can be drawn from these results. The second analysis (NICHD ECCRN 2000c) used a regression model of cognitive development to control for five family and child characteristics and site dummies in addition to the cumulative type, quantity, and quality of child care. The analysis included only children who were in nonmaternal child care at the time of the developmental assessments. This study found positive and statistically significant effects of child care quality on several measures of cognitive development at ages fifteen, twenty-four, and thirty-six months. A one-standard-deviation increase in child care quality, as measured by a positive caregiving rating scale, was estimated to cause increases in cognitive development of .07 to .16 standard deviations, depending on the measure of development and child age. A subset of positive caregiver behaviors specifically related to language stimulation was included as a regressor in another set of models (in which the overall positive caregiving scale was also included) and had effects of .06 to .25 standard deviations, with some tendency for smaller effects at the older ages. The corresponding effects of a summary measure of the quality of the home environment were in the range of .09 to .23 standard deviations.

The study of the effects of child care on behavior problems (NICHD ECCRN 1998b) controls for family income, psychological adjustment of the mother, child gender, child temperament, the quality of the home environment, the character of mother-child interactions, and the security of the child's attachment to the mother. The analysis includes only children who were in nonmaternal child care arrangements at ages twenty-four or thirty-six months. A wide variety of measures of behavior were analyzed. At age twenty-four months, the average quality of child care during the first twenty-four months of life was associated with a reduced incidence of caregiver-reported behavior problems but had no effect on mother-reported behavior problems. Greater stability of care arrangements was associated with lower rates of noncompliance by children in the child care arrangements. Mother and observer reports of child behavior were not associated with child care characteristics. Some of these effects were no longer present by age thirty-six months, but higher-quality care was still negatively associated with problem behavior in the child care arrangement. A study of the effects of child care quality on children's peer interactions (NICHD ECCRN 2000b) controlled for several family characteristics as well as the child's cognitive development, temperament, and the mother's sensitivity. The results showed weak effects of child care quality on most measures of peer interaction.

The NICHD ECCRN (2000a) analyzed the effects of child care inputs on child care quality. The regression analysis controlled for site dummies but did not include any measures of the characteristics of the children and their families, and it also did not include any measures of center characteristics. The only variables included were characteristics of the room and teacher, as well as indicators of the type of child care. The results showed that larger groups and higher child-staff ratios had negative and statistically significant effects on the quality of care at ages fifteen and twenty-four months, but not at thirty-six months. Caregiver education had positive and significant effects on the quality of care at ages twenty-four and thirty-six months, but not at fifteen months. Caregiver specialized training in early childhood education had a positive and significant effect on the quality of care at fifteen months, but not at twenty-four or thirty-six months. Caregiver experience in child care had positive and significant effects on the quality of care at ages twenty-four and thirty-six months, but not at fifteen months.

The results from these studies are more credible than most in the literature because of the longitudinal design of the SECC, the inclusion of children in all types of child care (in some but not all of the studies), and the availability of extensive information on non-child-care factors. However, despite the richness of the data and the reasonably large sample size, many of the same problematic statistical methods typical of the child development literature are used in these studies. Baseline measures of the outcomes are generally not included in the regression models. It would be very useful, for example, to analyze cognitive development and behavior problems at age three as a function of cognitive development and behavior problems at age two and the quality of child care experienced between ages two and three. This would control for unobserved confounding factors that might be associated with both the level of development at age two and the quality of child care experienced between ages two and three. Alternatively, controlling for development at birth—birthweight and other indicators of developmental delay—would make the analysis of the cumulative effects of child care quality on child development more convincing. Most of the studies exclude children who were not in child care at the time of observation. This could lead to biased estimates if such children are different from the included children in unobserved dimensions. Many of the variables included in the analysis as regressors are chosen by parents. If there are unobserved factors that affect both the child's development or behavior and the choice of child care arrangement, then such omitted variables will lead to biased estimates of the variables that are included. (For a more thorough discussion and critique of the SECC studies, see Duncan and Gibson 2000.)

Perhaps the most important limitation of the results from the SECC to date is that the results cover children only through thirty-six months of age. By following children through the preschool ages and beyond, the SECC could make a very important contribution to knowledge about the long-run effects of child care quality on the development of children.

The Cost, Quality, and Outcomes Study

The Cost, Quality, and Outcomes Study collected data from a sample of four hundred day care centers in four states in 1993. Observational measures of quality were recorded, along with rich data on inputs and costs. Children who were expected to spend another full year at one of the sampled centers and then enroll in kindergarten in the fall of 1994 were selected to be given developmental assessments. They were reassessed in kindergarten and second grade, but published results to date cover only the initial assessment. (For a summary of results through second grade, but without coefficient estimates, see Peisner-Feinberg et al. 1999.) The sample included 828 children, of whom 757 provided usable data.

Controlling for maternal education, child gender and ethnicity, and the teacher's rating of her relationship with the child, Peisner-Feinberg and Burchinal (1997) report a positive association between child care quality and mental development, reading and pre-math achievement, and the child's attitude. A one-unit increase in quality (ECERS) was associated with a two-point increase in the PPVT score, implying an elasticity of .09 at the sample mean. An elasticity of .09 means that a 1 percent increase in ECERS would lead to a .09 percent increase in the PPVT score. A one-unit increase in ECERS was also associated with about a 0.7 increase in the Woodcock-Johnson reading and math scores, implying an elasticity of .03 at the sample mean. These are suggestive findings, but the absence of information on the home environment and a baseline development assessment leaves considerable uncertainty about whether they represent causal effects.

Another study (Mocan et al. 1995) used the CQOS data to estimate a model of classroom quality as a function of child care inputs. Unlike most studies in this literature, a large number of control variables were included in the model. This makes it more likely that the effects of the inputs were estimated without bias. They found a statistically significant effect on quality of .022 per .01 increase in the staff-child ratio. This implies that an increase in the staff-child ratio of 0.1 (for example, from one teacher for every ten children to one for five) would increase child care quality by .22, or about 20 percent of a standard deviation. They found small positive effects of group size that were not significantly different from zero. They found a positive and statistically significant effect of the wage rate for teachers with low education (a .107 increase in ECERS per dollar increase in the wage), a positive and statistically significant effect of the proportion of staff with a college degree (a .43 increase in ECERS for a change in the proportion from zero to one), and a negative and statistically significant effect of lead teacher turnover ($-.28$ effect on ECERS for a change from no turnover to 100 percent turnover).

I reanalyzed the CQOS data to determine the robustness of these results (Blau 2000b). The CQOS data provide an unusual opportunity to control not only for many observable factors that might be confounded with the inputs but also for unobserved characteristics of centers that might be important. In most of the centers the quality of two classrooms was assessed. By comparing classrooms to each other *within centers*, the effects of observed and unobserved center-specific factors that affect all classrooms within a center are held constant. In a more typical *between-center* analysis, we can control for observed differences across centers that might be correlated with both the dependent variable (quality) and the inputs. Examples include whether a center is nonprofit, the type of curriculum, the tenure of the director, and so forth. But it is easy to conceive of other intangible factors that are much harder to measure and that might affect both quality and the inputs. For example, the leadership ability of the director and her energy, enthusiasm, and ability to motivate her staff may be important. Such factors are held constant in a within-center analysis because they do not vary within centers. However, if there are classroom-specific unobservables that are confounded with both quality and inputs, then even a within-center analysis will yield biased estimates. For example, if teachers who are less skilled in ways that are not measured in the data are assigned to smaller groups of children, then within-center estimates will be biased.

Table 7.1 shows an excerpt from the results reported in Blau (2000b). The dependent variable is a classroom's ECERS-ITERS score, which can range between 1 at the low end and 7 at the high end. In addition to the variables shown, all models included an intercept and a dummy variable indicating whether the room serves infants and toddlers rather than preschoolers. Models 4 and 5 included a large number of other teacher and family characteristics, listed in the note to the table. Models 1 through 4 use all variation in the data, including between-center and within-center variation, while model 5 uses only within-center variation.

Several points are worth noting about these results. First, the effect of group size is of the "wrong" sign: higher group size is estimated to *increase* classroom quality. The effect size is small and becomes insignificantly different from zero in the models with more controls. Second, most of the effects are smaller when more control variables are added, indicating that failure to control for the additional factors causes biased estimates. Third and most important, using only within-center variation (model 5) yields much smaller estimates of all effects, and only the effect of training workshops remains significantly different from zero. Apparently, even with the extensive set of control variables available in the CQOS, there are still many important center-specific unobservables that can cause biased estimates when using between-center variation. As noted earlier, these estimates do not control for classroom-specific unobservables, such as teacher energy and motivation, that may be even more important than center-specific unobservables. So the estimates in model 5 should not be taken as the "truth." Rather, the set of estimates as a whole indicates that the effects reported in typical studies that rely on between-center variation may not be robust. If the results from model 5 are accurate, they suggest that standard regulatable inputs are mostly unproductive, with recent workshop training the only exception.[9]

The National Longitudinal Survey of Youth

Several studies have used a large nationally representative data set, the National Longitudinal Survey of Youth (NLSY), to analyze the determinants of child development. These data have large samples of children,

Table 7.1. / Five Models of the Effects of Inputs on Child Care Quality
(ECERS-ITERS)

	1	2	3	4	5
Group size	.016 (.008)*	.015 (.007)*	.007 (.007)	.009 (.007)	−.001 (.001)
Staff-child ratio	2.15 (.45)*	2.04 (.44)*	1.26 (.43)*	.89 (.42)*	.03 (.46)
Training workshops	—	.36 (.10)*	.34 (.09)*	.41 (.10)*	.19 (.10)*
College degree	—	.47 (.10)*	.29 (.10)*	.35 (.12)*	.10 (.16)
Teacher's wage rate	—	—	.12 (.01)*	.05 (.02)*	−.01 (.03)

Source: Blau 2000b, Table 5.
Notes: Dependent variable is the ECERS-ITERS score. "Training workshops" is an indicator that the teacher has received workshop training in the past year. The mean ECERS-ITERS score in the sample of 548 classrooms used in the analysis is 4.1, with a standard deviation (SD) of 1.0. The means (and SDs) of the explanatory variables are 13.5 (6.3) for group size, .18 (.11) for staff-child ratio, .79 (.40) for training workshops, .19 (.36) for college degree, and 7.43 (2.76) for teacher's wage rate. All models include an intercept and an infant-toddler dummy. The additional variables included in model 4 are teacher age, race, experience, and tenure; average education, income, hours of work, and race of the room parents; and center characteristics: average staff turnover, whether the program is bilingual, offers before- and after-school care, is for-profit, is part of a national chain, receives substantial public funds, is publicly operated, is church-sponsored, or uses the Waldorf curriculum; and state dummies. Model 5 includes all of these except the center characteristics and state dummies, since these do not vary within centers.
Standard errors of the coefficient estimates are in parentheses.
*The coefficient estimate is significantly different from zero at the 5 percent level.

good measures of child development and home inputs, and repeated measures for the same children over time. Some studies have included in their specifications variables related to child care and maternal employment. However, most have used measures of the type of child care, the age at which the child entered nonmaternal care, or maternal employment indicators only (see Baydar and Brooks-Gunn 1991; Belsky and Eggebeen 1991; Blau and Grossberg 1992; Caughy, DiPietro, and Strobino 1994; Desai, Chase-Lansdale, and Michael 1989; Gamoran, Mare, and Bethke 1999; Greenstein 1993; Han, Waldfogel, and Brooks-Gunn 1999; Korenman, Miller, and Sjaastad 1995; Mott 1991; Ruhm 2000; and Vandell and Ramanan 1991). Parcel and Menaghan (1990), Studer (1992), and Blau (1999) are the only studies using the NLSY that included child care inputs. Parcel and Menaghan report that the staff-child ratio had a negative but statistically insignificant effect in a model of the PPVT score in an analysis of the 1986 cross-section. Studer combined group size and staff into an "index of quality," which had a positive but statistically insignificant effect on PPVT in a sample of ninety-five children from the 1986 wave.

I used the NLSY data in an analysis of the effects of child care inputs on child development that more fully exploits the richness and longitudinal nature of the data than previous studies (Blau 1999). The NLSY began with a sample of 12,652 individuals who were between the ages of fourteen and twenty-one in 1979. They have been surveyed regularly since then, and beginning in 1986 the children of female sample members have been given a battery of developmental assessments every other year. In addition, mothers are asked a series of questions about the home environment and home inputs to child development. And extensive data on child care are collected from the mothers as well. The main disadvantages of the NLSY are that there are no data on child care quality (because this would require visits to thousands of child care arrangements), and the child care input data are reported by the mother instead of being recorded by trained observers in visits to the child care provider. The advantages are the very large random sample of children, the availability of extensive measures of the home environment and inputs, and the availability of repeated measures of the inputs and developmental outcomes. Unlike most other studies (with the exception of the NICHD SECC), the sample is not limited to children in a single mode of child care.

The dependent variables are the PPVT score (a cognitive ability measure), Peabody Individual Achievement Test (PIAT) math and reading scores (achievement measures), and a Behavior Problems Index (BPI) derived from a series of about thirty questions asked of the mother about the child's behavior. The explanatory variables of interest are the group size, staff-child ratio, and teacher training experienced by the child in his or her child care arrangement, as reported by the mother. The analysis also controlled for the type of care, whether it was a paid arrangement and the amount paid per hour, and how many hours per week and months per year the child spent in the arrangement. The analysis controlled for a large number of family and child characteristics, including two summary scales measuring the cognitive stimulation and emotional supportiveness of the home environment.

Excerpts from three sets of models are presented in table 7.2. The results in panel A are from models that include all of the control variables but do not control for unobserved factors or the level of child development prior to enrollment in the arrangement. The only statistically significant effects of the inputs in these models is on the PIAT-reading score, for which the group size effect is of the "wrong" sign, as in the CQOS analysis discussed earlier.

To gain a sense of the implications of the estimates, consider a child care arrangement that has ten children cared for by one adult: group size is 10

Table 7.2 / Estimates of the Effects of Child Care Inputs on Child Development

A. Ordinary Least Squares Estimates of Effects of Infant-Toddler Child Care

	BPI	PIAT-Math	PIAT-Reading	PPVT
Group size	0.08 (0.16)	0.06 (0.11)	0.37 (0.10)*	0.05 (0.27)
Staff-child ratio	−0.00 (2.53)	3.05 (1.87)	5.00 (1.88)*	2.72 (2.21)
Training	2.25 (1.86)	1.92 (1.56)	−0.56 (1.74)	1.47 (2.19)
Cognitive stimulation	−.14 (.02)*	.08 (.01)*	.07 (.02)*	.09 (.03)*
Emotional support	−.10 (.02)*	.10 (.02)*	.08 (.02)*	.14 (.03)*
Sample size	4,031	3,515	3,464	2,504

B. Mother Fixed Effects Estimates of Effects of Infant-Toddler Child Care

	BPI	PIAT-Math	PIAT-Reading	PPVT
Group size	.10 (0.22)	0.30 (0.27)	0.30 (0.31)	0.13 (0.35)
Staff-child ratio	1.65 (2.01)	−1.72 (2.62)	−0.18 (3.20)	3.85 (2.88)
Training	−1.67 (1.75)	−1.69 (2.18)	−1.97 (2.53)	−2.48 (2.40)

C. Ordinary Least Squares Estimates of Effects of Child Care in the Past Two Years

	BPI	PIAT-Math	PIAT-Reading
Group size	0.21 (0.11)*	−0.13 (0.12)	−0.13 (0.12)
Staff-child ratio	−1.09 (1.99)	−1.70 (3.10)	−5.83 (3.06)
Training	−1.81 (1.59)	1.87 (2.23)	−2.68 (2.35)
Lagged dependent variable	.057 (.003)*	.471 (.058)*	.521 (.052)*

Source: Blau 1999.
Notes: Standard errors are in parentheses. A model for the effects of child care in the past two years on PPVT could not be estimated because there were too few cases with PPVT scores in adjacent assessment years. The means and SDs of the outcomes are 106.6 (15.1) for the BPI, 100.1 (13.1) for PIAT-Math, 103.8 (14.2) for PIAT-Reading, and 93.6 (19.0) for the PPVT. Teacher training is an indicator for whether the teacher had any training in child care or early childhood education. The sample mean is .20 for the infant-toddler years and .29 for the preschool years. Average group size is 4.2 (4.6) for infants and toddlers, and 7.1 (9.2) for preschoolers; average staff-child ratio is .51 (.30) for infants and toddlers, and .44 (.31) for preschoolers. The mean (and SDs) of the cognitive stimulation score is 99.7 (15.2), and of the emotional support score is 99.7 (15.0).
*The hypothesis that the coefficient estimate equals zero can be rejected at the 5 percent level of significance.

and staff-child ratio is 0.1. Adding a second adult increases the staff-child ratio from 0.1 to 0.2 and leaves group size unchanged. According to the estimates in panel A of table 7.2, this would cause the PIAT reading score to rise by 0.50, an increase of 4 percent of a standard deviation. Splitting the group in half and providing a teacher for each of the groups would also increase the staff-child ratio from 0.1 to 0.2 and reduce group size from 10 to 5. This would *reduce* the PIAT reading score by 1.35, or 10 percent of a standard deviation. The effects of these experiments on the other outcomes are much smaller and statistically insignificant. In contrast, the effects of the cognitive stimulation and emotional support variables are all significantly different from zero, and measured in terms of elasticities, their effects are three to five times larger than any of the child care effects. Home inputs are far more important determinants of child development than child care inputs.

Panel B of table 7.2 reports estimates from a model that uses only within-family variation in the outcomes and inputs. This is possible because many women in the NLSY have two or more children for whom all the necessary data are available. If there are unobserved family-specific factors that affect child development and are correlated with the child care inputs, then the results in panel A would be biased. By comparing children within families, the effects of any permanent family-specific unobservables are controlled. Note that as in the case of the within-center analysis discussed earlier, this approach is not a panacea for all sources of bias; for example, it does not account for child-specific unobservables within families. But it can tell us whether the models that ignore unobserved family heterogeneity are seriously misleading. The results show no statistically significant effects of the child care inputs on any of the outcomes. The effects for PIAT reading scores in panel A are not robust—they appear to be spurious correlations accounted for by some omitted family variables.

The final set of results in table 7.2 shows the impact of child care inputs experienced by a child during the two years between surveys, controlling for the level of the dependent variable at the previous survey date. The lagged dependent variable controls for child-specific unobserved variables that are correlated with development outcomes and that remain constant as a child ages (for example, genetic factors).[10] The results show a negative effect of the staff-child ratio on the PIAT reading score (an effect of the "wrong" sign), and a positive effect of group size on the BPI, an effect of the "right" sign. Cutting group size from 10 to 5 would reduce the BPI by 1.05 points, or 7 percent of a standard deviation. Increasing staff-child ratio from 0.1 to 0.2 would reduce the PIAT reading score by .58, or 4 percent of a standard deviation.

The general message of these results is that there is little evidence of robust effects of child care inputs on child development. The few precisely measured effects are small and not robust to controls for unobserved family and child-specific unobserved factors. Does this mean that large groups, few staff per child, and untrained teachers are in fact not harmful to child development?

There are at least three reasons to be cautious about drawing this conclusion from the NLSY results. First, the results are not based on a random assignment experiment, so there is always the possibility of bias arising from failure to control for some important variables. Second, the results apply only within the range of variation observed in the data. As group size increases to forty, fifty, sixty, or more, it seems very likely that providing developmentally appropriate care to preschoolers would become impossible. Third, the input data in the NLSY are reported by the mother, not recorded by trained observers, so bias resulting from measurement error is a distinct possibility. However, I have shown that even allowing for the possibility of a substantial amount of measurement error does not change the basic message of small effects of the inputs on child development (Blau 1999). Finally, the inputs may serve as useful signals of quality to parents, even if they do not have a causal impact on quality. If child care providers with small groups, high staff-child ratios, and well-trained staff also tend to have other more intangible inputs that contribute to child development, then parents can use the inputs as a basis for identifying high-quality child care.

Despite these caveats, the results are not encouraging from a policy perspective. It is not clear that regulating the inputs or subsidizing child care based on the inputs will succeed in improving child care quality. This point forms an important part of the basis for my policy proposal in chapter 10.

Early Childhood Intervention Programs

Evaluations of Head Start and other preschool intervention programs could in principle provide very useful information about the effects of child care inputs and quality on child development. However, virtually all evaluations of such programs compare outcomes for a group of children subjected to the "treatment" to a control or comparison group not treated, and therefore they do not estimate the impact of specific features of the program, such as group size and teacher training. (For recent evaluations of Head Start, see Currie and Thomas 1995, 1999; and for evaluations of the Perry Preschool Project and the Carolina Abecedarian Project, two well-known early intervention programs, see Barnett 1992, Campbell and Ramey 1994, and Campbell et al., in press.) Bryant and her colleagues (1994) analyze the effect of a summary indicator of Head Start classroom quality on child outcomes but do not study the effects of attributes such as group size and teacher training. Karoly and her colleagues (1998) thoroughly review the literature on the evaluation of early intervention programs. They conclude that such programs can have substantial impacts on the lives of disadvantaged children, and that the benefits of some of these programs far outweigh the costs. Thus, these appear to be highly worthwhile programs, and I discuss them in more depth in chapter 8. However, because of the treatment-control nature of the program interventions, we cannot determine how much each feature of a given program contributes to its success.

CONCLUSIONS

Developmental psychologists have devoted a great deal of effort to conceptualizing and measuring child care quality and analyzing its determinants and consequences. The concept of "process quality" is very useful in characterizing the interactions that take place between adults and children in child care. The widely used measures of process quality, such as the ECERS-ITERS scales, are well validated and seem intuitively reasonable—in a sense, they formalize what a well-educated parent might look for in a child care arrangement. It seems quite plausible that high-quality child care as measured by such instruments would have a beneficial impact on child development. And it is also plausible that better-trained teachers, smaller groups of children, and more adults per child would lead to higher-quality care and ultimately to better child development outcomes.

Unfortunately, the evidence on these points is relatively weak, especially in the latter case. Developmental psychologists have been quite successful in defining and measuring the quality of child care but have not convincingly analyzed its determinants and consequences. This is not to say that the hypothesized links between inputs, quality, and child outcomes do not exist. Rather, the evidence is simply inconclusive about whether the links exist and their strength.

With the half-dozen exceptions noted in this chapter, the literature is dominated by studies of small, convenience samples of children in child care arrangements that are often not representative of arrangements used in the population. Even in the studies with larger and more representative samples, the statistical analysis is often not convincing. These analyses typically focus on explaining variance or comparing groups rather than measuring effect sizes. They tend to err on the side of undercontrolling for potentially confounding factors rather than take the safer and more conservative approach of overcontrolling. They usually make little effort to determine how robust the findings are and whether they are affected by unobserved confounding factors, which are ubiquitous in non-experimental studies. These studies are useful for descriptive and exploratory purposes, such as establishing the reliability of an instrument or testing the design of a measure. But the information we need for policy purposes—unbiased estimates of the consequences for child development of changing each input and the quality of care—cannot be produced without careful attention to statistical issues and efforts to determine the sensitivity and robustness of the findings.

My conclusion from the evidence on the effects of child care inputs on quality is that teacher training in early childhood education enhances child care quality, but that smaller group size and higher staff-child ratio do not, at least within the range of variation observed in the data. The types of training that seem most productive are on-site workshops and courses in early childhood education designed for child care providers. College degrees and formal schooling in general seem less productive.

Eschewing false modesty, I believe the best available evidence on these effects is from my own analysis of the National Child Care Staffing Study and the Cost, Quality, and Outcomes Study (Blau 1997, 2000b). In the NCCSS data, I found robust evidence that having taken a college course in early childhood education in the past year increases teacher sensitivity by 16 percent of a standard deviation, reduces detached teacher behavior by 21 percent of a standard deviation, and increases appropriate caregiving behavior by 21 percent of a standard deviation. These are modest but not negligible effects, they are statistically significant, and they arise from models that exploit only within-center variation in quality and inputs. Many other measures of teacher education and training were included in the models, and none had consistent and robust effects. In results from the CQOS data discussed earlier, I found robust evidence that when a teacher has had recent workshop-based training, the classroom score on ECERS-ITERS increases by 23 percent of a standard deviation. This statistically significant effect is from a model that exploits only within-center variation in quality and inputs. Effects of other measures of teacher training were never statistically significant, and effects of formal teacher education were sometimes significant but not robust to changes in specification.

The lack of robust evidence of beneficial effects of small groups and high staff-child ratios is consistent with evidence from European countries, such as France, Germany, Spain, and Portugal, in which highly trained teachers provide care in relatively large groups. The group size used in preschool classrooms in these countries would not meet regulatory standards in many U.S. states, yet child development outcomes are in some cases better than in the United States (Bergmann 1996, Cryer et al. 1999).

The evidence on the effect of child care quality on child development suggests that there is an effect. The best available estimates in my view are from the NICHD Early Child Care Research Network (2000c) and Peisner-Feinberg and Burchinal (1997). These studies have the benefit of relatively large and somewhat representative samples, and good measures of most of the key variables. The estimates of Peisner-Feinberg and Burchinal imply an elasticity of child development with respect to child care quality of .09 for an IQ-like measure (the PPVT), and .03 for pre-reading and pre-math achievement. Estimates from the NICHD ECCRN imply elasticities of an IQ-like measure (Bayley) with respect to language stimulation of .04 to .09, and elasticities of language production and comprehension (MacArthur Communicative Development Inventory and Reynell Developmental Language Scale) of .07 to .27 with respect to language stimulation. These are modest but not inconsequential effects. Whether they turn out to be robust to further analysis is an important question.

Finally, my reading of the evidence on the net effect of the inputs on child development is that there is an effect of teacher training, but little evidence of effects of group size and staff-child ratio. I believe the best evidence on this issue is from the National Day Care Study (Ruopp et al. 1979). These researchers report that increasing the proportion of day care center classroom staff with child-related education and training from zero to one would cause an increase of 25 percent in the fall-to-spring gain in the Preschool Inventory score of children. Because this relatively large effect is based on a random assignment experiment, it is quite credible. My analysis of the NLSY suggests that home inputs are much more important to child development than child care inputs.

Despite the weaknesses of the evidence, an important point to take from this chapter is that high-quality child care can be beneficial for child development, especially for children raised in poverty. Home inputs may be more important than child care inputs, but the latter are likely to be more amenable to change through public policy. This point plays a decisive role in my proposal for a new child care policy in chapter 10.

Part of the intent of this book is to provide an evaluation of the evidence on issues that are crucial for the design of policies to deal with the child care problem. In this chapter, as in the other chapters presenting this evidence, it is important to emphasize the limitations of the evidence and the resulting uncertainty about how effective policy can be. But another role of the book is to point out that even with the limited evidence at our disposal, we cannot ignore the fact that there is a child care problem, that it may be causing harm to the development of many children, and that there may be something we can do about it. In the final three chapters of the book, I turn to a discussion of child care policy, first analyzing existing policy in chapters 8 and 9, and then presenting my own ideas in chapter 10.

Part III

CHILD CARE POLICY

Chapter 8

Child Care Subsidies

I n this chapter, I describe and analyze child care subsidy policy in the United States. Child care subsidies are one of the two major parts of U.S. government child care policy; the other is regulation, which I analyze in the next chapter.[1] It is important to understand the current child care subsidy system to determine whether it is sensible, and how it should be reformed, if at all.

I begin by providing an overview of child care subsidy policy. I take a broad view of child care subsidies, discussing not only subsidies tied to the employment of the parents but also early education subsidies such as Head Start and Title I-A. The latter are not typically thought of as subsidies for child care, and they do not require that the parents be employed. But any subsidy for nonparental care of children may influence both the employment of the parents and the quality of care received by the children. All such programs can be thought of as located on a two-dimensional spectrum with respect to the restrictions on the use of the subsidy. One dimension is the employment requirement of the program, with one end of the spectrum requiring full-time parental employment to receive a subsidy, and the other end not requiring any employment. The other dimension is the quality of child care required to be eligible for a subsidy, with one end of the spectrum having no restriction on the quality of care and the other extreme allowing the subsidy to be used only for care that meets detailed quality specifications. The choice of where to locate a program along this spectrum is a policy decision, so it is important to discuss together all programs that subsidize nonparental child care. I show in the next section that current policy is tilted toward subsidies with an employment requirement and few quality restrictions.

I then discuss the rationale for and goals of child care subsidies. I present and evaluate each of the main arguments for the government to subsidize child care. The evaluation includes both the logical coherence of the argument—given its premises, are child care subsidies a logical response?—and evidence on whether the premises specified in the argument hold in practice. I conclude that evidence supporting the rationale for employment-related child care subsidies is weak, while evidence in support of the rationale for quality-related subsidies is stronger. This conclusion plays a major role in the design of my proposal in chapter 10.

The last section examines evidence on the effects of child care subsidies on employment and child outcomes. Here I address the questions of how effectively child care subsidies increase employment and improve the quality of care and developmental outcomes of children. The evidence indicates that child care subsidies have a moderate effect on the employment of mothers. There is no direct evidence available on the impact of child care subsidies on the quality of child care demanded or supplied. However, there is reasonably convincing evidence that very high-quality child care for low-income children can have a substantial impact on their outcomes in adolescence and early adulthood.

U.S. CHILD CARE SUBSIDY POLICY

Child care subsidies help parents pay their expenses for nonparental child care and preschool and help child care providers pay the cost of providing such care. Some of the subsidy programs are restricted to employment-related child care expenses, while others have no employment requirement. The goals and structure of employment-related child care subsidy programs are quite different from those of early education preschool programs.

I argue in this book that society faces a trade-off in child care policy between the goals of improving child well-being and increasing the net return from employment for parents of young children. Thus, it is important to interpret child care subsidies broadly and to include in the discussion all programs that help defray expenses for the regular care of young children by adults other than their parents. A subsidy for work-related child care expenses may affect the quality of child care purchased, whether or not this is a goal of the subsidy program, and a subsidy for an early education program intended to improve child development affects the work incentives of the parents, whether by design or not.

The goals and provisions of the major U.S. child care and early education subsidy programs are summarized in table 8.1.[2] The first two programs listed are tax subsidies. The Exclusion (from taxable income) of Employer-Provided Dependent Care Expenses (EEPDCE) is a fringe benefit offered by some firms to their employees, in one of two forms. In the first, if the firm provides child care benefits to its employees in the form of subsidized on-site or near-site facilities or direct reimbursement of employee expenses, such benefits are treated as a form of nontaxable compensation, like health insurance. Only 4 percent of employees in private establishments had such benefits in 1995 to 1996 (U.S. Department of Labor 1998). Ten percent of private-sector professional and technical employees, 4 percent of clerical and sales employees, and 2 percent of blue-collar and service employees worked for an establishment that offers a direct child care subsidy. This suggests that firms that employ mainly low-wage workers are much less likely to offer such benefits. Medium-sized and large establishments (employing more than one hundred) are about four times as likely as small establishments to offer this benefit.

In the second form of tax subsidy, if the firm provides its employees with the option of a flexible spending or reimbursement account ("cafeteria plan") that can be used for child care expenses, the employee contribution to such an account is treated as nontaxable compensation. Twenty percent of private-sector workers in 1995 to 1996 worked for a company that allowed employees to establish a reimbursement account to cover child care expenses. Firms are not obliged to offer the EEPDCE as a benefit, but if they do offer it, they must make it available to all qualified employees. If, as a result of low income, an employee has no federal income tax liability, then the employee does not benefit from a reimbursement account. This suggests that firms with predominantly low-wage workers would be less likely to offer a reimbursement account. In 1997, 40 percent of private-sector professional and technical employees, 34 percent of clerical and sales employees, and 19 percent of blue-collar and service employees worked for a medium-sized or large establishment that offered a child care reimbursement account. The corresponding figures for small establishments in 1996 were 16 percent, 13 percent, and 5 percent (U.S. Department of Labor 1999a).[3]

The Dependent Care Tax Credit (DCTC) allows taxpayers with adjusted gross income (AGI) of less than $10,000 to receive a tax credit of 30 percent for child care expenses of up to $4,800 per year for two or more children ($2,400 for one child). The maximum subsidy for two or more children is $1,440 (30 percent of $4,800). The subsidy rate declines by one percentage point for each $2,000 increase in AGI, reaching 20 percent for AGI of $28,000. The subsidy rate remains constant for AGI above $28,000. This subsidy is *means-tested* in the sense that the subsidy rate and therefore the value of the subsidy declines as income increases. More important, however, the credit is not *refundable*, so the amount of credit available to low-income families is relatively small. A nonrefundable credit is limited to the amount of income tax liability; many low-income families have no federal income tax liability and therefore cannot receive any tax credit. One-quarter of the total amount of tax credit claimed in 1997 went to families with AGI of less than $30,000, but almost all of this amount was claimed by families with AGI between $15,000 and $30,000; only 1.8 percent of the total was claimed by families with AGI less than $15,000 (Internal Revenue Service 1998–1999).

In 1996 the Personal Responsibility and Work Opportunity Reconciliation Act (PRWORA) consolidated four existing employment-related child care subsidy programs for low-income families into a single child care

/ 151

Table 8.1 / The History, Goals, and Provisions of Major Federal Child Care and Early Education Programs

	Exclusion for Employer-Provided Dependent Care Expenses (EEPDCE)	Dependent Care Tax Credit (DCTC)	Child Care and Development Fund (CCDF)
Year began	1981	1954	1996[b]
Goal	Subsidizes employment-related dependent care expenses.	Subsidizes employment-related dependent care expenses.	Helps families who recently left welfare for work maintain self-sufficiency. Helps families who need child care in order to work and are at risk of going on welfare if child care is not provided.
Form	Amounts paid or incurred by an employer for dependent care assistance provided to an employee are excluded from the employee's gross taxable earnings.	Nonrefundable tax credit.	Block grant. States must meet maintenance-of-effort and matching requirements for some of the funds. States may transfer up to 30 percent of their TANF block grant funds into the CCDF. States may also use TANF funds directly for child care, without transferring them to CCDF.
Provisions	Up to $5,000 per year excludable. Expenses excluded from gross income are not eligible for the DCTC.	Thirty percent tax credit on expenses up to $4,800 for two children for adjusted gross income of $10,000 or less; subsidy rate falls to 20 percent for adjusted gross income of more than $28,000.	Sliding fee scale, but states may waive fees for families below the poverty line. At least 4 percent of funds must be spent on quality improvement and consumer education. Child care must meet state licensing and regulatory standards. Vouchers preferred over contracts. Relative care eligible if provider lives in a separate residence.
Eligibility criteria	None, other than being employed by a firm that offers this benefit.	Both parents (or only parent) must be employed.	Family income no more than 85 percent of state median income, but states can (and most do) impose a lower income eligibility limit. Children under age thirteen. Parents must be in work-related activities.

Source: Committee on Ways and Means 1998; U.S. Department of Education 1996.
[a]Less than 2 percent of the funds in the food program go to adult care centers.
[b]The CCDF combined four previous programs, two of which began in 1988 (Aid to Families with Dependent Children—Child Care and Transitional Child Care), and the other two of which began in 1990 (At-Risk Child Care, and the Child Care and Development Block Grant).
[c]Earlier provisions of the Social Security Act provided federal matching funds to the states for social services.

Table 8.1 / *Continued*

Title XX Social Services Block Grant (TXX-CC)	Head Start (HS)	Child and Adult Care Food Program (CCFP)[a]	Title I, Part A, of the Elementary and Secondary Education Act (Title I-A)
1975[c]	1965	1968	1965
Helps low-income families achieve self-sufficiency; prevents child neglect.	Improves the social competence, learning skills, health, and nutrition of low-income children age three to five.	Improves nutrition of low-income children. Part of the National School Lunch Act.	Provides programs and services for educationally disadvantaged children (children who are failing or at risk of failing student performance standards).
Block grant to states that can be used for many social services; 15 percent of funds on average used for child care.	Part-day preschool, health screening, nutrition, and social services.	Cash subsidies to the provider for meals and snacks in day care centers and family day care homes.	Grants to states based on number of children from low-income families and per-pupil education expenditures.
Child care must meet state regulatory and licensing standards.	Free.	Child care must meet state regulatory standards. Must serve mainly low-income children.	A school or local education agency may operate a preschool program.
States choose income eligibility. Employment required.	Children age zero to five (mainly three to five); 90 percent of enrollees must be below the poverty line. Ten percent of slots reserved for disabled children.	Subsidy amount depends on whether income is less than 130 percent of poverty line; 130 to 185 percent of poverty line; or more than 185 percent of poverty line.	Targets funds to schools with the highest percentage of children from low-income families.

block grant program called the Child Care and Development Fund (CCDF).[4] The goal of the consolidated program is to facilitate the transition of families from welfare to work and to help low-income parents maintain employment. One of the reasons for consolidating the four previous programs was to eliminate the fragmentation that existed under the previous system of multiple programs with varying rules and eligibility requirements. Under the new system, states can (but are not required to) allow a family that moves from welfare to work to continue to receive a child care subsidy without changing programs.

States can use CCDF funds to assist families with income up to 85 percent of state median income (SMI), but are free to use a lower income eligibility criterion. Parents must be employed, in training, or in school, although some exceptions are permitted. In general, priority for CCDF funds is supposed to be given to families with very low incomes and children with special needs. The CCDF also requires that part of the funds be used to assist working poor families who are not current or recent welfare recipients, and not likely to be in the future. As part of the general increase in flexibility provided by PRWORA, states are permitted to transfer up to 30 percent of their Temporary Assistance for Needy Families (TANF) block grant funds to the CCDF to be used for child care, and states can also use TANF funds directly for child care services without transferring the funds to the CCDF. States must offer "certificates" (formerly called vouchers) that allow families to purchase care from any provider that meets state regulations and licensing standards or is legally exempt from licensing, including relatives and baby-sitters. States can also contract to purchase slots in day care centers and family day care homes and provide such slots to eligible families.

The states have substantial flexibility in designing their CCDF programs, including the income eligibility limit, copayments by families, and reimbursement rates to providers. Only nine states set income eligibility at the maximum allowed by law—85 percent of state median income. Seven states set the income eligibility limit at less than 50 percent of SMI. States are permitted to waive fees (copayments) for families with income below the poverty line, and there is substantial variation across states in the use of this provision. Fees are determined in many different ways, including flat rates, percentage of cost, percentage of income, and combinations of these. States are required to have sliding scale fee structures, with fees that rise with family income. The amount of the subsidy is supposed to be based on a recent market survey, with the subsidy set so that it covers the fee charged by the provider at the seventy-fifth percentile of the market rate distribution. In practice, many states use out-of-date market surveys or set the subsidy below the seventy-fifth percentile (Adams, Schulman, and Ebb 1998, 23).[5]

The other main means-tested subsidy program with an employment focus is the Title XX Social Services Block Grant (TXX). This program subsidizes a wide variety of social services and gives states flexibility in how the funds are allocated across the various eligible services. On average, about 15 percent of TXX funds have been spent on child care in recent years. Child care funded by Title XX must meet applicable state standards and is often provided through slots in centers and family day care homes purchased through grants and contracts with state or local agencies. States choose the income eligibility limit.

The last three programs listed in table 8.1, Head Start, the Child and Adult Care Food Program (CCFP), and Title I-A of the Elementary and Secondary Schools Act, are intended to improve child well-being and have no employment or training requirement for the parents. Head Start provides part-day preschool, along with health, nutrition, and social services, to children from families in poverty. The goal of the program is to improve the social competence, learning skills, health, and nutrition of children. Head Start programs must meet a set of federal standards that are more stringent and oriented toward child development than most state regulations. The Child and Adult Care Food Program provides subsidies for meals meeting federal nutrition requirements served in licensed day care centers and family day care homes serving low-income children. Subsidy rates depend on the family income of the children served, with a maximum income of 185 percent of the poverty level. Title I-A provides services for educationally disadvantaged children who are at risk of failing to meet student performance standards. Most Title I-A funds go to schools serving students in kindergarten through twelfth grade, but state and local education agencies may use such funds to serve preschool-age children as well, in school-based or community-based programs. Title I-A programs must meet the Head Start standards.

Table 8.2 summarizes federal and state expenditures on child care subsidies in recent years and the numbers of children served by the subsidy programs. Assuming that fiscal year 1999 DCTC and CCFP expenditures are the same as in fiscal year 2000 (in real terms, adjusting for inflation), a rough figure for total federal and state expenditures on child care subsidies in fiscal year 1999 is $21 billion. A meaningful total for the number of children cannot be computed. The CCDF is the biggest program in terms of expenditures, at $9 billion. About half of CCDF spending was from the TANF block grant in 1999—states have taken advantage of the flexibility offered by PRWORA to spend large amounts on child care from the TANF block grant. Head Start is the best-funded program per child served, with annual expenditures of $5,403 per child in 1999 (Head Start 2001). The only subsidy programs that are open-ended entitlements are the EEPDCE and DCTC tax subsidies (in terms of the number of children served, not expenditures per child). The other programs are capped entitlements with no obligation to serve all eligible families. It is estimated that the CCDF serves only 12 to 15 percent of eligible children (Administration for Children and Families 1999, 2000a). Head Start is estimated to serve 34 percent of three- to five-year-old children in poverty.[6] No figures are available on the percentage of eligible children served by the other programs.

Table 8.2 / Federal and State Expenditures and Children Served by Major Federal Child Care Subsidy Programs

Fiscal Year	DCTC[a]	EEPDCE[b]	HS[c]	TXX-CC	CCFP	CCDF	Title I-A[o]
Federal and State Expenditures (Billions of Constant 1999 Dollars)							
2000	2.200	.984	5.056	.222[d]	1.624[g]	—	—
1999	—	.995	4.658	.285[e]	—	9.132[j]	2.015
1998	2.649	.910	4.443	—	—	6.540[j]	—
1997	2.464	.862	4.132	.384[f]	1.582[h]	4.535[j]	—
1996	2.663	.823	4.223	.374[f]	1.678[h]	—	—
1995	2.518	.792	3.862	.453[f]	1.603[h]	3.4[k]	—
Children Served (Millions)							
2000	—	—	.858	—	—	—	—
1999	—	—	.826	—	—	1.760[l]	—
1998	6.120	—	.822	—	2.6[i]	1.531[l]	—
1997	5.796	—	.794	—	2.2[i]	1.248[m]	—
1996	6.003	—	.752	—	2.4[i]	—	—
1995	5.964	—	.751	—	2.3[i]	1.445[n]	—

Notes: See table 8.1 for definitions of the program acronyms. Current dollar expenditures were converted to constant 1999 dollars using consumer price index values of 1.093, 1.062, 1.038, 1.022, 1.0, and 0.96 for 1995 through 2000, respectively.

[a]Committee on Ways and Means 2000, 816. The figure for 2000 is estimated (600). The 1998 figures are preliminary. Figures in the lower panel are number of returns filed claiming the credit, not the number of children. The figures are for calendar years, not fiscal years.

[b]Office of Management and Budget 1996, Table 5-1. These figures are for the calendar year. The method used to compute them is unclear, and in budget statements for subsequent years they are different. They are also different in Joint Committee on Taxation (1999). These are probably the least reliable figures in the table.

[c]Head Start Fact Sheet 2001.

[d]Thirteen percent of $1.775 billion, multiplied by .96 to convert to 1999 dollars (Committee on Ways and Means 2000, 600).

[e]Estimated at 15 percent of $1.9 billion for TXX from Committee on Ways and Means (2000, 634).

[f]Committee on Ways and Means 1998, 714, 720: 14.8 percent of total TXX funding of $2.800 billion, $2.381 billion, and $2.500 billion for fiscal years 1995, 1996, and 1997.

[g]Committee on Ways and Means 2000, 600.

[h]Committee on Ways and Means 1998, 679, 687.

[i]U.S. Department of Agriculture 2001.

[j]I computed these figures by summing all federal and state expenditures on the CCDF, either directly or through transfers to TANF, using data from the annual TANF reports to Congress (U.S. Department of Health and Human Services, various years) and reports from the Child Care Bureau (various years). The latter source provides allocations to the CCDF for fiscal years 2000 and 2001, but there are no data available on transfers from TANF for these years. Transfers to TANF constituted about half of CCDF spending in fiscal year 1999.

[k]U.S. General Accounting Office 1998, 4: total funding for the four programs later consolidated into the CCDF: AFDC-CC, TCC, ARCC, CCDBG.

[l]Administration for Children and Families 2000a.

[m]Administration for Children and Families 1998b, 1.

[n]Sum of AFDC-CC, TCC, ARCC, and CCDBG Administration for Children and Families 1995.

[o]U.S. General Accounting Office 1999, 6: Department of Education programs: Title I-A, Individuals with Disabilities Education Act, Even Start, Twenty-first Century Learning Centers. U.S. General Accounting Office (2000b) gives different figures, and an estimate of 341,000 preschool children served by Title I-A and Even Start.

WHY SUBSIDIZE CHILD CARE?

Four arguments have been used in support of government subsidies to child care. The arguments are based on alleviating shortages, attaining economic self-sufficiency, addressing child care market imperfections, and striving for equity.[7]

Alleviating Shortages

It is often claimed that there are shortages of child care of particular types, such as center care for infants, weekend and night-shift care, high-quality care, and care for sick children. Subsidies to providers of such types of child care might increase the quantity available. In economic terms, a shortage of a service exists if the amount of the service offered for sale at the market price is less than the amount consumers wish to purchase at that price. For example, if the market price in a particular city for full-time center care of a specified quality for infants is $100 per week, and there are more infants whose parents would like to purchase care at this price than there are spaces available in centers at this price, then a shortage exists at the price of $100. It is unlikely that such a shortage would persist indefinitely. If centers can expand their capacity and provide additional infant slots with the specified quality at a weekly cost of less than $100 per slot, we would expect them to do so since they can make additional profit. If parents would rather pay, say, $120 for care than not be able to purchase care at all, we would expect parents to offer a higher price, since they would prefer to have the care at a higher price than to not have it at all. In this case, firms that could not profitably offer care at $100 per week but could do so at $120 per week would be likely to enter the market, helping to alleviate the shortage. These standard arguments suggest that shortages are the exception rather than the rule, and that they are temporary when they do occur.

Assertions of shortages often implicitly or explicitly refer to a situation in which providers are not willing to supply much child care of a given type or quality at prices that most consumers are willing to pay. Referring to the previous example, suppose that most consumers feel they cannot afford to pay more than $100 per week for infant care—they would rather not purchase child care of the specified quality than purchase it for more than $100. They are therefore unwilling to bid the price up. Suppose also that the cost of providing additional slots for infants exceeds $100, because centers would have to raise wages to attract more staff. Perhaps a few slots for infants are available at a price of $100 or less in church-sponsored or other nonprofit centers that use donated space or labor. But additional slots would be available only at higher cost in for-profit centers, because the

/ 157

nonprofits cannot expand. There is no shortage of infant care, however, in this scenario; the absence of infant care slots simply reflects the fact that consumers do not feel they receive enough value from the service to be willing to pay a price that covers the cost of providing the service. In this situation, there is no rationale for the government to provide a subsidy *for the purpose of alleviating a shortage,* because there is no shortage.

Attaining Economic Self-sufficiency

Child care subsidies might help low-income families be economically self-sufficient. A "self-sufficient" family in this context means one in which at least one adult is employed and the family is not enrolled in a cash assistance welfare program, though perhaps is receiving in-kind subsidies such as food stamps, Medicaid, housing, or child care. Self-sufficiency is considered desirable because it may increase future self-sufficiency by inculcating a work ethic and generating human capital through on-the-job training and experience, and it may therefore save the government money in the long run (Robins 1991, 15).[8]

These arguments explain why many child care subsidies require employment or work-related activities such as education and training. Child care and other subsidies paid to employed low-income parents may cost the government more today than would cash assistance through TANF. But if the dynamic links suggested here are important, then employment-related subsidies may be more likely to result in increased future wages and hours worked, and lower lifetime subsidies, than the alternative of cash assistance, both today and in the future. Note that this argument has nothing to do with the effects of child care on children, and there are few restrictions on the type and quality of child care that can be purchased with employment-related subsidies such as the CCDF and DCTC. Note also that while child care subsidies clearly improve the well-being of recipients, cash transfers would presumably increase their well-being even more. But immediate improvement in well-being is not the rationale under consideration—rather, it is long-run self-sufficiency.

There is surprisingly little known about the wage growth of low-skill workers, but a recent paper by Gladden and Taber (2000) provides some useful evidence. They analyze the wage growth of individuals with at most a high school education, over the first ten years after completing schooling, using longitudinal data from the National Longitudinal Survey of Youth. They find that wages grow with labor market experience at similar rates for different skill groups. They define skill groups by education and family background (parent's education and income). The fact that the lower-skill groups have wage growth rates similar to those of higher-skill groups suggests that low-skill workers do gain higher wages as their work experience increases. But the actual wage growth rates with experience are modest for all skill groups and do not seem high enough to lift low-skill workers out of poverty. For example, high school dropouts averaged 4.4 percent real wage growth per year of actual work experience over the first ten years of work. Thus, if a high school dropout began working at the minimum wage of $5.15 an hour, after ten years of work experience her wage rate would have increased to $8.00 an hour on average. This increase is not negligible, but it is also not enough to reduce significantly her dependence on welfare. Gladden and Taber (2000, 189) conclude from their results that ". . . work experience is not a magic bullet. The . . . evidence indicates that low-skilled workers will not have huge wage gains from work experience."

Middle- and upper-income families are generally not at risk of going on welfare, so why should the government provide subsidies for the employment-related child care expenses of such families? One argument is that taxing labor income reduces the incentive to be employed, and that child care and other work-expense subsidies can help offset this distortion (Barnett 1993a; Joint Committee on Taxation 2000, 105–7). This is not a compelling rationale. Child care subsidies certainly increase employment incentives, but they introduce another distortion by providing an incentive to use paid rather than unpaid child care. If there is some kind of market imperfection that causes paid child care to be underutilized, then the appropriate remedy is a subsidy to paid child care, *independent of employment status*. This argument is spelled out in detail in chapter 10. In general, the best remedy for one government-induced economic distortion is not the introduction of another such distortion, but rather the removal of the initial distortion. For example, instead of taxing labor income, the government could tax consumption or production. In the absence of a compelling economic rationale for middle-class employment-related child care subsidies, the most likely explanation for the existence of such subsidies is that they are politically popular.

Addressing Market Imperfections

The third argument for child care subsidies centers on imperfections in the child care market. The imperfections often cited are the imperfect information available to parents about the quality of child care and the positive external benefits to society generated by high-quality child care. These considerations can be and are used to argue for child care subsidies to all families, since neither external benefits nor information problems are necessarily income-specific.[9] Walker (1991) spells out these points in detail, and the discussion here follows his arguments closely (see also Council of Economic Advisers 1997; Magenheim 1995; Robins 1991; Vandell and Wolfe 2000).

Imperfect information in the child care market exists because consumers are not perfectly informed about the identity of all potential suppliers, and because the quality of care offered by any particular supplier is not fully known. A potential remedy for the first problem is government subsidies to resource and referral (R&R) agencies to maintain comprehensive and accurate lists of suppliers. This may not solve the problem in practice because of very high turnover among informal child care providers and their unwillingness to reveal their identity. There are two reasons for the second information problem: consumers know less about product quality than does the provider, and monitoring the provider is costly to the consumer. This can lead to moral hazard (hidden action) or adverse selection, or both. Moral hazard is a plausible outcome in day care centers (for example, not changing diapers until just before pickup time). Adverse selection of providers is plausible in the more informal family day care sector. Family day care is a very low-wage occupation, so women with high wage offers in other occupations are less likely to choose to be care providers. If the outside wage offer is positively correlated with the quality of care provided, then women who choose to work in child care would offer lower-quality care than would the potential caregivers who have chosen other occupations.

Is there evidence that child care consumers are not well informed? Walker (1991) reports that 60 to 80 percent of child care arrangements made by low-income parents are located through referrals from friends and relatives or through direct acquaintance with the provider. This suggests that consumers may not be well informed about a wide range of potential providers, but it does not prove that a suboptimal amount of information is used by consumers. If parents have strong preferences for acquaintance with the provider, then limited information may be optimal from their perspective, though not necessarily from a social perspective if acquaintance is uncorrelated with the quality of care. Cryer and Burchinal (1995) report a direct comparison of parent ratings of various aspects of their child's day care center classroom with trained observer ratings of the same aspects, using data from the Cost, Quality, and Outcomes Study. The results show that parents give higher average ratings on every item than do trained observers, by about one standard deviation for preschool-age classrooms and by about two standard deviations for infant-toddler rooms. The instrument containing these items (ECERS-ITERS) is of demonstrated reliability when administered by trained observers, so this suggests that parents are not well informed about the quality of care in the arrangements used by their children.

Child care subsidies targeted at high-quality providers could induce parents to use higher-quality care by reducing the net price of such care compared to the price of lower-quality care. This would not necessarily solve the information problem, but it would deal with a consequence of that problem, namely, a level of child care quality that is suboptimal from the perspective of society. Head Start and Title I can be thought of as providing subsidies for high-quality child care for low-income children, while other subsidies generally place few restrictions on quality.[10]

The externality argument is a standard one that closely parallels the reasoning applied to education. High-quality child care leads to improved intellectual and social development, which in turn increases school readiness and completion. This reduces the cost to society of problems associated with low education: low earnings, unstable employment, crime, drugs, teenage childbearing, and so forth. If parents are either not fully aware of these benefits or consider only the private rather than the social benefits of high-quality child care, then they may choose child care with less than socially optimal quality. This argument could rationalize subsidies targeted to high-quality providers, such as Head Start, as well as similar programs for middle- and upper-income children.

Evidence on the effect of child care quality on child development is of two types, as noted in chapter 7. The first is from randomized assignment demonstrations that have evaluated the impact of high-quality preschool programs for disadvantaged children. A comprehensive review of early childhood interventions by Karoly and her colleagues (1998) concludes that such programs can provide significant benefits to participating children and reduce future expenditures on welfare, criminal justice, and related items. This evidence is compelling, but it is based mainly on very intensive and costly programs that are of higher quality even than Head Start. It is unclear whether child care of moderately high quality provides positive but proportionately smaller developmental benefits, or whether there exists a threshold of quality below which benefits are negligible. The second type of evidence is from observational studies of children placed by their parents in child care arrangements of varying quality. Such studies have generally not followed children long enough to determine whether any observed developmental gains are long-lasting and whether there are subsequent effects on school outcomes.

Another way of thinking about this issue is by analogy to public school. The government offers fully subsidized schooling for children age five to eighteen. The rationale for such massive public subsidies is an externality argument: many parents could not afford to invest in private schooling for their children (because of credit market constraints) or would not be willing to do so. The result would be a level of schooling below the social optimum, so the government intervenes. Free public schooling for five-year-old children in kindergarten is a relatively recent phenomenon in the United States and is justified by the same arguments that are applied to grades one through twelve: there are important benefits to society, and not all parents could or would make the investment on their own (Stoney 1998). We might well ask whether extending free public "schooling" (that is, developmentally appropriate child care) to four-year-olds and three-year-olds could be justified by similar arguments. Some states are in fact beginning to do this.[11]

Striving for Equity

The fourth argument for government child care subsidies is based on distributional considerations related both to cross-sectional equity at a given time and to the long-run benefits to children of high-quality child care. Bergmann (1996, 131) argues that high-quality child care can be thought of as a "merit good, something that in our ethical judgment everybody should have, whether or not they are willing or able to buy it." This would justify in-kind subsidies aimed at low-income families, but also those geared to middle- and upper-income families if positive externalities from high-quality child care are prevalent throughout the income distribution. In its pure form, this argument is based solely on the moral grounds that it is unethical to deprive any child of the optimum conditions for development if society has the resources to provide such conditions. It is not an economic argument and cannot be supported or disputed on economic grounds.

We can, however, point out possible economic *consequences* of the equity argument as a justification for child care subsidies. As noted earlier, high-quality child care may have external benefits to society at large in addition to the direct benefits to children and their families. Thus, providing subsidized child care for purely moral reasons may have the beneficial side effect of moving the child care market closer to the socially optimal ("efficient") level of child care quality. On the other hand, there could be an equity-efficiency trade-off. If the gains to society, in terms of reduced crime, increased employment, and so forth, from increased high-quality child care are not very large, then the resources used by the government to subsidize such care might have a higher payoff to society if used in some other way, such as greater subsidies to higher education or medical research. These are rather abstract arguments, and in practice there is not enough information to determine whether there is an equity-efficiency complementarity or an equity-efficiency trade-off for child care.

EFFECTS OF CHILD CARE SUBSIDIES

This section describes evidence on the effects of child care subsidies on employment and child care quality. The evidence discussed is from three types of studies: evaluations of experimental demonstration projects, evaluations of actual child care subsidy programs, and studies of the effects of the price of child care. The last type of study does not directly measure subsidies and their impact but infers the impact of subsidies from the estimated price effects. Studies of price effects are the least direct but by far the most common.

Experimental Demonstration Projects

Several demonstration programs designed to help low-income families achieve economic independence included child care subsidies along with other benefits and services. These programs were evaluated using randomized assignment methods, which greatly facilitate an evaluation of their effects. Random assignment of individuals eligible for a program to a treatment group that is offered the program services or a control group that is not offered the services makes it possible to estimate the average effects of the treatment on outcomes of interest without bias by simple comparisons of treatment and control group outcome averages. In each case, however, the child care subsidy was only one item in a package of several services provided as part of the program, so it is not possible to determine how much of the program impacts were due to the child care subsidy. I discuss one example of a demonstration program to illustrate the nature of the evidence from such programs.[12]

New Hope was a program intended to reduce poverty among the low-income population in Milwaukee (Bos et al. 1999). It operated from 1994 through 1998 with broad eligibility rules that made virtually anyone with low income eligible to enroll, regardless of employment and family status. The program was voluntary and provided an earnings supplement, affordable health insurance, a child care subsidy, and a full-time community service job if no other employment was available. The program required full-time employment (at least thirty hours per week) and provided benefits for up to three years. Participants made their own child care arrangements and were reimbursed for most of the expenses, with a copayment that increased with family income. Thirty-nine percent of participants with children used child care, at an average subsidy of $2,376 over two years.

An early evaluation based on two years of data from the program found that among individuals who were not employed at entry to the program, participation in the program increased employment by seven percentage points, boosted earnings by about $700 per year (13 percent), raised income by 12 percent, and had no impact on welfare participation. The program had no statistically significant effects on employment and earnings for those who were employed for at least thirty hours per week at entry, although the sample size was small (the point estimate of the earnings impact was −$571 per year). It did reduce AFDC and food stamp participation by 7 to 10 percent in the second year. The program increased the use of formal child care by 7.4 percent for boys and 12.5 percent for girls and resulted in improved academic performance, study skills, social competence, and behavior among boys, but not girls. Future evaluations of the long-run benefits and costs of the New Hope program may demonstrate that it is a worthwhile program, but it will be difficult to determine the relative contributions of the child care subsidy and the other services to the observed outcomes of program participants.

Child Care Subsidy Programs

Three studies have estimated the impact of actual child care subsidies on employment. Two evaluated means-tested state subsidies for low-income families funded by federal programs prior to welfare reform. The third evaluated the labor supply effects of the implicit child care subsidy provided by free public school. This is not a means-tested subsidy (and is not usually thought of as a child care subsidy at all), but information about its impact could be useful for evaluating the effects of means-tested child care subsidies with a similar structure. There was no random assignment in these studies, and as a result it is likely that the subsidy recipients were self-selected. That is, those individuals who had the most to gain from receiving a subsidy were the ones most likely to be in the program. The studies recognize and attempt to deal with the resulting possibility of selectivity bias.[13]

Berger and Black (1992) evaluated the employment impact of two Kentucky child care subsidy programs funded by Title XX in 1989. Both programs subsidized slots in licensed day care centers only and imposed a work requirement of at least twenty hours per week. One program reimbursed day care centers directly for up to $40 per week, depending on family income, and had an income eligibility limit of 60 percent of state median income; the corresponding figures for the other program were $50 and 80 percent. The two programs were treated by Berger and Black as a single program. The first evaluation strategy used by these researchers was to compare the employment of single mothers who were subsidy recipients with the employment of single mothers who were on the waiting list for a subsidy. Controlling for the effects of other variables, the employment rate of mothers on the waiting list was 85.5 percent, and the employment rate of subsidy recipients was 97.5 percent, implying a (statistically significant) subsidy impact of twelve percentage points.

Berger and Black recognize that if program administrators select recipients on the basis of characteristics not observed by the researchers, then the waiting list would not be a valid comparison group for the subsidy recipients. For example, if administrators want the program to appear as successful as possible, they may systematically select from the waiting list those applicants who have the greatest chance of remaining employed. If the researchers cannot measure all of the factors used by administrators in making this decision, then a comparison of recipients with individuals on the waiting list would yield an upward-biased estimate of the employment effect of the subsidy.

Their second evaluation strategy was to compare the employment rate of subsidy recipients before and after beginning to receive a subsidy. This approach controls for any fixed unobserved differences across individuals and is therefore less susceptible to omitted-variable bias. This comparison yields an estimate of the subsidy impact of 8.4 percentage points, which suggests that there is some upward selection bias in the comparison of recipients and the waiting list group.

The employment rate of those in the waiting list group was 16.9 percentage points higher after they applied to the program and entered the waiting list compared to before entering the waiting list. Berger and Black suggest that this could be either a selection effect (their employment rate would have increased even if they had not applied to the program) or an impact of the subsidy as mothers went to work in anticipation of needing to meet the work requirement upon being selected for a subsidy from the waiting list. If the 16.9 figure is treated as part of the impact of the subsidy, then the full subsidy effect is 25.3 (16.9 plus 8.4) percentage points from an average weekly subsidy of $45.62. Assuming this was a 100 percent subsidy, and taking the employment rate of subsidy recipients as 97.5 percent, this implies an employment rate of 72.2 percent in the absence of the subsidy, yielding an employment effect of 35 percent and an elasticity of .35. If the 16.9 is treated as due entirely to selection effects, then the corresponding elasticity estimate is .094 (8.4 divided by [97.5 minus 8.4]). One caveat to generalizing from the study is that the subsidy was available only for use in day care centers, while most current programs provide vouchers that can be used in any paid arrangement. It is also not clear whether Kentucky is reasonably representative of the United States.

Meyers, Heintze, and Wolf (2000) use data from a sample of California AFDC recipients in four counties to analyze the determinants of receipt of a child care subsidy and the impact of subsidy receipt on employment. Individuals were randomly selected from AFDC administrative records in November 1992, interviewed about eighteen months later, and interviewed again eighteen months after the first interview. By the time of the second interview, 25 percent were no longer receiving welfare. Those still receiving welfare were eligible for subsidies under a variety of different programs, and assuming that the nonrecipients still had relatively low income, they were also likely to have been eligible for a subsidy under various California programs.

Meyers and her colleagues used a subsample of 903 single mothers who responded to the second interview to estimate a statistical model explaining whether the mother received a child care subsidy conditional on using nonparental child care. They computed the predicted probability of subsidy receipt from the subsidy receipt model for each mother and used it as an explanatory variable in a model of the mother's labor market activity. The mother was coded as engaged in labor market activity if she was employed or participating in job preparation activities. The predicted subsidy probability had a positive coefficient, significantly different from zero, in the labor market activity model. Simulations indicated that increasing the probability of subsidy receipt from 0.0 to 0.5 caused the employment probability to increase from .210 to .727. Data on the subsidy amounts and child care expenditures were not available, so an elasticity cannot be computed.

A problem with drawing inferences from this study is that no natural control or comparison group is available. The authors are aware of the possibility of self-selection: "The unobserved factors associated with the receipt of a subsidy are likely to be correlated with the unobserved factors associated with the decision to be employed" (Meyers, Heintze, and Wolf 2000, 11). But in the absence of a useful comparison group, such as the waiting list group or the subsidy recipients before they received a subsidy in Berger and Black's (1992) study, there is no reliable way to produce estimates that solve this problem. Hence, we cannot be confident that the estimates represent causal effects of receiving a subsidy rather than unobserved differences that led some mothers to be both more likely to gain a subsidy and employed.

Gelbach (1999) estimated the impact on employment of the implicit child care subsidy provided by free public kindergarten for five-year-old children. Public kindergarten can be thought of as providing free child care of a given quality for a fixed number of hours. Child care outside school hours must be purchased by the family or supplied by informal providers. Gelbach notes the likely possibility that mothers with a stronger unobserved preference for employment will be more likely to enroll a child in school at the earliest possible age. Thus, a simple comparison of the employment rates of mothers of enrolled and non-enrolled five-year-old children would yield an upward-biased measure of the impact of the subsidy.

To deal with this, Gelbach exploits variation in birth dates of children and the fact that all states impose a date-of-birth requirement for entry to kindergarten. For example, if a child must have had his fifth birthday by December 31 in order to enter kindergarten in the year in which he turns five, a mother whose child was born in the fourth quarter of the year will have access to the subsidy for that school year, while a mother whose child was born in the first quarter of the next calendar year will not, independent of labor supply preferences (assuming quarter of birth is not chosen by parents with this issue in mind). Gelbach uses only the part of the variation in enrollment that is caused by quarter of birth to explain employment outcomes. He uses data from the public use sample of the 1980 census (quarter of birth was not collected in the 1990 census) on 10,932 single mothers whose youngest child was five at the time of the census on April 1, 1980.[14]

Gelbach's estimates indicate that access to free public school increased the employment probability by five percentage points at the interview date and by four percentage points during calendar year 1979. He also finds positive effects of about 2.0 on hours of work per week, 3.6 on weeks worked per year, $932 on wage-salary income in 1979, and a four-percentage-point-lower probability of receiving public assistance in 1979. All the estimates are significantly different from zero. Gelbach was not able to estimate the value of the subsidy, so the elasticity of employment with respect to the subsidy could not be computed. Gelbach's approach is creative and provides credible evidence of the impact of a child care subsidy on the employment of mothers whose youngest child is five years old. However, it is unclear whether his results can be generalized to children younger than five.

A final point about these three studies is that the drastic nature of the 1996 welfare reform may make the pre-reform results of these studies less relevant for predicting behavior in the post-PRWORA era. Less emphasis was placed on moving welfare participants into employment before PRWORA. A low-income mother might have been able to turn down a child care subsidy offer before PRWORA and remain out of the labor force without losing her welfare benefit. A mother who turned down a child care subsidy today would be more likely to lose eligibility for welfare. It seems plausible that a mother who is going to lose her welfare eligibility in any case would be likely to accept a subsidy offer and join the labor force.

Inferences on the Impact of Subsidies Based on the Effects of the Price of Child Care

More than a dozen studies have estimated the effect of the price of child care on the employment behavior of mothers. Results from these studies were summarized in chapter 4. One of the motivations for this literature is to infer how child care subsidies would affect employment decisions. Whether inferences about the effects of subsidies drawn from this literature are useful depends on two factors. First, if there are substantial costs to taking up a subsidy—in the form of either the time costs required to negotiate the subsidy bureaucracy or the psychic costs ("stigma") of participating in a means-tested program—then price effects on employment may not be a reliable guide to subsidy effects. Second, the price effects estimated in this literature are generally assumed to be constant per hour of child care, while many subsidies are variable. For example, the CCDF subsidy program imposes sliding scale fees that cause the effective price of an hour of child care to increase as the number of hours of care purchased increases. This does not alter the fact that a child care subsidy will increase the incentive to be employed, but it could affect the magnitude of the employment effect. Thus, estimates of linear price effects could be an unreliable guide to the effects of typical nonlinear subsidies.

The evidence discussed in chapter 4 suggested that the most plausible estimates of the elasticity of employment of mothers with respect to the price of child care were relatively small, in the range of $-.09$ to $-.20$. My elasticity estimate of $-.20$ implies that a subsidy that reduces the effective price of child care paid by consumers by 50 percent would cause the employment rate to increase by 10 percent (for example, from 60 percent to 66 percent). There is some evidence from the literature that the elasticity may be larger in absolute value for lower-income families. That is, the employment of mothers in low-income families may be more sensitive to the price of child care than in other families. The only direct comparison that can be made between this estimate and estimates based on actual subsidies is to Berger and Black (1992), who, as noted earlier, estimated an elasticity of employment with respect to child care subsidy dollars of .09 to .35. This is of the same order of magnitude as my estimate of the price elasticity of $-.20$.

A crude estimate of the number of mothers with children under six who were employed in 1995 and who would *not* have been employed had all employment-related child care subsidies been eliminated is 355,000, or 3.0 percent of the actual number employed. The calculations underlying this figure are based on strong assumptions, and the result should be treated as no more than a ballpark figure.[15] Overall, the evidence indicates that child care subsidies increase employment, but the magnitude of the effect is modest.

Effects of Child Care Subsidies on Child Development

There are no studies that have examined the effect of the price of child care or employment-related child care subsidies on child development outcomes. However, a substantial literature evaluates the child development effects of Head Start and other early intervention programs. Since these programs can be interpreted as child care subsidies, their effects on child development are of interest. This large literature has been reviewed by Karoly and her colleagues (1998), Barnett (1992, 1995), Currie (2001), and Waldfogel (1999), among others, and is summarized briefly here.

Karoly and her colleagues (1998, xiii) conclude that "in some situations, carefully targeted early childhood interventions *can* yield measurable benefits in the short run and that some of those benefits persist long after the program has ended." This conclusion is based on evaluations of nine early intervention programs with randomized assignment to treatment, including the well-known Perry Preschool, Carolina Abecedarian, and Infant Health and Development Projects. Most of the programs produced short-run gains in IQ, but only one program, the Abecedarian Project (Campbell et al., in press), has produced IQ gains that lasted past age twelve. However, short-run improvements in academic achievement caused by the programs did persist in most of the programs through the latest age at which achievement was measured (age twenty-one). The Perry Preschool evaluation, which has followed its subjects longer than the other intervention evaluations, found substantial improvements through age twenty-seven in high school graduation, crime and delinquency, income, and welfare participation. No effects on grade repetition and teen pregnancy were found. The mechanisms through which these effects occur are not well understood, because it is clear that they are not a result of long-run improvements in IQ, except possibly in the case of the Abecedarian Project (Campbell et al., in press).

There have been many evaluations of Head Start, but they have been hampered by two factors: none have been based on randomized assignment, and Head Start is not a single "program" but rather an umbrella for a large number of programs that vary in design and quality while presumably meeting the main requirements for a Head Start program (Karoly et al. 1998).[16] Evaluations of Head Start have almost uniformly found substantial positive short-run impacts on IQ that have subsequently faded out within a few years after exit from the program. About half of the Head Start evaluations found short-run positive effects on reading and mathematics achievement that faded out within a few years, and the others found no short-run effects. However, Head Start evaluations that have examined effects on grade retention (seven studies), special education (four), and high school graduation (one) have sometimes found positive effects on these outcomes (Barnett 1995).

The only Head Start evaluation that has found effects on cognitive ability that have *not* faded out over time is Currie and Thomas (1995), who found this result for white children but not for black children. Like other Head Start evaluations, theirs was not based on a randomized design. But unlike other evaluators, they were able to control for at least some potentially confounding unobserved factors by exploiting two facts: the National Longitudinal Survey of Youth contains data on multiple children in the same families, and there are substantial numbers of families in which one child attended a Head Start program and another child did not. Using an estimator that identifies the effect of Head Start only by within-family differences between siblings who did and did not attend Head Start, Currie and Thomas found substantial positive short-run effects on cognitive ability (the Peabody Picture Vocabulary Test) for whites and blacks that do not fade out for whites but do for blacks, and no short- or long-run effects on grade retention for blacks, but a substantial positive effect for whites that fades only a bit over time. Currie and Thomas note that their method relies on the assumptions that assignment of children to Head Start within families is "random" (uncorrelated with child-specific unobservables), and that there are no spillover effects of Head Start attendance by one child on other children in the family. The first assumption would be valid if, for example,

Head Start slots were rationed by some method that did not favor the siblings of children who had already attended Head Start, or if family income changed over time in a way that was unrelated to child-specific factors and led to one child in the family being eligible for the program and another not being eligible. They argue and present evidence that if child-specific unobservables and spillover effects do exist, they tend to bias the within-family estimates of the effect of Head Start toward zero.

An important issue concerning early childhood interventions that involve a child care component is whether the benefits of the intervention exceed the costs. The interventions tend to be expensive relative to typical market child care because they are designed to provide very high-quality services to help overcome the developmental disadvantages faced by low-income children. But the benefits are potentially large as well, if academic achievement, higher earnings, lower crime, and lower welfare participation are permanent results of the intervention. The data needed to perform a credible and thorough benefit-cost analysis of Head Start and other early intervention programs do not exist. Cost data are readily available, but many of the benefits are intangible, and others that could in principle be quantified are spread over long time periods and require data that have not been collected.

Karoly and her colleagues (1998) have used data from studies by Barnett (1993b, 1995) to perform what they call a "cost savings" analysis of one early intervention program, the Perry Preschool Project. This analysis does not attempt to measure all of the benefits of the program to the participants or society but rather tries to determine whether the program results in direct savings to the government that exceed the cost of the program to the government. If the answer is yes, government funding of the program can be justified purely as a way for the government to save money without even considering other possible benefits of the program. This is a conservative approach to evaluating a program, but Karoly and her colleagues argue that it is the only approach available given data limitations, and even for this approach the data needed are available for only one program. The finding that the cost savings are smaller than the cost of the program does *not* necessarily mean that funding the program is a bad idea.

Table 8.3 illustrates the calculations made by Karoly and her colleagues (1998), based on Barnett's figures, using data through age twenty-seven of the participants, and expressed in 1996 dollars discounted at a 4 percent annual rate of interest to the date of birth of the child.

These calculations do not place any value on the decrease in tangible and intangible losses to crime victims, or the increased earnings of the program participant. Even this very conservative approach that costs out only tangible cost savings to the government leads to the conclusion that the Perry Preschool Project was a highly worthwhile investment by the government.

Table 8.3 / "Cost Savings" Analysis of the Perry Preschool Project

Item	Program Cost	Government Savings	
		Through Age Twenty-Seven	Projected, Ages Twenty-Eight to Sixty-Five
Cost of preschool, ages three to four	$12,148	—	—
Reduced special education costs	—	$6,365	—
Increased taxes on earnings	—	3,451	$3,115
Decreased welfare payments	—	1,968	341
Decrease in criminal justice costs	—	7,378	2,817
Total	12,148	19,162	6,273

Source: Karoly et al. 1998, based on figures from Barnett 1993b, 1995.

CONCLUSIONS

Child care subsidies can be designed to encourage employment or to enhance the quality of child care. These goals are generally in conflict: policies that are most likely to encourage employment would allow parents flexibility in the choice of the quality of care, and policies that are most likely to encourage the use of high-quality care would not impose an employment requirement. Current policy is tilted toward employment-related subsidies: about 60 percent of subsidy dollars in 1999 had an employment requirement.

My reading of the evidence leads me to conclude that the rationale for employment-related child care subsidies is not very compelling. Employment-related child care subsidies substitute in-kind benefits for cash benefits and increase the incentive for low-income mothers to be employed. But there is no evidence that such programs increase the long-run economic self-sufficiency of low-income families, where self-sufficiency is defined as not being enrolled in a means-tested program. The rationale for quality-related subsidies is more compelling. There is evidence, albeit not a large amount, that parents lack information about how to identify high-quality child care, and that very high-quality care has important long-run benefits to children and society. These observations form the basis for the recommendations I make in chapter 10.

The evidence reviewed in this chapter suggests that employment-related child care subsidies for low-income mothers may have a modest positive impact on their labor force participation rate. Estimates of the effects of fully subsidized child care on the employment rate of low-income single mothers range from four to five percentage points (Gelbach 1999) to eight to twenty-five percentage points in Kentucky (Berger and Black 1992). However, this evidence predates the 1996 welfare reform, which changed the rules of the game in important ways. We lack solid evidence of the employment impact of child care subsidies in the post-reform era. This is an important area for research. To be useful for this purpose, surveys must explicitly ask respondents who are not receiving a child care subsidy whether they applied for a subsidy, whether they were offered a subsidy, why they were turned down if not offered a subsidy, and why they did not accept a subsidy if offered one.

We also lack evidence on the effects of subsidies on the demand for and supply of quality in child care, another important area for research. A random assignment demonstration program that focused exclusively on child care as the "treatment" would be a very useful approach to learning more about the effects of different types of child care subsidies on employment and child outcomes of low-income families.

Chapter 9

Child Care Regulations

R egulation would appear at first glance to be the most direct way for the government to influence the quality of child care. Many service industries and occupations are regulated and licensed to ensure that low-quality service is not offered. But if regulations impose only minimum standards or are not supported by vigorous enforcement, then they may not be as effective at improving quality as other approaches.

Increased regulation of child care is favored by some non-economists who advocate policy reform, while most economists who have proposed new child care policies favor subsidies over regulations (see chapter 10). Economists tend to be skeptical of the effectiveness of regulations, particularly in an industry with hundreds of thousands of small providers that have little market power.[1] Enforcing regulations in such an industry requires major resources, which are often not provided by the legislative bodies that impose regulations. Policymakers tend to view regulations as a relatively inexpensive policy, since the government does not bear most of the cost, but effective regulations require resources for enforcement and can impose substantial costs on consumers and firms.

This chapter describes the child care regulatory structure in the United States and analyzes the impact of child care regulations on the quality of care and other outcomes in the child care market. There is substantial variation in regulations across states and over time within states. This variation can be exploited to determine whether tougher regulations affect child care quality in the intended manner and whether they affect other outcomes, such as the price of child care, as predicted by economic theory. The results of the analysis can help us determine whether regulations can be a useful part of child care policy.

The main finding from the empirical analysis is that regulations have small effects on the quality of child care and other outcomes in the child care market. Thus, regulations are currently not an effective tool for improving the quality of child care, although the results do not rule out the possibility that tougher and more effectively enforced regulations could significantly improve child care quality. My proposal in the final chapter is based on subsidies, not regulation, though I do not advocate dismantling the current regulatory structure.

In the overview of child care regulations in the United States that opens the chapter, my focus is on regulations related to the developmental appropriateness of care. The next section discusses the rationale for regulation of child care. The main argument for regulating child care is imperfect information: consumers may not know how to recognize the quality of care, and regulation can attempt to ensure that consumers do not inadvertently use low-quality care. This argument and its implications are spelled out in detail. The bulk of the chapter describes the empirical approach and presents the results.

OVERVIEW

Child care is regulated by the states in an effort to reduce the risk of harm to children from exposure to child care. The risks that regulations address include developmental impairment, injury, and the spread of disease (Morgan and Azer 1997). Regulations require child care providers to be licensed or registered and to meet minimum standards for safety, hygiene, and structural features. Providers that fail to meet the minimum standards can be fined and denied a license to operate. Most states regulate the ratio of children to staff in a group, the education and training of the staff and director, building and equipment safety (for example, access to exits, crib dimensions, ventilation, pest control, playground equipment), sanitation, fire drills, staff background checks, discipline practices, food safety, immunization, and other program features.

Three aspects of regulations are especially important. First, they are determined by state governments, not the federal government. The federal government can impose standards that child care providers must meet to be eligible for federal subsidies, but the federal government is not authorized to regulate child care.[2] Child care regulations therefore differ across states, sometimes substantially. Second, child care regulations impose minimum standards but do not define or attempt to enforce "optimal" standards (Morgan and Azer 1997). Thus, it is possible for a child care provider to comply with all state regulations but nevertheless receive a low score on quality rating scales. Child care regulations in many states are quite different from standards for "optimal" care such as those specified by the National Association for the Education of Young Children. Third, regulations differ for day care centers and family day care homes, and in most states some providers are legally exempt from regulation. For example, many states exempt family day care homes that provide care for only a few children. This means that such providers are not required to register or obtain a license, though they must comply with some health and safety standards. Some states exempt church-affiliated day care centers from regulatory requirements.

Table 9.1 summarizes a few of the many child care regulations, by state.

(Text continues on p. 178.)

Table 9.1 / Selected State Child Care Regulations, 1997

State	Day Care Centers						Family Day Care Homes	
	Infants		Four-Year-Olds		Pre-Service Education, Experience, and Training Requirement for Teachers	Number of Annual Inspections	Child-Staff Ratio	Minimum Size for Licensing
	Child-Staff Ratio	Group Size	Child-Staff Ratio	Group Size				
Alabama	6:1	6	20:1	20	—	1	6:1	1
Alaska	5:1	—	10:1	—	—	NA	8:1	4
Arizona	5:1	—	15:1	—	—	1.3	5:1	1
Arkansas	6:1	—	15:1	—	—	3	10:1	6
California	4:1	—	12:1	—	Twelve semester hours in early childhood education (ECE) or related field	1	6:1	1
Colorado	5:1	10	12:1	24	—	0.5	6:1	2
Connecticut	4:1	8	10:1	20	—	0.5	6:1	1
Delaware	4:1	—	15:1	—	Sixty hours' training in ECE and one year's experience	2	6:1	1
District of Columbia	4:1	8	10:1	20	Nine credit hours in ECE and one year's experience	2	5:1	1
Florida	4:1	—	20:1	—	Thirty clock hours' training in ECE	4	10:1	1
Georgia	6:1	12	18:1	36	Ten clock hours' training within one year after hire	2	4:1	3
Hawaii	4:1	6	16:1	—	Bachelor's degree; twelve credits in ECE; six months' experience	2	6:1	1

(Table continues on p. 176.)

Table 9.1 / *Continued*

State	Infants Child-Staff Ratio	Infants Group Size	Four-Year-Olds Child-Staff Ratio	Four-Year-Olds Group Size	Pre-Service Education, Experience, and Training Requirement for Teachers	Number of Annual Inspections	Family Day Care Homes Child-Staff Ratio	Family Day Care Homes Minimum Size for Licensing
Idaho	6:1	—	12:1	—	—	0.5	6:1	1
Illinois	4:1	12	10:1	20	Six credits in ECE	1.3	12:1	4
Indiana	4:1	8	12:1	—	—	1.5	12:1	6
Iowa	4:1	—	12:1	—	—	3	6:1	1
Kansas	3:1	9	12:1	24	Twelve credits in ECE and six months' experience	1	3:1	1
Kentucky	5:1	10	14:1	28	—	2	10:1	4
Louisiana	6:1	—	16:1	—	—	2	6:1	1
Maine	4:1	12	10:1	30	—	1	8:1	3
Maryland	3:1	6	10:1	20	Six semester hours in ECE	1	8:1	1
Massachusetts	3:1	7	10:1	20	High school vocational program in child care	1.5	6:1	1
Michigan	4:1	—	12	—	—	1.5	6:1	1
Minnesota	4:1	8	10:1	20	Twenty-four college credits in ECE and two years' experience	1	10:1	1
Mississippi	5:1	10	16:1	16	—	3	5:1	6
Missouri	4:1	8	10:1	—	—	2.5	10:1	5
Montana	4:1	—	10:1	—	Eight hours' ECE training in first year of employment	2.3	6:1	3
Nebraska	4:1	—	12:1	—	—	2	8:1	4
Nevada	6:1	—	13:1	—	Three hours' ECE training in first six months	3	6:1	5

State							
New Hampshire	4:1	12	12:1	24	Seventy-two hours of workshops	1.3	9:1	1
New Jersey	4:1	20	15:1	20	Fifteen child-related college credits	1.3	5:1	1
New Mexico	6:1	—	12:1	—		3	6:1	5
New York	4:1	8	8:1	16		1.5	6:1	3
North Carolina	5:1	10	20:1	25		1	5:1	3
North Dakota	4:1	—	10:1	—		3	7:1	4
Ohio	5:1	12	12:1	28		2.5	6:1	1
Oklahoma	4:1	8	15:1	30		3.5	7:1	1
Oregon	4:1	8	10:1	20		2	10:1	4
Pennsylvania	4:1	8	10:1	20		2	6:1	4
Rhode Island	4:1	8	10:1	20	Bachelor's degree and meet standards for RI early childhood certification	2	4:1	4
South Carolina	6:1	—	18:1	—		2.5	6:1	1
South Dakota	5:1	20	10:1	20		2	12:1	1
Tennessee	5:1	10	15:1	20		4	7:1	5
Texas	4:1	10	20:1	35	Eight hours' ECE training	1	6:1	1
Utah	4:1	8	15:1	25		3	6:1	4
Vermont	4:1	8	10:1	20	Thirty-hour ECE course in first six months	2	6:1	2
Virginia	4:1	—	16:1	—		2	8:1	6
Washington	4:1	8	10:1	20		1.3	12:1	1
West Virginia	4:1	—	12:1	—		0.5	6:1	4
Wisconsin	4:1	8	13:1	24	Eighty hours' ECE training	2.5	8:1	4
Wyoming	5:1	—	15:1	—		2	6:1	3

Source: Center for Career Development in Early Care and Education at Wheelock College 1998; U.S. General Accounting Office 2000a; National Child Care Information Center 2000; unpublished data provided by Joseph Hotz and Rebecca Kilburn.

Notes: Blank cell indicates no regulation. NA indicates the information is not available.

The regulations are typically very detailed. For example, in most states the maximum group size and child-staff ratio standards differ by single year of child age, and staff training requirements differ by type of position. The regulations shown in the table represent a small excerpt from the regulatory structure of each state, but comparisons across states on the basis of the examples shown are a reasonable guide to the overall relative standards of different states. The maximum child-staff ratio for infants younger than one year old in day care centers ranges from three children to one teacher in Kansas, Maryland, and Massachusetts to six to one in eight states. Maximum group size for infants ranges from six to twenty and is not regulated at all in nineteen of the states. The maximum child-staff ratio for four-year-old children in centers ranges from ten to one in seventeen states to twenty to one in four states, and the maximum group size for four-year-olds ranges from sixteen in Mississippi to thirty-six in Georgia. Thirty-two states have no pre-service child care experience or early education or training requirement for teachers in day care centers. In these states it is legal to employ a teacher with no education, training, or experience in child care or early education. Many of these states do impose an education requirement that is not specific to child care, such as a high school diploma. In the other states pre-service requirements range from ten clock hours of training in child care within the year following the date of hire in Georgia, to a bachelor's degree in any field, twelve credits in early childhood education, and six months' experience in Hawaii.

Many child care providers would comply with regulations even if they were not enforced by the state, but enforcement efforts based on inspections and responses to consumer complaints may be an important determinant of compliance with regulations and therefore of the effects of regulations on the child care market. As part of enforcing child care regulations, states inspect child care providers and give them information on how to comply with regulations. Table 9.1 shows a summary measure of state enforcement: the average annual number of inspections per day care center. This varies from a low of every other year (0.5) in four states to a high of four per year in Florida and Tennessee and three or three and a half in eight states. Interestingly, most of the states with three or more annual inspections have no pre-service training requirement for staff, suggesting that frequent inspections might be viewed as a substitute for a minimum training standard.

The last two columns of table 9.1 show the maximum allowed child-staff ratio in family day care homes and the minimum number of children in a family day care home for which a license is required. In many states the maximum child-staff ratio varies by age; the table shows the maximum for preschool-age children. This ranges from a low of three to one in Kansas to a high of twelve to one in four states and ten to one in six others. About half the states require all family day care homes to be licensed or registered, while four states exempt those caring for fewer than six children, and four others exempt those caring for fewer than five children.

This brief overview shows that regulatory standards vary widely across states. This is a source of concern to many child care policy analysts who believe that lax child care regulations allow low-quality child care to persist in many states. The heterogeneity of state child care regulations is also a source of variation that can be exploited in statistical analyses to identify the effects of imposing alternative regulatory standards on outcomes in the child care market. This is the main topic of this chapter, but first I discuss the rationale for child care regulations in more depth.

WHY IS CHILD CARE REGULATED?

The main argument for government child care regulation is imperfection in the child care market. The imperfections usually cited are lack of information to parents about the quality of care, and negative external benefits to society generated by low-quality child care. The problems caused by these imperfections were discussed in chapter 8 in the context of subsidies. Regulations can in principle deal with information problems, to some extent, by ensuring that all providers offer care of minimum quality. By eliminating the lowest-quality providers, regulations can reduce the possibility that poorly informed consumers will stumble upon child care that is harmful to their children. Walker (1991) points out that the monitoring required to enforce regulations may be costlier for the government than for consumers. He also notes that the conditions under which regulations are beneficial to consumers may not be satisfied in the child care market. These conditions are that consumers place a relatively high value on child care quality, and that the cost of improving quality is relatively small.

Walker's discussion is based on applying Shapiro's (1986) model of occupational licensing to the case of child care. It is worth taking a closer look at the implications of Shapiro's model because it seems quite applicable to child care.[3] In his model, the seller of a service chooses the quality of the service by investing in human capital. A large investment in human capital (extensive training in early childhood education) increases the quality of the seller's service but has direct costs (tuition) and opportunity costs (lost earnings during the training period) to the seller. The seller knows the quality of her service (which for simplicity is assumed to be completely determined by her human capital investment and cannot be changed once she has completed her training), but consumers cannot discover the quality of a seller's service until she has been in the market for a while and developed a reputation. Until the seller's reputation is established, the price that her service commands in the market will not reflect the quality of her service. Shapiro shows that as a result of this lack of information to consumers, the equilibrium price for all recent entrants to the market, whether of high or low quality, will be based on the average quality of care provided by new entrants. Thus, until a high-quality seller has established a reputation, the price she receives will be lower than would be warranted if her quality were known to consumers, and the price received by a low-quality provider will be higher than would be warranted if her quality were known to consumers. Another key feature of the model is that consumers are heterogeneous in their preferences for child care quality: some are willing to pay a lot for improved quality, and others are willing to pay only a little. The market is assumed to be perfectly competitive: there are many potential sellers at each level of quality, and many consumers for each level of quality. Finally, licensing is interpreted as imposing a minimum level of human capital investment. Sellers who would have chosen less investment than the licensing standard will be forced to either upgrade their quality or not enter the market. Sellers who would have chosen investment in excess of the licensing standard are not affected directly.[4]

The essence of Shapiro's model is imperfect information. This causes average quality in the market to be lower in equilibrium than it would be if consumers could observe quality perfectly. As a result, a seller has an incentive to acquire a low level of human capital, produce a low-quality service, and receive a price that reflects average market quality (which is higher than the low-quality service chosen by the seller) during the pre-reputation phase. All sellers face this incentive, so quality will be lower than if perfect information were available. Some sellers will nevertheless provide high-quality service because some consumers are willing to pay for it. But Shapiro shows that the consumers with strong preferences for quality pay a higher price for the high-quality service than in the perfect-information equilibrium because the high-quality sellers must be compensated after establishing a reputation for the relatively low price they received during the pre-reputation phase. So consumers who have strong preferences for quality in effect subsidize consumers with weak preferences for quality.

In this model, a licensing requirement causes an increase in the price of low-quality services in order to cover the cost of the increased investment forced on low-quality providers by the minimum investment standard. Licensing also reduces the *marginal cost* of increasing quality beyond the lowest level, by reducing the gap between the investment needed to be a high-quality provider and that required to be a low-quality provider. The investment needed to be a high-quality provider is not affected by regulation, but the investment required to be a low-quality provider is increased, so the *additional* (marginal) investment needed to move from low to high quality is reduced. This lower marginal cost induces more sellers to undertake the additional investment and become high-quality providers. In perfect competition, price is determined by marginal cost, so by reducing marginal cost the regulation causes the price of high-quality services to fall and increases the average quality of the service provided. Thus, regulation benefits consumers with strong preferences for quality and hurts consumers with weak preferences for quality.

Does this mean that licensing is a good idea? Not necessarily: it depends on our value judgments. Licensing makes consumers with strong preferences for quality better off and reduces the well-being of consumers with weak preferences for quality. If we place no weight on the well-being of consumers with weak preferences for quality, then licensing is clearly beneficial. We might take such a view if we think of consumers with weak preferences for quality as misguided parents who do not know what is best for their children. However, if we place any weight at all on the well-being of consumers with weak preferences for quality, then we must consider the harm caused by forcing them to consume higher-quality child care than they would prefer at a higher price than in the absence of regulation. We might adopt this view if, for example, most such consumers have low income and are forced to make difficult trade-offs between child care quality and housing, food, transportation, and so forth. Shapiro demonstrates that the net benefit to society of regulation, weighing both the benefits to some consumers and the costs to others, is more likely to be positive if the marginal cost of increasing quality is low, if it takes a long time to establish a reputation, and if the proportion of consumers who prefer high quality is large.[5]

THE EFFECT OF REGULATIONS ON THE CHILD CARE MARKET: THEORY

Economic theory suggests that regulations affect the child care market by driving out low-quality providers or by inducing low-quality providers to increase the quality of care. There are two central issues that determine the magnitude of the effects of child care regulations: Are the regulations binding? And if so, are the regulations enforced?

If child care regulations are not binding on many providers, then we would not expect them to have much impact on the child care market. A regulation that is not binding has no bite. For example, if a center that would have chosen a group size of ten in the absence of a regulation faces a maximum group size regulation of fifteen, then the regulation does not force the center to alter its behavior.[6] Child care providers are very heterogeneous, of course, so the real question is: What proportion of providers face binding regulations? The smaller the proportion of providers on which regulations are binding, the smaller will be the effects of regulations on the market. And even if regulations are binding on some providers, they will nevertheless have no impact on the child care market if they are not enforced. As documented earlier, most states do not inspect child care providers very often, and it seems quite possible that it would be feasible for providers facing binding regulations to choose to not comply with them.[7] If parents have little knowledge of the precise regulations, then they are unlikely to be helpful in enforcement except in the case of egregious violations. Providers could comply voluntarily in the absence of strict enforcement, but this is by no means certain.

To the extent that regulations are binding and enforced, theory predicts that tougher regulations reduce the quantity of licensed child care and increase the average quality and price of licensed care (Leland 1979; Shapiro 1986). Theory also predicts that if regulations are binding and enforced, then providers tend to be concentrated at the regulated standard. For example, if half of the day care centers in a state would have chosen a group size greater than fifteen in the absence of regulation, then a well-enforced regulated maximum group size of fifteen will cause up to half the centers to choose a group size of exactly fifteen. Some centers may go out of business rather than comply, so we would not necessarily expect half of all the centers that remain in business following the imposition of the regulation to choose a group size of fifteen. The key point is that those centers that remain in business and would have preferred a group size greater than fifteen have no incentive to reduce group size below fifteen. To minimize their cost and still comply with the regulation, they will find that a group size of exactly fifteen is optimal.

EMPIRICAL APPROACH

I take two approaches to analyzing the impact of child care regulations. The first approach might be termed microscopic: I use data from the Cost Quality and Outcomes Study (CQOS) and the National Child Care Staffing Study (NCCSS) to examine the distributions of two key regulated variables within the nine states covered in these data: group size and child-staff ratio. These data provide direct observations by trained observers (as well as reports by the center director) of group size and child-staff ratio in samples of day care centers. Because the distributions of these variables within each state can be compared directly to the regulations governing the variables, we can make a straightforward analysis of the extent to which regulations are binding, and the degree of compliance. It is also possible with these data to analyze the impact of regulations on the price and quality of care, using the data on the Early Childhood Environment Rating Scale and its infant-toddler counterpart that are available in these samples.

The second approach is more macroscopic: I use data from all fifty states over a fourteen-year period to examine the effects of regulations on a more limited set of outcomes that can be measured consistently over time and across states. These outcomes include the proportions of women who choose to be employed as child care workers and workers in other sectors, and the wage rates of child care workers and other women workers.

A key issue that arises in both approaches is how to identify the effects of regulations. The most obvious source of variation in child care regulations is across states, as documented in table 9.1. With data that include observations from multiple states, it is a straightforward matter to analyze statistically the association between cross-state variation in regulations and cross-state variation in child care market outcomes. This strategy may yield biased estimates, however, if there are other differences across states that are correlated with both regulations and child care market outcomes.[8] For example, residents of Connecticut may on average have strong preferences for high-quality child care compared to residents of North Carolina. Such differences in preferences could be the reason why Connecticut has more stringent regulations than North Carolina, and it could also be the reason why child care quality is higher on average in Connecticut than in North Carolina. In this scenario, the more stringent regulations in Connecticut do not cause the higher-quality child care (or at least, they are not the only cause); rather, residents of Connecticut are willing to pay for high-quality care and would be willing to do so even if regulations were much more lax.[9]

One approach to handling this problem is to exploit a different source of variation: changes in child care regulations over time within states. Most states have changed some of their child care regulations at least once in the recent past. (For example, see the discussion of the Florida case in chapter 7.) If child care market outcomes can be observed before and after the change in regulations, then within-state variation in regulations can be used to identify the effects of regulations. This approach controls for *any* permanent differences across states that might affect both the regulations and child care market outcomes. This approach in effect throws out the cross-state variation and uses only within-state variation, so it is relatively inefficient. Nevertheless, it is presumably less biased than an approach that exploits both sources of variation.

However, this approach does not account for the possibility that *changes* in regulations in a state could be the result of unobserved changes in the state that might also independently affect child care markets. Continuing the earlier example, residents of North Carolina might be spurred to increase their demand for high-quality care by reading news stories about the harmful effects of low-quality child care. And North Carolina politicians might respond to the changed sentiments of voters by tightening child care regulations. In this scenario, the change in regulation and the change in demand for quality are both caused by a third factor; they are not cause and effect.

There is one additional source of variation in child care regulations that might be exploited to deal with the problem of time-varying unobserved heterogeneity across states. Group size and child-staff ratio regulations are typically specific to the age of the child, as illustrated in table 9.1. The *difference* in regulations by child age differs across states, fairly dramatically in some cases. For example, as will be seen in table 9.3, the child-staff ratio regulations in Phoenix for one- and two-year-old children in centers are six to one and eight to one, respectively, while in California they are four to one and twelve to one, and in Detroit they are four to one and four to one. In two of the three data sets that I analyze, outcome variables can be observed separately by child age. This makes it possible to control both for fixed unobserved differences across states (state fixed effects) and for time-varying unobserved differences across states, relying only on within-state-and-year differences in regulations by child age to identify the effects of regulations. Even this method may yield biased estimates if the differences in regulations by child age are due in part to unobserved heterogeneity across states. But by using this approach and comparing the results to those of the other approaches, it is at least possible to get a sense of whether the results are robust.

EMPIRICAL RESULTS

Cost, Quality, and Outcomes Study

The CQOS data provide information on one hundred day care centers in each of four states in 1993: California, Colorado, Connecticut, and North Carolina. There is no variation over time in this data source, so I rely on cross-state differences in regulations and within-state differences in regulations by child age to identify the effects of regulations. The outcomes I analyze are group size, child-staff ratio, price, and quality. The data provide four measures each of group size and child-staff ratio.

The director of each center filled out a roster listing the number of children by age and the number of staff in each room in the center. The director also indicated on the roster how many children and staff were present at the center on the day of the survey in each room. I refer to the measures derived from these rosters as "enrolled" and "present" group size and child-staff ratio. These are available for every room in each center. In addition, two rooms in each center were randomly selected to be observed for the purpose of measuring quality with the ECERS or ITERS instrument. Completing this instrument takes most of the morning, and during the observation period the observer recorded the number of staff and children present in the room every half-hour. I use the average of these measures recorded during the observation period and the "prime-time" observation recorded at or near 11:00 A.M. These are available for at most two rooms per center, and only for rooms with infants, toddlers, or preschool-age children.

Figures 9.1 through 9.8 show the frequency distributions of two of the four measures of child-staff ratio, enrolled and prime-time, by state for

(Text continues on p. 193.)

Figure 9.1 / California, Enrolled Preschooler-Staff Ratio

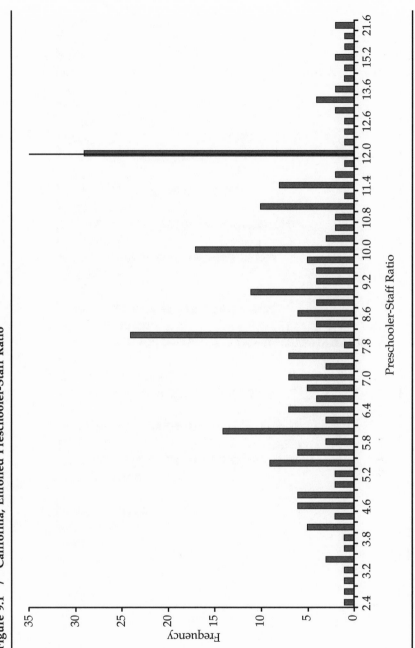

Source: Cost, Quality, and Outcomes Study.

Figure 9.2 / California, Prime-Time Preschooler-Staff Ratio

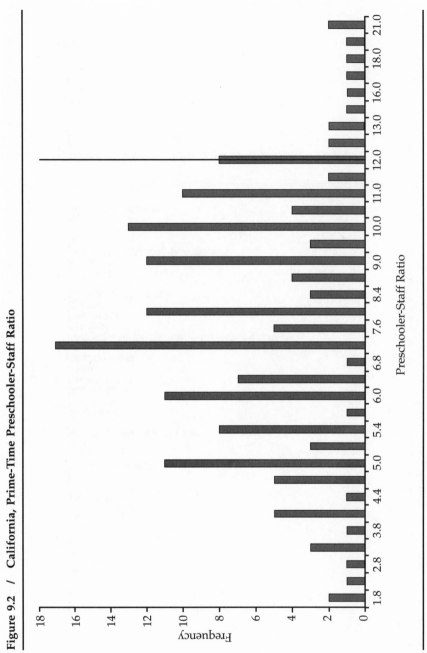

Source: Cost, Quality, and Outcomes Study.

Figure 9.3 / Colorado, Enrolled Preschooler-Staff Ratio

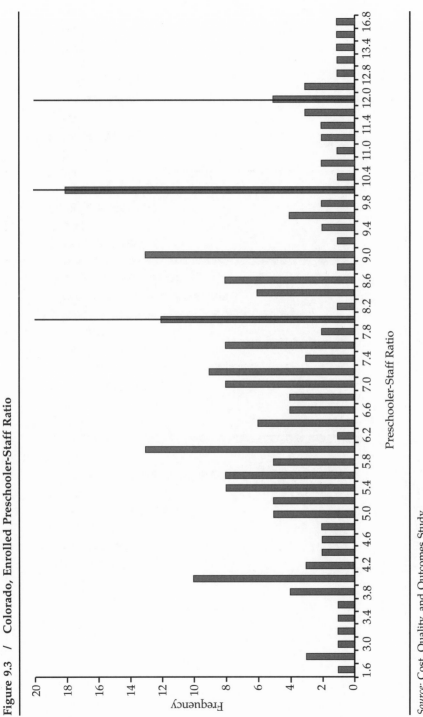

Source: Cost, Quality, and Outcomes Study.

Figure 9.4 / Colorado, Prime-Time Preschooler-Staff Ratio

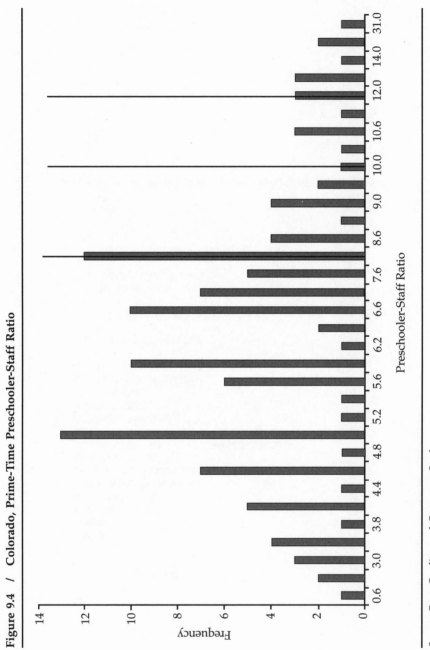

Preschooler-Staff Ratio

Source: Cost, Quality, and Outcomes Study.

Figure 9.5 / Connecticut, Enrolled Preschooler-Staff Ratio

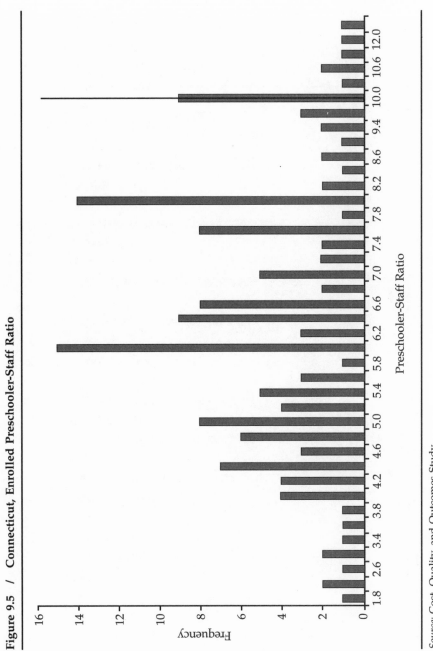

Source: Cost, Quality, and Outcomes Study.

Figure 9.6 / Connecticut, Prime-Time Preschooler-Staff Ratio

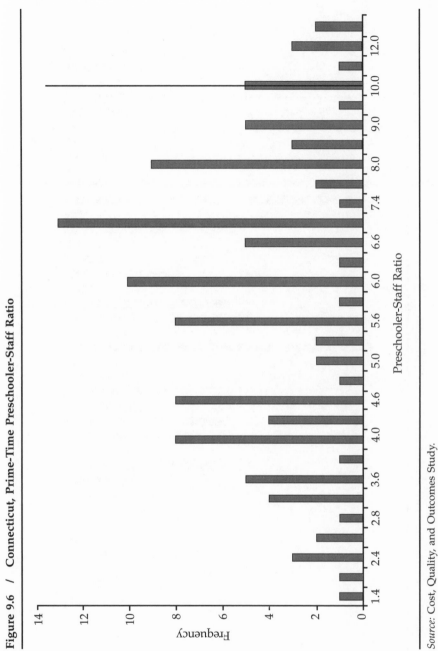

Source: Cost, Quality, and Outcomes Study.

Figure 9.7 / North Carolina, Enrolled Preschooler-Staff Ratio

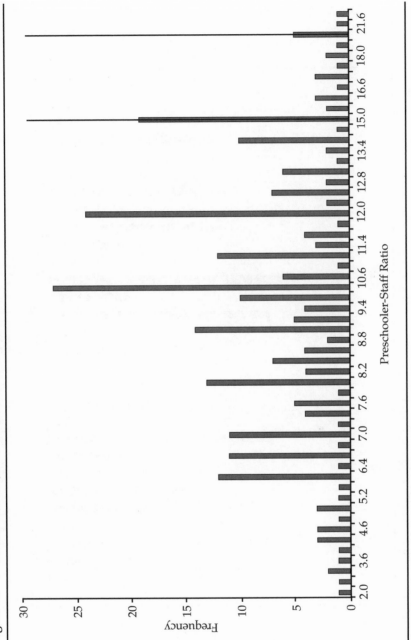

Source: Cost, Quality, and Outcomes Study.

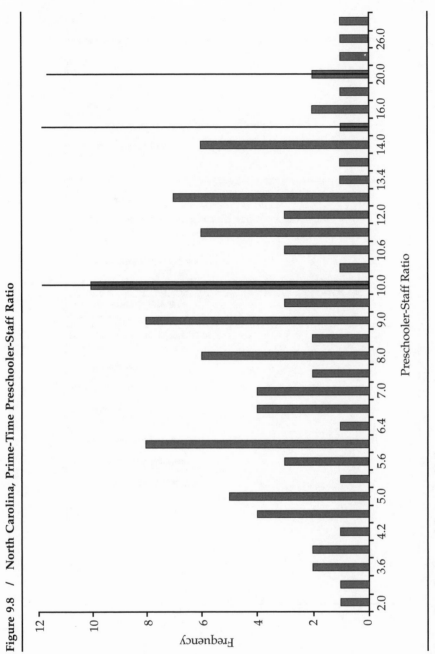

Figure 9.8 / North Carolina, Prime-Time Preschooler-Staff Ratio

Source: Cost, Quality, and Outcomes Study.

preschool-age children. In the CQOS data, I do not know the exact age of each child in a room, just the age group: infant-toddler (zero to thirty-six months), preschooler (thirty-seven to sixty months), and kindergarten or school age (sixty-one months or older). Superimposed on each figure is a vertical line that identifies the regulated maximum value of the child-staff ratio for preschoolers in the state in 1993. In several cases, two or three such lines in a figure indicate that the regulations differ by single year of age, which I cannot identify in the data.

Several features stand out in these figures (and in figures for the other measures of child-staff ratio and group size). First, day care centers are extremely heterogeneous, even within states and age groups. The distributions of child-staff ratio are very spread out, with a range of between two to one and twenty-two to one in California, between one to one and thirty-one to one in Colorado, between two to one and twelve to one in Connecticut, and between two to one and twenty-seven to one in North Carolina. Second, the great majority of centers are in compliance with the regulations regardless of the measure of group size and child-staff ratio used. That is, most of the distribution is to the left of the regulation line in each figure. Noncompliance is summarized in table 9.2 for all four measures of child-staff ratio and group size. Violation ranges from 11 to 20 percent on average across states, with the highest rate of noncompliance based on the enrolled measures, and the lowest rate based on the present and prime-time measures.

A third feature is that most of the centers that comply with a regulation are *not* right at the regulated value. The figures show that there is usually a spike in the distribution at the regulated value, but there are often even larger spikes at other values, and in some cases there is no evidence at all of a spike at the regulated value. Even in the cases in which there is a large spike at the regulated value, many rooms are far from the regulated value. Averaged across the four states, the percentage of rooms that are right at the regulated value *as a percentage of all rooms in compliance* is 2 to 8 percent for measures other than "enrolled," and 11 percent for the enrolled measures.[10] There appears to be little systematic difference across the four states in the percentage of compliers that are right at the regulated value.

A fourth feature of the distributions is that many of the rooms in violation of the regulations are fairly close to the regulated value, while some are quite far from the regulated value. Finally, the distributions are generally similar across the two different measures of child-staff ratio (and across the others not shown). The main difference is that noncompliance is systematically higher when measured by enrollment than by the other measures, by four to eight percentage points. This could indicate that centers "overbook" groups based on the expectation that there will be absences on a typical day.

The figures suggest that regulations are not binding on most day care

Table 9.2 / Day Care Center Rooms That Exceed, Meet, or Violate Regulations: Cost, Quality, and Outcomes Study

	Child-Staff Ratio			Group Size		
	Exceed the Regulation	Exactly Meet the Regulation	In Violation of the Regulation	Exceed the Regulation	Exactly Meet the Regulation	In Violation of the Regulation
All States						
Enrolled	72%	9%	19%	71%	9%	20%
Present	83	5	11	80	6	14
Average observed	83	2	15	82	3	15
Prime time	81	7	12	83	6	12
California						
Enrolled	72	11	16	—	—	—
Present	83	6	11	—	—	—
Average observed	91	1	8	—	—	—
Prime time	85	7	7	—	—	—
Colorado						
Enrolled	76	9	15	—	—	—
Present	89	4	7	—	—	—
Average observed	85	1	14	—	—	—
Prime time	81	4	15	—	—	—
Connecticut						
Enrolled	84	9	6	71	13	16
Present	90	6	4	82	8	10
Average observed	69	7	24	82	3	15
Prime time	86	8	6	82	6	12
North Carolina						
Enrolled	63	6	30	70	6	24
Present	75	5	20	78	4	18
Average observed	77	2	21	82	3	15
Prime time	73	7	20	83	5	12

Source: Cost, Quality, and Outcomes Study.

Notes: "Enrolled" and "present" measures are derived from room rosters. "Average observed" and "prime time" measures are based on direct observation of selected rooms.

centers, and that of the relatively small proportion of centers for which they are binding, the rate of noncompliance is quite high. With the exception of the enrollment-based measure, the data in table 9.2 indicate that the regulations are binding on fewer than 20 percent of rooms; for the enrollment measure, the regulations are binding in fewer than 30 percent of rooms. Of the rooms in which the regulations are binding, compliance ranges from a low of 12 percent for average observed child-staff ratio to a high of 37 percent for prime-time child-staff ratio, averaged across states.[11] There are clear differences in compliance across states, with the compliance rate noticeably higher in Connecticut and noticeably lower in North Carolina. If this inference is correct, then it is unlikely that child care regulations currently have much impact on the child care market. If 80 percent or more of providers satisfy the regulation with room to spare, it is hard to imagine how the observed outcomes of these providers could have been substantially affected by regulation.

It is of course possible that regulations affect the market mainly by causing low-quality providers to exit the market or to not enter. The data in the figures are consistent with this possibility, since such providers would not appear in the figures. But if only 12 to 37 percent of the providers that we do observe facing a binding regulation are in compliance with the regulation, it is hard to see why other low-quality providers would have been discouraged by the regulations from entering or remaining in the market. Some providers might be able to evade the regulations more easily than others, so perhaps the providers that find it hardest to evade the regulations were induced to drop out. In any case, while the visual impression from the figures is quite suggestive, it is important to conduct a more formal statistical analysis to determine whether and how regulations affect the child care market.

Two sorts of analyses seem worthwhile. First, I estimate regression models to explain variation across centers in observed child-staff ratio, group size, quality (ECERS-ITERS scores), and price as a function of regulations and other center characteristics, with and without controlling for state fixed effects. Second, I examine the issue of compliance in more depth by estimating models that explain the choice of centers among the three discrete alternatives shown in table 9.2: exceeding the regulation (that is, choose a value of group size or child-staff ratio less than the regulated value), complying exactly with the regulation, or violating the regulation. These models also contain the regulation as an explanatory variable along with other center characteristics (and the state fixed effects in some versions). One issue that arises in the statistical analysis is deciding which value of the regulation to use for cases in which there are multiple regulation values. Recall that this issue arises because the regulations differ by single years of age in some states, but I observe only the age group (infant-toddler, preschool, kindergarten and older) of each room. Table 9.3 de-

Table 9.3 / Child-Staff Ratio and Group Size Regulations in the CQOS and NCCSS Cities

	CQOS States, 1993				NCCSS Cities, 1988				
	California	Colorado	Connecticut	North Carolina	Atlanta	Boston	Detroit	Phoenix	Seattle
Child-staff ratio, by age									
Zero	4	5	4	5	7	3	4	5	4
One	4	5	4	6	10	6	4	6	7
Two	12	8	4	10	12	6	4	8	10
Three	12	10	10	15	15	10	10	13	10
Four	12	12	10	20	18	10	12	15	10
Five or older	12	15	10	25	20	15	12	20	10
Group size, by age									
Zero	—	—	8	10	—	7	—	—	8
One	—	—	8	12	—	9	—	—	14
Two	—	—	8	20	—	9	—	—	20
Three	—	—	20	25	—	20	—	—	20
Four	—	—	20	25	—	20	—	—	20
Five or older	—	—	20	25	—	30	—	—	20

Source: Unpublished data provided by Joseph Hotz and Rebecca Kilburn.
Notes: California, Colorado, Georgia, Michigan, and Arizona did not regulate group size in 1988.

scribes the exact child-staff ratio and group size regulations for the four CQOS states.[12] I chose the age-zero regulation for the infant-toddler group and the age-three regulation for the preschool group because these are the tightest regulations for each group. (There were no cases of multiple regulations for the kindergarten and older group.)

Table 9.4 summarizes the estimated effects of regulations on each of the four measures of child-staff ratio and group size and on quality and price. The entries in the first two rows of panel A are the coefficient estimates (and standard errors) on the regulation variable in regression models that included child age group dummies and other variables listed at the bottom of the table. The specification in the first row of panel A also includes state fixed effects (dummy variables for states) that control for the unobserved differences across states that affect the outcomes.

The coefficients in the child-staff ratio and group size equations are all positive, and in six out of eight cases the hypothesis of a zero effect can be rejected at the 5 percent level in both rows of panel A. These estimates imply that regulations matter a lot: a one-unit decrease in the child-staff ratio regulation (from ten to one to nine to one, for example) causes child-staff ratio to fall by 1.09 to 1.18 for the enrolled measure, by .71 to .75 for the "present" measure, and by .32 to .54 for the average and prime-time observations. A one-unit change in the group size regulation causes a change in actual group size of .47 to .70 on average with state fixed effects, and .13 to .38 without state fixed effects. These are surprisingly large effects in view of the apparent lack of visual evidence that regulations matter. Including state fixed effects dampens the effect of child-staff ratio regulations for the direct observations but increases the effect of group size regulations for all measures of group size. If providers attempt to signal their quality to consumers by exceeding regulations, as suggested by Queralt and Witte (1997), this could explain why regulations affect providers even when the average provider exceeds the regulation.

If regulations have caused many centers to reduce their child-staff ratio and group size, then they also should have caused increases in both quality and price. Quality would increase if lower child-staff ratio and group size lead to higher quality, and price would be affected because reducing child-staff ratio and group size increases cost. So we would expect negative coefficients on regulations in the price and quality models. The last two columns of table 9.4 show the estimated effect of the child-staff ratio regulation on quality and price.[13] Negative effects do appear when state fixed effects are omitted, but positive effects appear when state effects are included. The results with state fixed effects imply that tighter regulations lead to *lower* quality and price. This finding is implausible, and it suggests that relying solely on variation in age differences in the regulations, as the state fixed effects estimates do, is not a good way to identify the regulation effects. Regulations are tighter for younger children, but quality is lower

Table 9.4 / Effects of Regulations: Cost, Quality, and Outcomes Study

Dependent Variable	Child-Staff Ratio				Group Size					
	Enrolled	Present	Average Observed	Prime Time	Enrolled	Present	Average Observed	Prime Time	Quality	Price
	A. Coefficient on Regulation in Ordinary Least Squares Regression									
With state fixed effects	1.18*	.71*	.32*	.38*	.61*	.60*	.70	.47	.071	.027*
	(0.17)	(.12)	(.12)	(.15)	(.28)	(.25)	(.37)	(.39)	(.039)	(.006)
Without state fixed effects	1.09*	.75*	.52*	.54*	.34*	.38*	.22	.13	−.077*	−.030*
	(0.12)	(.09)	(.08)	(.10)	(.17)	(.16)	(.19)	(.22)	(.024)	(.007)
Sample size	1,600	1,533	591	585	895	845	287	287	650	796
	B. Coefficients on Regulation in Multinomial Logit Without State Fixed Effects									
Coefficient in "exactly meet"	−.09*	−.13	.01	−.16	−.34*	−.42*	−.58	−.55	—	—
	(.04)	(.08)	(.26)	(.14)	(.10)	(.15)	(.30)	(.33)		
Coefficient in "in violation"	.05	.04	−.19	−.04	−.25*	−.19	−.22	−.28	—	—
	(.03)	(.04)	(.11)	(.10)	(.10)	(.11)	(.14)	(.15)		

C. Predicted Probability of Exactly Meeting the Regulation for Alternative Values of the Regulation

Reg = 4	.14	.10	.02	.12	.61	.77	.81	.83	—	—	—
Reg = 8	.10	.06	.03	.07	.49	.59	.63	.62	—	—	—
Reg = 16	.05	.02	.03	.02	.18	.13	.12	.10	—	—	—

D. Predicted Probability of Violating the Regulation for Alternative Values of the Regulation

Reg = 4	.14	.09	.27	.14	.32	.14	.12	.11	—	—	—
Reg = 8	.17	.11	.16	.13	.34	.18	.17	.20	—	—	—
Reg = 16	.23	.15	.04	.11	.24	.16	.17	.19	—	—	—

Notes: Entries in panels A and B are the coefficient estimate and standard error on the regulation variable. Other variables included in the models are the percentage of white children in the center, full-time enrollment in the center, dummies for for-profit, national chain, and church-sponsored, the age of the center, the county unemployment rate, dummies for the age group served, and state dummies (only in the row "With state fixed effects"). The dependent variable in the logit models is a categorical indicator of whether the room exceeds the regulation, meets it exactly, or violates it. Exceeding the regulation is the reference category. The predicted probabilities in panels C and D are computed for each observation, setting the regulation alternatively to 4, 8, and 16, with the other explanatory variables taking on their actual values and averaged over the sample. Quality is the ECERS-ITERS score. Price is in dollars per hour.

*The hypothesis that the coefficient estimate equals zero can be rejected at the 5 percent level of significance.

for younger children (as documented in chapter 2) and price is higher. It is highly unlikely that the tighter regulations for younger children caused lower quality and higher price. Rather, the "technology" of caring for infants and toddlers causes both the lower quality and higher cost. The estimates without state fixed effects imply that a one-unit reduction in the child-staff ratio regulation (for example, from ten to one to nine to one) increases quality by .077 points (8 percent of a standard deviation), and price by three cents per hour.

The estimates that exclude state fixed effects may be subject to omitted variable bias but are clearly more plausible than the estimates that include the state fixed effects. Therefore, I focus on estimates that exclude the state fixed effects in the rest of the table.

The lower part of table 9.4 shows coefficient estimates and predicted probabilities from multinomial logit estimates of models that explain whether a room exceeds, exactly meets, or violates the regulation. The coefficient estimates on the regulation in the "meet" and "violate" categories are mostly negative, though not often significantly different from zero at the 5 percent level. Thus, looser regulations reduce the incidence of exactly meeting and violating the regulations. This is sensible: in the extreme, very lax regulations will not be binding on any provider, so they will not be exactly met or violated by any provider. The predicted probabilities at the bottom of the table indicate that relaxing the child-staff ratio regulation from four to one to eight or sixteen to one would cause moderately large reductions in the probabilities of exactly complying with and violating the regulation. The group size effects are large in some cases but also somewhat anomalous as a result of insufficient variation in regulations. (Recall that only Connecticut and North Carolina have group size regulations.)

National Child Care Staffing Study

The NCCSS collected data from 227 centers during 1988 in five cities: Atlanta, Boston, Detroit, Phoenix, and Seattle. Like the CQOS, the NCCSS includes both direct observations of child-staff ratio and group size in selected rooms and a complete roster reported by the director. I have access to the data from the direct observations and from the average child-staff ratio and group size by child age from the director reports, but not the individual rooms from the roster. The averages are reported for three groups: infants, young toddlers, and older toddlers and preschoolers. The direct observations are available by single years of child age. I omitted from the analysis rooms that had multiple age groups, since it is not clear which regulation applies to such rooms. The sample sizes in the NCCSS are too small to make frequency distributions disaggregated by city and age useful, so I do not present them.

Table 9.5 describes compliance rates in the NCCSS data. The percentage

Table 9.5 / Day Care Centers and Rooms in Compliance with Regulations: National Child Care Staffing Study, 1988

	Child-Staff Ratio			Group Size		
	Exceed the Regulation	Exactly Meet the Regulation	In Violation of the Regulation	Exceed the Regulation	Exactly Meet the Regulation	In Violation of the Regulation
All Cities						
Center	69	4	27	69	4	27
Room	83	7	10	83	8	9
Atlanta						
Center	85	4	11	—	—	—
Room	89	5	6	—	—	—
Boston						
Center	90	1	9	60	6	34
Room	93	0	7	78	13	9
Detroit						
Center	49	5	46	—	—	—
Room	85	9	6	—	—	—
Phoenix						
Center	43	5	52	—	—	—
Room	69	12	19	—	—	—
Seattle						
Center	75	6	19	80	2	18
Room	85	10	5	88	2	10

Source: National Child Care Staffing Study 1988.

of centers that exceed the regulation is generally high, and the percentage precisely at the regulation is low. In some cases, the disparity between the center average and the selected rooms is quite large, with the center averages showing a much greater rate of noncompliance than the room-specific figures. For example, in Detroit and Phoenix, the center averages show about half the centers in violation of the child-staff ratio regulation, while the room-specific figures show only 6 percent in violation in Detroit and 19 percent in Phoenix. The room-specific figures show noncompliance rates very similar to those in the CQOS, while the center average noncompliance rates are much higher in several of the NCCSS cities than in any of the CQOS states. The reason for this difference between the CQOS and NCCSS is unclear, but the room-specific data are probably more reliable since they are based on direct observation. Table 9.3 documents the regulations in force in the NCCSS states at the time of the survey. As in the CQOS states, the regulations vary substantially across the five NCCSS states, including large variations in age differences by state. For example, the gap between the child-staff ratio regulations for two- and three-year-olds is different in each of the states and ranges from zero to six.

Table 9.6 presents the results of statistical analyses of the effects of the regulations. The evidence that regulations affect child-staff ratios and group size is much weaker in the NCCSS than in the CQOS. Only one of the four coefficient estimates in the regressions with city fixed effects is large and significantly different from zero: .51 for child-staff ratio at the room level. As in the CQOS analysis, I find that lax regulations reduce quality, as would be expected if regulations are effective. In this case, the results are robust to inclusion of the state fixed effects, unlike in the CQOS results. A one-unit decrease in the child-staff ratio regulation, from ten to one to nine to one, for example, is predicted to increase the ECERS-ITERS score by .11 to .15, or about 10 percent of a standard deviation. As in the CQOS, the price effect is positive with city fixed effects and negative when city fixed effects are excluded. Price in the NCCSS is measured in weekly terms. If hours of child care average forty per week, then the coefficient estimate in the price equation without city effects of -5.39 implies an effect of $-\$0.13$ on the hourly fee per unit change in regulation, compared to $-\$0.03$ in the CQOS.

The multinomial logit analysis yields results similar to the CQOS: looser regulations reduce the probability of violation and exact compliance. Moving from a regulated value of four to sixteen for child-staff ratio or group size is predicted to reduce the violation rate from 12 to 14 percent to 5 to 6 percent based on the room-level analysis, and from 59 to 84 percent to 2 to 6 percent in the center-average analysis.

Table 9.6 / Effects of Regulations: National Child Care Staffing Study, 1988

	Child-Staff Ratio		Group Size		Quality		
	Center	Room	Center	Room	CARE	ENV	Price
		A. Ordinary Least Squares Regression					
With city fixed effects	−.01 (.10)	.51 (.17)*	.09 (.14)	−.06 (.19)	−.15* (.08)	−.11 (.07)	3.12 (2.11)
Without city fixed effects	.39 (.09)*	.47 (.08)*	−.01 (.16)	−.03 (.17)	−.16 (.04)*	−.12 (.04)*	−5.39 (.80)*
Sample size	478	606	173	227	535	535	381
		B. Multinomial Logit Without City Fixed Effects					
Coefficient in "exactly meet"	−.16 (.15)	−.23 (.15)	−.22 (.26)	−15.1* (.07)	—	—	—
Coefficient in "in violation"	−.45 (.09)*	−.10 (.08)	−.51 (.15)*	−.36 (.22)	—	—	—
		C. Predicted Probability of Exactly Meeting the Regulation for Alternative Values of the Regulation					
Reg = 4	.04	.15	.02	.63	—	—	—
Reg = 8	.04	.07	.03	.33	—	—	—
Reg = 16	.02	.02	.02	.02	—	—	—
		D. Predicted Probability of Violating the Regulation for Alternative Values of the Regulation					
Reg = 4	.59	.12	.84	.14	—	—	—
Reg = 8	.28	.09	.61	.15	—	—	—
Reg = 16	.02	.05	.06	.06	—	—	—

Source: National Child Care Staffing Study 1988.
Notes: Entries in panels A and B are the coefficient estimate and standard error on the regulation. Other variables included in the models are full-time enrollment in the center, dummies for for-profit, national chain, and church-sponsored, dummies for urban location and middle- and upper-income neighborhood location, dummies for the age group, and in the first row only, city dummies. The dependent variable in the logit models is a categorical indicator of whether the room exceeds the regulation, meets it exactly, or violates it. The omitted category in the logit is exceeding the regulation. The predicted probabilities in panels C and D are computed for each observation, setting the regulation alternatively to 4, 8, and 16, with the other explanatory variables taking on their actual values, and averaged over the sample. Quality is measured by two subcomponents of the ECERS-ITERS score, appropriate caregiving (CARE) and appropriate environment (ENV). Price is measured in dollars per week.
*The hypothesis that the coefficient estimate equals zero can be rejected at the 5 percent level of significance.

Current Population Survey

The CPS provides a time series of cross-section samples of the population that can be used to track outcomes of interest over time and across all fifty states and the District of Columbia. This is a significant advantage compared to the CQOS and NCCSS, in which centers in only nine states are observed at one point in time. Following states over time makes it possible to analyze the effects of changes in regulations, controlling for state fixed effects that capture permanent unobserved differences across states. It is also possible to study the effects of a broader range of regulations than those governing child-staff ratio and group size.

The disadvantage of the CPS is that it has fewer outcomes of interest pertaining to child care. I use the CPS to estimate the impact of regulations on the supply and wage rates of child care workers. If regulations reduce the supply of child care and cause the price of child care to increase, then we would expect to see a negative impact of tighter regulations on the supply of child care labor. The effect of tighter regulations on the child care wage rate is not as clear. A smaller supply of child care reduces the demand for child care labor, tending to lead to lower child care wages, while the higher quality of care caused by tighter regulations increases the quality of child care labor demanded, tending to increase the child care wage.

The regulation data for this analysis were assembled by V. Joseph Hotz and M. Rebecca Kilburn, who generously made it available to me. The data contain information from 1983 through 1996 on more than one hundred regulations governing all aspects of child care for each state. One question that immediately arises is deciding which of the many regulations to include in the analysis. States with tight regulations on one aspect of child care may tend to have tight regulations on other aspects as well. This could make it difficult to distinguish which specific regulations affect the outcomes of interest. There are very high correlations among the child-staff ratio regulations for different ages and the group size regulations for different ages. The correlation between the child-staff ratio and group size regulations for given ages is only .12 to .17, so it appears that group size and child-staff ratio regulations are distinct enough that both can be incorporated. Most of the correlations among other regulations are low enough to make it possible to estimate the impact of a fairly large number of regulations.

Table 9.7 presents the results of the analysis. The first column shows selected results from a multinomial logit model of the choice of women age eighteen to sixty-four to be a child care worker, to work in a sector other than child care, or not to work (the base category). The last column shows results from a log wage equation for child care workers, estimated by ordinary least squares (OLS) regression with a correction for self-selection into

Table 9.7 / Coefficient Estimates on Regulations in Child Care Choice and Wage Equations: Current Population Survey, 1983 to 1996

Regulation	Multinomial Logit Coefficients for Choice of Child Care		Log Child Care Wage Regression	
Group size	.0001	(.0020)	−.0002	(.0007)
Child-staff ratio	.0004	(.0045)	−.0005	(.0017)
Health	.05	(.18)	.01	(.07)
Crime check	.26	(.12)*	.055	(.043)
Years of education	−.01	(.02)	−.0053	(.0057)
Years of experience	.05	(.21)	.04	(.07)
Annual hours of training (100)	−.03	(.09)	.028	(.032)
First aid	−.20	(.12)	−.095	(.041)*
Curriculum	.15	(.24)	−.06	(.09)
Equipment	−.22	(.47)	−.01	(.16)
Food	−.06	(.28)	.19	(.10)
Square feet of space per child (100)	−.24	(.68)	.032	(.024)
Insurance	−.40	(.33)	.09	(.12)
Number of annual inspections	.05	(.14)	.02	(.04)
R^2			.14	
Sample size	19,654		8,520	
Test of the hypothesis that all regulation effects = 0	$42 \sim \chi^2(28)$: reject at 5 percent, don't reject at 1 percent		$1.10 \sim F(14, \infty)$: don't reject at 5 percent	

Source: Current Population Survey 1983 to 1996.
Notes: There are three categories in the logit model: "not employed," "employed in an occupation other than child care," and "employed in child care." "Not employed" is the reference category, and the coefficients for "employed in another occupation" are not shown. Other variables included in the logit model are dummies for central city and urban location, family size, Hispanic, black, other race, marital status, education, age, number of children, nonwage income and its square, and dummies for each state. Other variables in the wage models are the same except for nonwage income and its square. Standard errors are in parentheses.
*The hypothesis that the coefficient estimate equals zero can be rejected at the 5 percent level of significance.

child care. Both sets of models include state fixed effects, and the hypothesis that the coefficients on the state dummies are jointly equal to zero is strongly rejected. The hypothesis that the regulation coefficients are all equal to zero is rejected at the 5 percent level of significance, but not the 1 percent level, for the logit model, and it is not rejected even at the 10 percent level of significance in the wage model. This implies that regulations as a whole have at most weak effects on the outcomes that can be measured in the CPS, particularly child care wages.

Most of the regulation coefficients in the logit model are small and not significantly different from zero. The only exception is a positive effect of criminal background checks on the probability of being a child care worker.

Calculations based on the logit estimates indicate that the effect of criminal background checks is to increase the probability of choosing to be a child care worker from .016 to .019, a 19 percent increase. The effects of changing from no experience requirement to the requirement of two years' experience is to reduce the probability of labor force participation from .75 to .60, an implausibly large effect. When the state dummies are omitted from the logit model, the effect of criminal background checks changes very little.

The log wage regression results in table 9.7 show two cases in which individual regulation coefficients are significantly different from zero for child care workers. Imposing a training requirement in first aid for teachers is associated with a 9 percent reduction in child care wages, and imposing nutritional requirements for meals and snacks is associated with a 19 percent increase in wages. These effects are robust to exclusion of the state dummies. Both effects seem implausibly large and hard to explain. Given that the regulation effects as a whole are insignificantly different from zero, I discount these two effects.

The effects of child-staff ratio and group size regulations are very small and insignificantly different from zero in the logit and wage models in table 9.7. This was true in many other model specifications that I estimated, including models in which each regulation was included by itself, models in which state fixed effects were omitted, and models in which regulations for different age groups were used. Hence, it seems to be a robust finding and suggests that the relatively strong effects of group size and child-staff ratio regulations found in the CQOS analysis do not carry over to other Outcomes.

CONCLUSIONS

The evidence in this chapter presents a mixed picture of the effects of regulations on the child care market. Since the majority of centers voluntarily exceed state regulations governing group size and child-staff ratio, it is likely that these regulations have little impact on the market. But regression analysis of the CQOS data shows that they apparently do have some rather sizable effects on actual group size and child-staff ratios observed in the data, and some modest but nonzero effects on price and quality. In the National Child Care Staffing Study sample, the analysis shows no effect of group size regulations on actual group size, but a sizable effect of child-staff ratio regulation on observed child-staff ratio, with small but nonzero effects on price and quality. The analysis of CPS data shows no evidence that child-staff ratio and group size regulations affect the supply of child care labor or wages, and little evidence that other child care regulations affect these outcomes. The evidence from the CPS could differ from the other evidence because different outcomes are analyzed and a different source of variation is used to identify the effects of regulations. Further evidence is clearly needed before it will be possible to draw any firm conclusions about the effects of child care regulations. I conjecture that regulation effects are in fact modest, because I place somewhat greater weight on the visual evidence in the figures than on the statistical analysis, given some of the anomalous statistical findings. But this is just speculation.

Even if regulations do turn out to have small effects, this does *not* necessarily mean that child care regulations are inherently ineffective. The small effects could simply result from lack of effective enforcement and from standards that are relatively loose. Effective enforcement and tougher standards could affect child care markets. However, the evidence presented here does not reveal any direct effect of enforcement, as measured by the annual number of inspections (see table 9.7). It is possible that this is not a good measure of enforcement.

Other studies of the impact of regulation have found more consistent evidence that regulations affect the child care market. Gormley (1991) and Lowenberg and Tinnin (1992) find that tighter child-staff ratio regulations tend to reduce the number of child care slots available per child in licensed facilities. Rose-Ackerman (1983), Hotz and Kilburn (1994), and Hofferth and Chaplin (1998) find that tighter regulations are associated with lower rates of use of nonparental child care, and the latter two studies also find an association with a higher price of child care per hour. On the other hand, Fuller, Raudenbush, Wei, and Holloway (1993), Hofferth and Chaplin (1998), and Queralt and Witte (1997) find no evidence that a tighter child-staff ratio regulation affects the average child-staff ratio observed in the Profile of Child Care Settings and National Child Care Survey data. Chipty and Witte (1997) find that a more stringent child-staff ratio regulation for infants reduces the proportion of centers that serve infants, while more frequent inspections increase the proportion. They also report finding a negative effect of the child-staff ratio regulation on observed child-staff ratios, in contrast to the expected positive effect.

Overall, the bulk of the evidence suggests that regulations do not have much impact on the child care market. One reason why policymakers may like regulations, and why economists often dislike them, is that their costs are hidden. Imposing a regulation does not have a direct cost to the government, unlike a subsidy. If the regulation has an impact, the cost is borne by consumers and firms and may be too difficult to quantify and compare to the benefits. This is the main reason why I do not favor tighter regulations as a way of increasing child care quality. Another reason is my aversion to policies that directly intervene in markets, as opposed to policies that give market participants incentives to alter their behavior without forcing them to do so. This is a personal preference, but it is grounded in substantial evidence that direct attempts by government to regulate behavior in markets often have adverse consequences.

Chapter 10

What Should We Do About the Child Care Problem?

In this chapter, I present my ideas on what should be done about the child care problem. These ideas are based on findings from the research described in previous chapters, and on my judgment about the goals that child care policy should seek to accomplish.

The descriptions of research findings in previous chapters often emphasized that there is much that we do not know, and that many of the research findings may not be robust. As is often the case in social science research, we have an abundance of empirical correlations among variables, but a paucity of solid evidence on causal effects. In this chapter, I step back from describing empirical results in detail, with all the caveats and doubts that go along with them, and summarize the general nature of what I think can be learned from existing research. This discussion is necessarily somewhat subjective, and it is no substitute for the more detailed descriptions in chapters 4 through 9. Moreover, some readers may disagree with my interpretation of the facts. Nevertheless, it is important to attempt such an interpretation as a basis for formulating policy.

My proposal is also based on my views about what child care policy should try to accomplish. Some readers may agree with my interpretation of the facts but have different views on the appropriate goals of child care policy. Again, I try to delineate my views as explicitly as possible so that the reader can determine whether his or her disagreement with my approach stems from a different view of the facts, from different value judgments about the role of government in child care, or from both.

In the first part of the chapter, I provide my interpretation of the facts and their implications. The second part discusses in general terms the rationale for child care policy, and the third part spells out a set of principles that I believe should guide child care policy. In the fourth part, I review the existing proposals for reform. The fifth part then describes the specifics of my own proposal and presents illustrative calculations of the cost. The conclusion to the chapter suggests how to proceed from here.

A SUMMARY OF EVIDENCE ON THE CHILD CARE MARKET AND IMPLICATIONS FOR POLICY

What have we learned about the child care market from the evidence discussed in this book?

1. When the quality of child care is measured by the developmental appropriateness of the care, consumers on average are willing to pay only a modestly higher price for higher-quality child care than for lower-quality care. There is considerable variation in willingness to pay across markets, and in the majority of markets studied consumers on average are unwilling to pay even a small amount more for higher-quality care than for lower-quality care.

2. Consumers are moderately sensitive to the price of child care when deciding among child care and employment options. Consumers show willingness to substitute among types of care in response to differences in their relative prices, and to substitute between paid and unpaid care in response to the price of care. A higher price of child care discourages mothers of young children from working, but only by a relatively small amount. Low-income families may be more price-sensitive than other families.

3. The real (inflation-adjusted) price of child care increased slowly during the past twenty to twenty-five years, despite a large increase in demand for child care. Part of the explanation for why the price did not rise more rapidly is an elastic supply of child care labor; the slow rise in prices was also due to an unexplained increase in child care supply. With a booming economy and a tight labor market, the elasticity of supply could be smaller in the future. Further substantial increases in demand may cause sharper increases in the real price of child care.

4. The cost of improving the quality of child care in day care centers is moderate. But centers have relatively little financial incentive to offer substantially higher-quality care, because consumers are not willing to pay much more for higher-quality care on average.

5. Higher-quality child care is associated with better developmental outcomes for children. This is probably a causal effect, but the evidence is not yet clear enough to rule out the possibility that the association is spurious. The benefits of high-quality child care are probably larger for children who are at risk of developmental delays as a result of living in poverty.

6. The most important determinants of the quality of child care are intangible characteristics of providers, such as their energy, enthusiasm, and motivation. Easily measured factors such as group size, staffing patterns, years of education, and years of experience in providing child care are correlated with the quality of care but do not appear to be

important causal factors. Training in early childhood education does appear to be a causal factor in the quality of child care.

7. Current child care regulations in the United States have small effects on the price and quality of care. This is probably due in part to the difficulty of enforcement and in part to the fact that regulations are set at the state level and reflect underlying preferences for the quality of child care in each state.

What are the implications of these findings for policy? Child care subsidies that require employment increase the quantity of child care demanded but do not increase the quality of care demanded. Improving the quality of child care is not very expensive, though it could become more costly if there is a large increase in the amount of high-quality child care demanded. Demand for high-quality child care will not increase unless consumers have better information about child care quality and stronger incentives to purchase higher-quality care. Tougher child care regulations are unlikely to result in substantial improvements in quality. Regulations govern child care *inputs*, and the main regulated inputs do not seem very productive in enhancing quality. And tougher regulations may substantially reduce the supply of child care by increasing cost without a compensating increase in revenue. The quality of child care is not the most important determinant of child development and well-being, but it is an important factor, particularly for low-income children, and it may be more amenable to change through policy than factors such as the home environment.

THE RATIONALE FOR CHILD CARE POLICY

Basic principles of welfare economics suggest that government intervention in the child care market would be warranted if the child care market allocated resources inefficiently, feasible policies existed that could improve the allocation of resources, and the benefits of such policies exceeded their costs. An inefficient resource allocation in this context means that the net well-being of society could be improved by a different allocation of resources. The first condition might be met if high-quality child care has beneficial effects on child development that "spill over" to affect society at large in addition to providing private benefits to the child and family. Even if there are no external effects of child development, if parents lack information about the private benefits of high-quality child care or about how to identify and find high-quality care, then resources are likely to be allocated inefficiently in the child care market. In either case, and assuming the other two conditions are also met, a government subsidy that leads to higher-quality child care could be financed by a tax on income or consumption, and in principle the benefits to society would exceed the cost of the tax.

There is little evidence either for or against the proposition that high-quality child care has external benefits to society beyond the benefits that accrue directly to the child and family. The small amount of evidence available shows that very high-quality preschools, along with other social services for children from poor families, can reduce the rate at which these children commit crimes in adolescence and improve their education and labor market outcomes (Karoly et al. 1998). But we do not have any evidence that preschools of moderately high quality (equivalent to Head Start, for example) either do or do not have similar long-run benefits for low-income children or other children. So the externality argument to justify government intervention in the child care market cannot be grounded on strong evidence that such externalities exist.

What about the possibility of an information problem in the child care market? If high-quality child care does have developmental benefits for children, then it is hard to understand why so many parents are unwilling to purchase high-quality child care. Parents may be either poorly informed about the benefits of high-quality care or unable to tell the difference between high-quality and low-quality care. As noted by Walker (1991), most parents search very little for child care. Cryer and Burchinal (1995) document that parents substantially overestimate the quality of care provided in their child's arrangement. If parents do not understand the benefits of high-quality child care, or if they cannot discern the quality of care, then the allocation of resources in the child care market would be inefficient. Government policies that improve parents' understanding of the benefits of quality and their ability to recognize quality would be worth considering if feasible policies with benefits in excess of cost could be found. However, another possibility is that parents are generally aware of the developmental benefits of high-quality child care but do not value those benefits as much as other things they can buy. For example, parents may feel that their own influence on the development of their children can make up for the effects of low-quality child care, or that the developmental outcomes measured by standard assessments are less important than, say, religious values, respect for authority, and other intangible attributes. The evidence suggests that there may be an information problem in the child care market, but the evidence is not definitive.

The majority of child care subsidy funds in the United States are available only to employed parents, and it is not immediately obvious what sort of inefficiency in the child care market is related to employment. The possible inefficiencies discussed earlier are related to the quality of child care, not the employment status of parents. Consider first the case of the tax-based employment-related child care subsidies that are available to middle- and upper-income families, the Dependent Care Tax Credit (DCTC) and the Exclusion of Employer-Provided Dependent Care Expenses (EEPDCE). These subsidies place no restrictions on the quality of child care, so it cannot be argued that one of their goals is to improve quality. They are politically popular because the majority of families with children are eligible for benefits. But there is no obvious economic inefficiency in the child care market for which these subsidies are a logical remedy. They encourage the employment of both parents in two-parent families and of the single parent in one-parent families, but it is not clear why society should wish to provide such encouragement. They increase the well-being of families in which both parents are employed, but they do not provide benefits to families in which one parent stays home to take care of children.

One argument used to justify employment-related child care subsidies is that taxing labor income creates a disincentive to be employed, especially for the second earner in a family, and that a child care subsidy can help offset this disincentive (Joint Committee on Taxation 2000). But an employment-related child care subsidy creates a distortion in the child care market to correct a distortion in the labor market. It may very well be true that the income tax is a disincentive to work, but a logical solution is to substitute a tax that does not have this feature, such as a consumption tax, rather than create a tax-induced distortion to child care incentives to offset a tax-induced distortion to labor supply incentives.

Another argument for employment-related child care subsidies is that they benefit women more than men (since mothers are usually the primary caregivers in the home), thereby helping to reduce the degree of economic inequality between the sexes. I am skeptical of this justification, again because it is a very indirect approach to a worthy goal. An employment-related child care subsidy probably does benefit women more than men, but it benefits only some women—those who choose to work outside the home—and it causes a distortion in child care incentives toward paid care. As argued by Fuchs (1989), a more appropriate remedy for the inequity between men and women caused by children is a subsidy for children, not for child care.

Employment-related child care subsidies for low-income families are apparently easier to rationalize. The goal of such subsidies is to help families achieve and maintain economic self-sufficiency as an alternative to dependence on welfare. Employment is not very financially rewarding for low-wage parents, and the cost of child care and other work-related expenses can make the net financial reward from employment so low as to make welfare a more attractive alternative. However, low wages are a result of low skills, a problem that child care subsidies do not directly address. If child care subsidies make employment more attractive, and if skills improve through the on-the-job training and experience gained by being employed, then child care subsidies would indirectly address the problem of low skills, which is the source of the welfare dependence problem. In this case, child care subsidies would help families escape poverty and welfare dependence in the long run.

There is no evidence, however, that the typical low-wage job provides training and experience that lead to improved skills. If skills do not improve much as a result of being employed in the typical jobs held by low-skilled workers, then wages do not rise much with employment experience. In this case, the child care subsidy must be continued indefinitely to make employment attractive, and the goal of economic independence is not achieved. Dependence on one form of government assistance, a cash benefit, is simply replaced by dependence on another form, a child care subsidy. A policy that deals with the direct cause of welfare dependence, low skills, would be more appropriate. As discussed in chapter 8, Gladden and Taber (2000) found that wage growth rates with experience are modest for low-skill groups and do not seem high enough to lift low-skill workers out of poverty. Thus, there is no evidence that child care subsidies increase economic self-sufficiency, defined as nonparticipation in means-tested government programs.

The new welfare system created by the Personal Responsibility and Work Opportunity Reform Act of 1996 imposes employment requirements and time limits on receipt of cash benefits. In the context of this system, employment-related child care subsidies might appear to be quite sensible. If welfare recipients are forced to accept employment at low wages, child care subsidies can help make employment more financially rewarding. But other policies, such as the Earned Income Tax Credit (EITC), can accomplish this as well, without the unintended consequences, such as increased use of low-quality child care, caused by employment-related child care subsidies. There is no logical connection between requiring employment and providing child care subsidies: if employment is to be required, and if employment at the typical jobs available to low-skilled individuals provides less net income than cash assistance, then a wage subsidy such as the EITC is a more direct remedy that does not induce distortions in child care incentives. The point I want to make here does not depend on the nature of the welfare system. The point is that employment-conditioned child care subsidies cannot be justified by the claim that the child care market is inefficient. The child care market may very well be inefficient, but not for reasons associated with employment.

It can be argued that equity considerations justify intervention in the child care market. The poor have less money than the nonpoor to spend on child care and are therefore likely to end up with lower-quality care in the absence of government intervention. I am sympathetic to this argument, but it is important to note that it is not specific to child care: the poor are likely to end up with lower-quality medical care, education, food, shelter, and other things that might affect child development. The problem is that the poor do not have enough money, not that they do not have enough money to afford high-quality child care. The government could of course provide subsidies to the poor for all of the goods and services deemed essential to healthy child development, and this is in fact the basis of most government policy toward the poor (Medicaid, food stamps, housing subsidies, and so forth). It would be simpler to transfer cash to the poor instead of subsidizing many different goods and services, but many people feel that the poor cannot be trusted to spend the cash on items deemed essential for the well-being of their children. This is a general issue, not one that is specific to child care. Later in the chapter, I discuss the issue of whether parents can be trusted to make the right decisions for their children.

WHAT PRINCIPLES SHOULD GUIDE CHILD CARE POLICY?

The following principles are based both on my reading of the evidence and on the goals that I believe a child care policy should attempt to achieve. Those goals are obviously based on my opinions and my values.

1. *Child care policy should be neutral with respect to employment.* There are no compelling economic or moral reasons for society to encourage the employment of both parents in a two-parent middle-class family. Many parents may feel that two incomes are necessary to attain a reasonable standard of living. This is a legitimate view, but there is no reason why parents who feel this way should be provided by society with a subsidy to defray the child care costs associated with achieving the standard of living they consider reasonable. There is a more compelling case for society to encourage single parents to achieve economic independence through employment, but a child care subsidy is at best an indirect and at worst an ineffective approach to accomplishing this goal. A wage subsidy such as the EITC and a job skills training program are more direct approaches to dealing with the underlying source of welfare dependence: low skills and the resulting low wages. Instead of subsidizing the employment of parents, government should, if anything, subsidize the costs of raising children, without favoring market child care costs over the forgone earnings cost of a parent who stays home to care for a child.

2. *Child care policy should inform parents about the benefits of high-quality child care and about how to discern the quality of care.* In my view, quality is the crux of the child care problem. If parents lack information about the benefits of high-quality child care or do not know how to recognize it, then children suffer as a result. The evidence on these points is not overwhelming, but it is persuasive enough to me that I would prefer to see the government take action rather than risk harm to children. Effective and low-cost policies to provide information, if they could be designed, would be a good approach because they would directly address one source of the inefficiency.

3. *Child care policy should provide incentives for parents to choose high-quality care.* Policies that provide financial incentives to choose high-quality care are worthwhile because, as noted earlier, some parents who are

fully informed about the benefits of high-quality child care may nevertheless fail to choose it. Financial incentives may be a remedy for this problem.

4. *Child care policy should help providers learn how to improve the quality of care.* If consumers are given incentives to choose high-quality child care, providers will have an incentive to offer such care. This is the essential feature of a competitive market: firms can prosper only by offering the services that consumers are willing to pay for. Thus, direct subsidies to providers are not proposed. For-profit providers will have an incentive to increase quality in response to consumer demand but may lack the knowledge and resources to upgrade quality. Hence, a government policy to help providers learn how to improve quality may be worthwhile.

5. *Child care policy should be progressive: benefits should be larger for children in poor families.* Children in poor families are at greater risk of experiencing developmental delays and the problems that result from such delays. The benefits of high-quality child care are therefore likely to be larger for poor children. Equity considerations also favor a progressive child care policy.

6. *Child care policy should be based on incentives, not regulations.* Regulating an industry with a few large firms, such as long-distance telecommunications or power generation, is difficult enough. Regulating an industry like child care with hundreds of thousands of providers is likely to be either very costly or ineffective. I would not discourage the states from regulation, but I would not base federal child care policy on regulation. Financial incentives are more flexible than regulations and, if designed well, can be self-enforcing rather than requiring a monitoring bureaucracy.

7. *Child care policy should be based on the presumption that well-informed parents will make good choices about the care of their children.* Government can provide the best available information to inform parental decisionmaking and can provide incentives to parents to make good choices for their children. But government should not limit the freedom of parents to arrange care for their children as they see fit, subject to caveats about neglect and abuse. Not all parents will want to take advantage of subsidized high-quality child care in preschools and family day care homes. Some will prefer care by a relative or close friend, some will prefer care in a church-based setting that emphasizes religion, and some will prefer a baby-sitter in their own home. These choices may not be optimal from a child development perspective, but government should not coerce parents to raise children in a particular way. As long as safety and general well-being are assured, parents should be the decisionmakers. Government policy should inform parents of the benefits of high-quality child care and should encourage the use of high-quality child care, but should not require it.

From the perspective of these principles, what are the problems with current child care policy? The majority of child care subsidy dollars are independent of the quality of care under current child care policy. Most of the child care subsidies provided under the Child Care and Development Fund are in the form of certificates (vouchers) that can be used for any legal child care arrangement. The DCTC and the EEPDCE are also unrestricted subsidies that are not tied to the quality of care. The Child Care and Adult Food Program does not impose any quality standards beyond existing state regulations. Head Start and Title I-A are the only major subsidy programs that require high quality. The latter two programs account for about one-third of all child care subsidies, and a much smaller proportion of all children in subsidized child care.

The reason for this is clear: most child care subsidies are intended to defray work-related child care expenses. Head Start and Title I-A are usually not even thought of as child care subsidies but rather as early education programs for disadvantaged children. They are not designed to facilitate parental employment and are therefore generally not classified as child care programs. But setting aside labels, employment-related and child development–related programs both subsidize care of a child by someone other than the parent, thus reducing the cost to the parent of being employed, whether by design or not. And they affect child development through the quality of the care provided, again whether or not this was intended. Because they have the explicit goal of facilitating employment, "child care" subsidies emphasize care that is convenient for employment—that is, full-day care—and are neutral with respect to quality. "Early education" programs emphasize quality rather than facilitating employment and as a result are often part-day. Conceptually they are the same kind of programs, located at different points on the two-dimensional spectrum of quality and employment facilitation. Viewed in this way, the problem with federal child care policy is clear, at least to me: two-thirds of subsidy dollars require employment but not quality. This is too heavily weighted toward employment, in my view.

EXISTING PROPOSALS FOR REFORM

Proposals for the reform of child care and early education subsidy programs fall into two groups. One set of proposals, mainly by economists, is focused on the low-income population, emphasizes freedom of choice for parents, and is more employment-oriented than child development–oriented. These include Barnett (1993a), Bergmann (1996), Robins (1990), and Walker (1996). The other proposals are mainly by child development experts and emphasize universal coverage, supply-side subsidies that are tied closely to the quality of care rather than to employment, and regulations.

Examples include Kagan and Cohen (1996) and Zigler and Finn-Stevenson (1999).[1]

Barnett (1993a) calls for a unified federal child care subsidy program for preschool-age children that would replace all other child care subsidies except Head Start. A baseline subsidy would be available to all families, with a supplemental subsidy for families in which the mother is employed. The subsidy would be universal but would decline in value from $6,000 per child, plus $2,000 if the mother works, for the poorest 25 percent of families, to $3,500, plus $4,500 if the mother works, for the next poorest quarter of families, to $1,000 per child, plus $1,000 if the mother works, for the upper half of the family income distribution. Barnett argues that the $6,000 subsidy for families in the lower half of the income distribution reflects the cost of high-quality child care. The subsidy could take the form of vouchers, contracts, or "credit accounts" (a kind of child care credit card). Barnett's proposal explicitly relies on parents to monitor quality and on the market to respond to increased demand for high-quality care by supplying more such care. He is willing, however, to consider limiting use of the subsidy to child care providers who meet high-quality standards. He estimates the cost of his proposal at about $60 billion per year in 1993 dollars, after accounting for the elimination of funding for the subsidies that would be replaced by his program. The goals of Barnett's proposal are to make high-quality child care affordable for all families and to increase the financial rewards from employment for women.[2]

Bergmann (1996, 126) proposes a subsidy for child care in the form of a voucher worth $4,800 per child, with the value of the voucher reduced as income rises and phased out at 60 percent of median family income.[3] The proposed voucher would replace the DCTC (and presumably other child care subsidies) and could be used at licensed facilities that meet certain quality standards. She estimates the cost of the child care subsidy at $54 billion per year.

Robins (1990) advocates making the DCTC refundable, more progressive, and more generous. Refundability would make the tax credit of value to low-income families by paying a credit to families with no tax liability. His proposed schedule for the DCTC would have an 80 percent subsidy rate (instead of the current 30 percent) for families with adjusted gross income under $10,000; the subsidy rate would be phased down gradually to zero at adjusted gross income over $60,000. He would also increase the maximum amount of child care expenses for which a credit could be claimed by 50 percent. He estimates that making the credit refundable would increase its cost by about 20 percent, and making it more generous and progressive would increase its cost by another 55 percent. Given current expenditure on the DCTC, this would increase its cost by only between $1 billion and $2 billion. He also proposes a "safety net" system of publicly funded day care centers for poor families who cannot take advantage of the DCTC for some reason.

Walker (1996) would replace several existing programs with a child allowance for low-income families and expanded parental leave that is not conditional on employment. The amount of the child allowance would depend on a family's income and the number and ages of its children but would not require the mother to be employed. The maximum allowance per family would be $7,600 for a family with three children under six years old and income less than 150 percent of the poverty line, and about half that level for three children over age six. The subsidy would be cut in half for families with income between 150 and 175 percent of the poverty line, and eliminated for those with income in excess of 175 percent of poverty. The estimated cost of $45 billion per year would be financed without raising taxes by eliminating the DCTC, cash assistance welfare programs, all other child care subsidies (except Head Start), and the income tax exemption for children. Eliminating the DCTC and the income tax exemption for children would significantly redistribute benefits from higher- to lower-income families. The other part of Walker's plan is a parental leave account (PLA), funded by an increase in the payroll tax on employees of three and a half percentage points. Parents could draw funds from their PLA to finance a leave from work for up to one year after the birth of a child, retaining the right to their old job when they return to the labor force. Low-interest loans from the government would be made available through the account to families who have not accumulated enough funds to finance a leave of the desired length, with the loan repaid by subsequent payroll taxes.[4]

Zigler and Finn-Stevenson (1999) propose a "Schools of the Twenty-first Century" plan that would use public schools as a setting to provide care for children age three to five and before- and after-school care for children age six to twelve.[5] The child care provided in the schools would be of high quality and available to all families regardless of income. By providing child care in schools, Zigler and Finn-Stevenson also hope to professionalize the child care occupation and raise pay for providers.[6] Child care in the schools would be financed mainly by sliding-scale parent fees. They argue that the fee for high-quality child care in the schools need be no higher than the fee for average-quality care in other settings because administrative, occupancy, and utility costs would be absorbed by the school system, leaving only staff and materials costs to be financed by parent fees. Start-up costs, such as building renovation and expansion, would be financed by a combination of federal, state, and local government funding and private foundations. They do not provide estimates of the total cost of their proposal. They suggest that funding would come from a variety of sources, and that it would mainly be new funding rather than funding reallocated from existing programs. (They do propose to reallocate funding from existing prekindergarten programs.) Given the large scope of the program, it seems likely that it would be at least as costly as the Barnett and Bergmann proposals.

Kagan and Cohen (1996) discuss a "vision" for reinventing the early care and education system in the United States. They emphasize the principles of a new system but do not propose a specific program. However, they do make some specific proposals related to licensing. They propose that individual staff who care for children in centers and family day care homes be required to hold a license that can be obtained only by completing a high level of education and training and demonstrating competency. All education and training would be provided in a setting in which academic credit would be earned. They also propose eliminating most existing licensing exemptions, such as those for church-sponsored day care centers in some states and for small family day care homes. They do not provide an estimate of the cost of their proposals, and they propose funding them mainly through new revenue.

The key element of the plans proposed by economists is allowing parental choice of child care. These proposals rely on parents to use subsidies to purchase child care of high quality. Barnett and Bergmann recognize the possibility that higher subsidies may not result in demand for higher-quality care, and they suggest that the use of the subsidies could be restricted to designated high-quality facilities. With the exception of Walker, facilitating the employment of mothers is an important goal of the proposals by economists. Allowing parents flexibility in using the subsidies is likely to be helpful in achieving this goal. The child allowance proposed by Walker allows flexibility to parents who wish to use the allowance to purchase child care.

The key features of proposals by child development experts are "supply-side" subsidies and regulations tied to the quality of care. Zigler and Finn-Stevenson would attempt to ensure high quality by locating child care in schools, where the environment and pay would promote high-quality care. Kagan and Cohen are less specific about location and funding issues, but they do emphasize much tougher licensing standards and enforcement as a way of raising the quality of child care. It seems likely that these approaches would be successful in improving the average quality of child care supplied in the United States. The emphasis on the public supply of child care raises the possibility, however, that the problems that are thought to be prevalent in many public schools could affect child care as well. These include absence of incentives for efficient use of resources, resulting in high cost and low productivity. Standard economic analysis of regulations that restrict entry to a service occupation suggests that such regulations will raise the cost of the service, reduce the supply, and increase the "underground" supply of the service. This seems especially likely in the case of family day care, in which the proportion of unlicensed providers is estimated to be as high as 90 percent (Hayes, Palmer, and Zaslow 1990, 151).

A NEW PROPOSAL FOR REFORM

The proposals discussed here contain some creative and useful ideas. I borrow from them liberally and add some ideas of my own. There are four elements to my proposal. I describe these in general terms and then discuss the cost of the proposal based on a specific set of numbers for benefit levels, including savings from eliminating some existing programs. The goals of the proposal are to increase consumer knowledge about the benefits of high-quality child care, encourage consumers to use high-quality child care, encourage providers to offer high-quality care, and provide increased flexibility to parents of young children in making choices about employment. The proposal is tailored specifically to accomplish these goals, but I cannot offer any reliable evidence about how effective the program would be.

1. *Provide a means-tested child allowance.* Each family would receive an allowance from the federal government for up to two children, from birth through age seventeen. The allowance could take the form of a refundable tax credit, requiring that a family file a tax return to claim the allowance. Refundability would make families with no tax liability eligible for the credit, so it would be of value to low-income families. The value of the allowance would decline as the level of family income rises, and it would be phased out entirely for high-income families. There would be no restrictions on the use of the allowance, since it would be in the form of cash. It could be used to pay for child care, food, housing, medical care, or other items that directly benefit children, but it could just as easily be used for other purposes. It could be used to subsidize non-employment by one of the parents, enabling the parent to stay home to care for children. The principle behind a cash allowance is that parents care about the well-being of their children and are in the best position to decide how to allocate additional resources to improve their children's well-being. I suggest that the allowance be limited to two children per family to avoid providing strong pronatalist incentives. This feature of my proposal is very similar to Walker's proposed child allowance. The rationale for subsidizing child-rearing costs is twofold: on moral grounds, children should be taken care of as well as possible; and on efficiency grounds, children are future workers and citizens, and society has an interest in their healthy development.

2. *Subsidize the cost of accreditation to child care providers.* The National Association for the Education of Young Children (NAEYC) charges a fee to day care centers and preschools that seek to become accredited as excellent-quality providers. Organizations such as the NAEYC should

be subsidized to provide accreditation services to child care providers at no cost to the providers. A system with two levels of accreditation seems sensible to me, so that providers unable to qualify for the highest level of accreditation could nevertheless be certified as providing care of good quality by meeting an intermediate set of standards. In the system I have in mind, each provider would be (a) unaccredited, meaning not certified as offering high-quality care, though it might satisfy state regulatory standards; (b) accredited as offering care of good quality; or (c) accredited as offering care of excellent quality. Participation by providers would be voluntary; a provider that does not wish to become accredited is not required to do so. A similar system for family day care homes and professional baby-sitters is feasible as well. However, relatives would not be included in such a rating system because they are generally not professional child care providers, even if they are paid for care. Most relatives provide care for a specific child, not more widely for other children. As discussed later, providers would have an incentive to offer excellent-quality or good-quality child care, and to be accredited as such.

3. *Inform all new parents of the benefits of high-quality child care and train them in recognizing and finding high-quality care.* The simplest way to accomplish this would be to give a booklet and video with such information to mothers when they are in the hospital to give birth. The booklet and video would describe and illustrate in vivid terms what a high-quality child care arrangement is like and contrast it with a low-quality arrangement. The consequences for child development of high- and low-quality care would be described, without making claims that could not be supported by scientific evidence. The booklet and video would describe the accreditation system and emphasize that accreditation is certified by independent agencies. They would also contain information on how to contact local resource and referral agencies and other sources of information about the local child care market.

4. *Provide a means-tested child care voucher with a value that depends on the quality of the child care provider at which it is redeemed.* The voucher would be worth more if it was used at an accredited provider. For example, a low-income family might receive a subsidy of 30 percent of the average cost of unaccredited child care if they use unaccredited care, 60 percent of the average cost of care if they use a provider accredited as of good quality, and 100 percent of the average cost of care if they use care accredited as of excellent quality. This gives families an incentive to seek care of high quality, and it gives providers an incentive to offer high-quality care in order to attract consumers. The value of the voucher would be smaller for higher-income families, and it would be phased out entirely at high income levels. The voucher would be of no value if the family did not purchase child care or paid a relative for child care. This is a disadvantage, but it is unavoidable if the system is to contain incentives for the use of high-quality care. Parents who do not use the voucher still receive benefits from the child

allowance part of the system. The child care voucher does not require employment, so it would encourage the use of high-quality care by both employed and non-employed mothers to enhance child development.

This proposed system is consistent with all of the principles described earlier. All of the elements of the system are neutral with respect to employment, are consistent with freedom of parental choice, and rely on incentives rather than regulations. The child allowance and voucher make the system progressive, providing greater benefits for low-income families. The voucher and technical assistance subsidies provide incentives for improving the quality of the care demanded and supplied. The video and information booklet provide parents with the information they need to make well-informed decisions.

This system would replace the entire current federal child care subsidy system. Employment-related child care subsidies, including the DCTC, the EEPDCE, the CCDF, and Title XX, as well as the CCFP, would be eliminated. Head Start and Title I-A programs could be integrated into the new system. These programs would be evaluated and accredited (or not) by the same standards applied to other programs and would be eligible for vouchers accordingly. Funding for these programs would be integrated into the new subsidy system. Head Start and Title I-A establishments could choose to maintain their special status as being designated exclusively for children from low-income families, or they could choose to accept other children as well. The system would also replace all current tax deductions and credits for children, including the income tax exemption for children and the child tax credit. The proposed child allowance serves the same purpose as these programs, so they would be redundant. Finally, the proposed new system would also replace Temporary Assistance for Needy Families. TANF provides cash assistance to low-income families with children, and the child allowance portion of my proposal does the same. My proposal does not include, however, the employment requirements and time limits of TANF. This is a deliberate choice: the child allowance benefit that I propose is means-tested, but it is not welfare, and I suggest that it be phased out at a relatively high level of income. Other policies could be used to encourage employment of low-income parents if this is considered desirable.

Because the proposed system is neutral with respect to employment, it would not replace programs that are explicitly intended to reward employment, such as the EITC and job training and education programs. If society considers it desirable for low-income single mothers to be employed, the voucher part of the child care system I propose provides considerable resources that such mothers could use for child care. Unlike the current child care system, the proposed new system does not encourage employment, and if such encouragement is desired, it would have to come from another source. Another employment-related policy that would be compatible with the proposed system is the paid parental leave system proposed by Walker. His parental leave proposal has many good features, but I do not include it in my proposed system because it is essentially an employment-related program, not a child care program. If a paid parental leave program is considered desirable, it would not conflict with the child care system I propose and would in fact complement it quite well.

The cost of the proposed new child care policy depends on a number of factors that are difficult to quantify, so the estimates I present here are no more than illustrative. I try to justify the specific numbers used in the calculations, but the considerable amount of arbitrariness in them is unavoidable. Hence, the cost estimates are no more than educated guesses and should not be treated as reliable guides to the actual cost of the proposed policy.

I propose a child allowance of $5,000 per child age zero to seventeen for families below the poverty line; $3,500 per child age zero to seventeen for families with income between one and two times the poverty line; $2,000 per child age zero to seventeen for families with income between two and four times the poverty line; and no allowance for families with income over four times the poverty line. The allowance would be provided for at most two children per family. Table 10.1 displays the average family income of each of these four groups in 1998, and the numbers of children by age in each income group. The figures in the last three rows of the table show the number of eligible children, accounting for the maximum of two per family.

Row 3 of table 10.2 shows the annual cost of the child allowance, assuming that all eligible children receive it. This cost is $131.6 billion.

The base amount of the proposed child care voucher is $6,000 for a preschool-age child in a low-income family using excellent-quality care. This figure is an estimate of the cost of providing day care in a high-quality center.[7] The value of the voucher is adjusted down by one-third for good-quality care and by two-thirds for unaccredited child care. The value of the voucher is reduced by one-sixth for families between one and two times the poverty line and by one-half for families between two and four times the poverty line. It is reduced by two-thirds for children age six to twelve. Table 10.2 illustrates these adjustments.

The most speculative part of the calculation is estimating the take-up rate of the voucher. The research findings discussed in chapter 4 unfortunately provide no sound basis for doing this, so my estimates are arbitrary. I assume that within each income group 65 percent of eligible children will use excellent-quality care, 15 percent will use good-quality care, 10 percent will use unaccredited care, and 10 percent will use no child care and therefore will not redeem the voucher. The value of the voucher to

Table 10.1 / **Number of Children and Average Income by Income-to-Needs Ratio, 1999**

	0.00 to 0.99	1.00 to 1.99	2.00 to 3.99	4.00 or more
Average annual family income	$7,911	$23,800	$46,516	$108,350
All children (millions)				
Number of children age zero to five	4.688	4.854	7.085	5.539
Number of children age six to twelve	5.499	6.146	9.554	7.337
Number of children age thirteen to seventeen	2.932	3.565	6.511	5.965
Maximum of two children age zero to twelve per family (millions)				
Number of children age five or younger	4.402	4.683	6.911	5.443
Number of children age six to twelve	3.829	4.808	8.169	6.596
Maximum of two children age zero to seventeen per family (millions)				
Number of children age zero to seventeen	9.919	11.938	20.115	17.759

Source: Tabulations from the March 1999 Current Population Survey.
Notes: The income-to-needs ratio is total family income divided by the poverty standard for the size and structure of the family. The figures in rows 5 and 6 were computed as follows: If there were at least two children under age six, then the number of children under age six was set to two and the number of children age six to twelve was set to zero. If there was one child under six and at least one child age six to twelve, then the number under six and the number age six to twelve were both set to one. If there were no children under six and at least two children age six to twelve, then the number of children age six to twelve was set to two. Income is for calendar year 1998.

poor families is quite high compared to existing subsidies (except for Head Start), so it seems sensible to assume that it will have a high take-up rate. For the other eligible income groups, I assume that the reduced value of the voucher is compensated by higher income, and that the information dissemination part of the program convinces large numbers of families to use high-quality care. This is plausible because the value of the voucher is much higher than current child care subsidies available to families in this income range.[8] Row 18 of table 10.2 shows the implied cost of the vouchers: about $75 billion. The costs of the other two parts of the system are minuscule compared to the cost of the allowance and the voucher. Shown in table 10.2, these amount to $110 million.[9]

The total cost of the proposed new system is $207 billion per year. However, as shown in table 10.2, eliminating programs that would be redundant with the new system saves $111 billion per year. After accounting for savings due to eliminating TANF, child care subsidies, the tax exemption for dependent children, and the child tax credit, the net annual cost of the

Table 10.2 / Illustrative Cost Calculations for a Proposed New Child Care System

	Family Income-to-Needs Ratio				Total Cost (Billions)
	0.00 to 0.99	1.00 to 1.99	2.00 to 3.99	4.00 or more	
1. Allowance per child age zero to seventeen	$5,000	$3,500	$2.000	0	—
2. Number of children age zero to seventeen (from row 7, table 10.1)	9.919	11.938	20.115	17.759	—
3. Cost of the child allowance (row 1 × row 2)	$49.595	$41.783	$40.230	$0	$131.608
Child care voucher per child age zero to five					
4. Excellent quality	6,000	5,000	3,000	0	—
5. Good quality	4,000	3,333	2,667	0	—
6. Others	2,000	1,667	1,333	0	—
Estimated number of voucher users age zero to five[a]					
7. Excellent quality (.65 × row 5, table 10.1)	2.861	3.044	4.492	—	—
8. Good quality (.15 × row 5, table 10.1)	.660	.702	1.037	—	—
9. Others (.10 × row 5, table 10.1)	.440	.468	.691	—	—
10. Total cost of vouchers, age zero to five (row 4 × row 7 + row 5 × row 8 + row 6 × row 9)	$20.686	$18.340	$17.163	$0	$56.189
Child care voucher per child age six to twelve[a]					
11. Excellent quality	2,000	1,667	1,000	0	—
12. Good quality	1,333	1,111	850	0	—
13. Others	667	556	440	0	—
Estimated number of voucher users age six to twelve[a]					
14. Excellent quality (.65 × row 6, table 10.1)	2.489	3.125	5.310	—	—
15. Good quality (.15 × row 6, table 10.1)	.574	.721	1.225	—	—
16. Others (.10 × row 6, table 10.1)	.383	.481	.817	—	—
17. Total cost of vouchers, age six to twelve (row 11 × row 14 + row 12 × row 15 + row 13*row 16)	$5.999	$6.278	$6.711	$0	$18.988

(Table continues on p. 226.)

Table 10.2 / *Continued*

	Family Income-to-Needs Ratio				Total Cost (Billions)
	0.00 to 0.99	1.00 to 1.99	2.00 to 3.99	4.00 or more	
18. Total cost of vouchers, age zero to twelve (row 10 + row 17)	26.685	24.617	23.873	0	$75.176
19. Technical assistance[b]	—	—	—	—	.075
20. Information booklet and video[b]	—	—	—	—	.035
21. Gross total cost of the child care system (rows 3 + 18 + 19 + 20)	—	—	—	—	206.894
Savings from eliminating (billions)					
22. TANF[c]	30.4	—	—	—	30.4
23. Child care subsidies[d]	—	—	—	—	21.0
24. Tax exemption for dependent children[e]	0	6.008	17.800	14.500	38.3
25. Child tax credit[f]	—	—	—	—	21.6
26. Total savings	—	—	—	—	111.3
27. Net total cost of the child care system	—	—	—	—	95.594

Source: Tabulations from the Current Population Survey, based on the assumptions described in the notes to the table.

[a]Assumes that 65 percent of eligible children within each income group will be in high-quality child care, 15 percent in good-quality care, 10 percent in other care, and 10 percent not in child care (and therefore not using the voucher).

[b]The cost calculations for technical assistance and information distribution are described in the text.

[c]TANF cost is computed from Administration for Children and Families (2000b) and includes FY1999 state and federal funds available, net of transfers to the CCDF and direct spending from TANF on child care (table A, part 1: total available federal funds of $22.948 billion minus transfer to CCDF of $2.432 billion; plus table B, total state maintenance-of-effort spending of $10.397 billion minus child care spending of $1.135; plus table C, state spending on separate state programs of $.865 billion minus child care spending of $.257 billion).

[d]Child care subsidies are from table 8.2, assuming that items not available for 1999 are the same in 1999 as in the most recent year for which they are available.

[e]Savings from eliminating the tax exemption for children are based on the assumption that all children age zero to seventeen are claimed as dependents. The calculation here uses the deduction from income of $2,750 per child and assumes that families in poverty pay no income tax, families between one and two times the poverty line are in the 15 percent tax bracket, and other families are in the 28 percent bracket. The figures in row 24 take all children age zero to seventeen (sum of rows 2, 3, and 4 of table 10.1) multiplied by $2,750, multiplied by the appropriate marginal tax rate.

[f]Child tax credit figure is from Committee on Ways and Means (1998, 840).

new system is $95.6 billion. This is obviously a very large sum and may not be politically feasible. In comparison, food stamp expenditures were $21.2 billion, the EITC cost the government $30.0 billion, and Medicaid expenditures were $189.5 billion in 1999, while the deduction for mortgage interest on owner-occupied housing was $236.0 billion in 1997 (Committee on Ways and Means 2000; IRS 1997).

Readers who have trouble swallowing a cost this large can use the information in table 10.1 to compute the cost of subsidies of smaller magnitudes or with lower assumed take-up rates. The proposed system is highly progressive but does provide substantial benefits up to an income level of four times the poverty line, which is about $64,000 for an average size family in 1999. Hence, benefits are spread quite far up the income distribution, and about 75 percent of all children would be eligible for subsidies, based on the figures in table 10.1. Assuming that the additional taxes needed to finance the cost of the system are raised in proportion to the current distribution of the income tax burden by income group, the system would still be highly progressive even accounting for higher taxes. Other possibilities for reducing the net cost of the system would be to eliminate some other means-tested programs for families with children, such as food stamps and subsidized housing. I do not pursue this possibility here because I want to keep the focus on programs that are specifically child-oriented.

The main losers under the proposed system are high-income families with children, who will lose the tax exemption, child care tax credit, and exclusion of employer-provided dependent care expenses with nothing gained in return. In my judgment, these families can afford this loss with little hardship and should still be able to purchase child care of high quality. I have no objection in principle to providing benefits to all families regardless of income, but a universal system is much more expensive than a means-tested system, particularly if the value of the voucher and child allowance is not reduced at higher income levels.

Table 10.3 illustrates net income gains under the proposal for families with two preschool-age children in each of the four income groups. For the lowest income group, I use Alabama and Connecticut figures for child care subsidy and welfare benefits, since these two states are at the extremes of the distributions for these benefits.[10] The lowest-income employed families gain $7,683 to $13,871, while the next-lowest-income families gain more ($13,953), since they give up the much less generous DCTC subsidy instead of the CCDF subsidy. The gain falls to $6,102 for the third-lowest-income group, and the highest-income-group loses $6,025, a figure that accounts for not only loss of subsidies but the higher taxes needed to finance the new benefits. The gains are higher for non-employed families since these families would not have been receiving child care subsidies under the old system but will gain them under the new system. These figures are merely illustrations of the magnitudes and should not be taken too seriously. They

Table 10.3 / Net Annual Income Gain in the New Child Care System for Families with Two Preschool-Age Children

	Family Income-to-Needs Ratio			
	0.00 to .99	1.00 to 1.99	2.00 to 3.99	4.00 or More
Loss				
Tax exemption for children[a]	$0	$825	$1,540	$1,540
Child tax credit[b]	0	1,000	1,000	1,000
Child care subsidy[c]	8,112/14,300	1,104	960	960
TANF[d]	1,968/6,516	—	—	—
Increased taxes to finance the new system[e]	17	118	398	2,525
Total loss if employed (includes child care subsidy, no TANF)	8,129/14,317	3,047	3,898	6,025
Total loss if not employed (no child care subsidy; includes TANF)	1,985/6,533	1,943	2,938	5,065
Gain				
Child allowance	10,000	7,000	4,000	0
Child care voucher[f]	12,000	10,000	6,000	0
Total gain	22,000	17,000	10,000	0
Net gain if employed	13,871/7,683	13,953	6,102	−6,025
Net gain if not employed	20,115/15,467	15,057	7,062	−5,065

[a]$2,750 per child, multiplied by assumed marginal tax rates of 0, .15, .28, and .28 for the four income groups, respectively.
[b]$500 per child. The lowest-income group is assumed to have no tax liability and is therefore ineligible.
[c]Assumes a CCDF subsidy for the lowest-income group, using benefits from Administration for Children and Families (1998a) for Alabama and Connecticut, assuming one infant and one preschooler and year-round care. Assumes a DCTC subsidy for the other three groups, with a subsidy rate of .23 for the second-lowest-income group, and .20 for the other two groups, and $4,800 in expenses. Head Start and other non-employment-related subsidies are ignored.
[d]TANF benefit for a family of one adult and two children with no other income, in Alabama and Connecticut, from Administration for Children and Families (2000b).
[e]The $95.594 billion total net cost from table 10.2 is allocated to the income groups in proportion to their shares of income tax paid in 1998, from Internal Revenue Service (1998). These shares were .0064, .0334, .1304, and .8298 for the four groups, assuming income ranges for the four groups of $0 to $12,999, $13,000 to $24,999, $25,000 to $49,999, and $50,000 or more, respectively. The total for each group was divided by the number of returns filed for the group: 34.906 million, 27.099 million, 31.328 million, and 31.411 million, respectively.

highlight the generous benefits to low-income families and the large amount of redistribution under the proposed new system.

Many practical issues would arise if such a system were implemented. Here I briefly discuss only two of them. First, how does the voucher get delivered to eligible families? The voucher is means-tested, but three-quarters of all children would be eligible, so it seems unlikely that the stigma associated with the use of a voucher would be a significant deterrent to its use. Nevertheless, because the child care subsidy is not universal, the voucher must somehow be delivered to eligible families, and securing a voucher could take a long time for some families. One way to avoid delays might be to deliver the voucher to families through the Internal Revenue Service, based on their tax return for the previous calendar year and an estimate by the family of changes in income and eligibility for the subsequent year. After filing a tax return for calendar year 2001 in, say, March 2002, the family receives from the IRS in April a child care voucher good for one year with a value based on income in 2001, the age distribution of children anticipated in year 2002, and any adjustments to expected calendar year 2002 income and age distribution of children noted by the family on the tax return. If income for 2002 turns out to be substantially different than anticipated, the value of the voucher for the following year can be adjusted accordingly. The voucher is redeemed by the family at the chosen provider, and the provider returns it to a designated government office for compensation. This procedure may require that either the provider or the consumer extend temporary credit.

A second practical issue is the possibility of a shortage of high-quality child care during the transition to the new system. If tens of millions of families receive substantial new child care subsidies targeted for use in high-quality child care, the child care market may not be able to respond quickly with large increases in capacity to provide high-quality care. One way to smooth the transition is to delay the distribution of vouchers until about a year after the new system becomes law, in order to give centers and family day care homes time to expand and upgrade quality. Any shortages caused by implementation of the new system are likely to be transitory, since providers will have strong incentives to expand capacity and upgrade quality in order to attract consumers with vouchers.

A final issue that should be discussed is the relationship between the proposed new system and state and local child care policy. The current child care subsidy system gives states considerable flexibility in how they use federal CCDF and TXX subsidies, both of which are disbursed as block grants. States can choose the income eligibility criterion, the sliding scale fee, and other features of their CCDF-funded programs, within limits. States would lose some flexibility in the new system, because both the income eligibility and quality guidelines would be uniform federal standards. In fact, state bureaucracies that administer federally funded child care subsidies would no longer be needed, since all subsidies would be disbursed through the federal income tax system. However, many states have their own child care subsidy programs funded entirely by state funds. The proposed new system would not interfere with these programs. Such programs vary widely, ranging from state child care tax credits and mini-

CCDF-style programs to teacher training initiatives and quality improvement subsidies.[11] States would be free to fund whatever child care programs they like or to discontinue such programs if they are found to be no longer necessary as a result of the expanded federal system.

CONCLUSIONS

Child care is a problem in the United States because the quality of care is low on average. Current child care policy does little to address the problem because most child care subsidies are designed to encourage employment rather than enhance child development. The tension between these alternative goals ensures that debate and discussion of child care policy issues will continue for the foreseeable future.

There is no consensus on the goals of child care policy or on the means to achieve those goals. This is due in part to conflicting views on the proper role of the government in a domain that was mainly left to families as recently as a generation ago. My proposal is squarely on the side of enhancing child development, and this stance will no doubt be controversial. Arguments about child care policy are also partly a reflection of lack of knowledge about the magnitudes of important parameters that affect the costs and benefits of alternative policies. Careful empirical studies that produce reliable estimates of such parameters would make a significant contribution to the policy debate. I gave examples of topics that deserve research attention in previous chapters. I conclude here with a summary of the reasons why I believe my proposal should be seriously considered and a discussion of whether it is politically feasible.

There are three reasons I think my proposal deserves serious consideration. First, it takes advantage of the market for child care instead of trying to ignore it. Like many economists, I believe that government policy often works better when it operates through a market than when it tries to replace or circumvent a market. That is, policy works better when it provides incentives and information to induce market participants to change their behavior than when it attempts to affect behavior directly through price controls, quantity controls, regulation, or government takeover of an industry. Direct government intervention often has undesired adverse consequences and creates entrenched bureaucracies with little incentive to strive for efficiency and adaptability. This is the reason for the market-oriented nature of my proposal, and I suspect it underlies the market-oriented nature of the child care policy proposals by other economists described earlier. In my view, there is no evidence of fundamental *internal* failures of the child care market, such as market power concentrated in a few firms or systematic failure of firms to provide the type of care for which consumers are willing to pay. The in-kind child care subsidies that I propose provide greater benefits when they are used for higher-quality care. This is an example of policy working through the market by providing the means and the incentive for families to increase their willingness to pay for higher-quality child care. The evidence presented in chapter 5 suggests that the supply of higher-quality care will respond to increased demand. I believe the market-oriented policy approach has significant advantages over the non-market-oriented approaches of Zigler and Finn-Stevenson, Kagan and Cohen, and others.

Second, my proposal addresses head-on what I believe to be the main problem with the child care market: low quality. Most child care subsidies proposed by economists (Walker is an exception) are partly or fully restricted to employed parents. As discussed earlier, I do not believe that the child care problem originates in the labor market. The *employment* problem is that workers with low skills earn low wages, especially after accounting for child care and other costs of employment. The employment problem should be addressed by employment policies such as wage subsidies and training and education. The cost of child care also reduces the disposable income of middle-income two-earner families, but I do not see this as a social or economic problem. I see the high cost of raising children as a problem, and that is why I include in my proposal a child allowance that benefits all low-to-middle-income families regardless of employment status. Economists who propose employment-related child care subsidies may believe that there is an important employment problem and that child care subsidies can alleviate the problem. I agree that there is an employment problem for low-income families, though not for middle-income families, but I think that using child care subsidies to address the employment problem is likely to worsen the child care problem by increasing the use of low-quality care.

Third, my proposal attempts to deal with an important source of the child care problem: lack of information by parents. To my knowledge, there has never been a major nationwide public effort to educate parents about the quality of child care. My proposal tackles this problem directly by providing all new parents with the information they need to recognize the quality of child care and to understand the benefits of higher-quality care for their children. The cost of this part of the proposal is tiny compared to the child allowance and child care subsidies, but that should not obscure its potential importance.

Is this proposal politically feasible or just a pie-in-the-sky wish list? I don't know the answer. The high cost of the proposal will discourage some from considering it. I do not have a firm scientific basis for the specific value of the child allowance part of the proposal, but a $10,000 allowance for a poor family with two children does not seem excessive compared with the support provided by the current welfare system. The $6,000 per child voucher for excellent-quality child care for a poor family does not seem excessive either compared with the cost of providing such care. Nevertheless, these costs do add up to a large figure.

One political advantage of the proposal is that it is scalable: the value of the child allowance and voucher could be reduced without compromising the basic idea of the proposal. Another advantage is that the proposal is not inherently biased toward one or the other ideological end of the "family values" political spectrum. Supporters of traditional values and supporters of gender equity should both be pleased by the child allowance. Supporters of efforts to give poor children the resources they need to achieve their potential should find the quality-biased child care voucher valuable. On the other hand, supporters of welfare reform who believe that employment of low-income mothers is an important goal will probably dislike the proposal. The child care voucher will provide mothers with a work incentive, but there is deliberately no work *requirement* for the voucher, and I believe that imposing a work requirement would be a mistake. In the current political environment, this may be the biggest obstacle to serious consideration of the proposal.

The Child Care and Development Fund is up for congressional reauthorization in 2002. I have no illusion that my proposal will leap off the pages of this book directly into the debate over child care policy. But if the book has any impact on thinking about a solution to the child care problem, then it will have served its purpose.

$\mathcal{N}otes$

CHAPTER 1

1. Data from the National Child Care Staffing Study and the Current Population Survey, assembled by the National Child Care Information Center, available at: *ericps.crc.uiuc.edu/nccichome.html*.

2. "The Economics of Family Child Care," cited by the National Child Care Information Center (see note 1).

CHAPTER 2

1. Most of the published tables produced from the 1995 SIPP double-count children who are in more than one child care arrangement. Publications from earlier years designate one arrangement as the primary arrangement and count each child in only one category. This makes comparisons across years difficult.

2. The National Survey of America's Families (NSAF) collected information on child care in 1997, but the published summaries of the data are not strictly comparable to the SIPP. Capizzano, Adams, and Sonenstein (2000) report that 32 percent of children under five with an employed mother in the NSAF were in center-based care, 16 percent were in a family day care home, 23 percent were cared for by a relative, 24 percent were cared for by a parent, and 6 percent were in the care of a baby-sitter. These figures are quite similar to the comparable categories in the fall 1994 SIPP.

3. In March 1997, 60 percent of all black families with children were headed by a single parent, compared to 22 percent of white families. Thirty-one percent of Hispanic families with children were headed by a single parent, compared to 27 percent of non-Hispanic families (tabulations from the March 1997 Current Population Survey; for CPS data online, see: *www.bls.census.gov/cps/pub/1997/int _race.htm* (and *www.bls.census.gov/cps/pub/1997/int_hisp.htm*).

4. In March 1999, the employment rate of mothers with children under age six was virtually identical in the South and other parts of the country, but among employed mothers, the rate of full-time employment (thirty-five or more hours per week) was 68.0 percent in the South and 60.7 percent in the rest of the nation (tabulations from the March 1999 Current Population Survey).

5. The 1995 SIPP included information on the child care arrangements used by non-employed mothers. However, as noted earlier, the published tables produced from this survey double-count children placed in more than one arrangement.

6. The Consumer Expenditure Survey does not report child care expenditures in the published tables, but it does report expenditure on other items. Husband-

wife families with children spent the following on other items in 1995: food, 11.9 percent; housing, 26.1 percent; apparel, 4.6 percent; transportation, 16.7 percent; health care, 3.9 percent; and entertainment, 4.3 percent. The corresponding figures for single-parent families were: food, 18.3 percent; housing, 41.7 percent; apparel, 8.4 percent; transportation, 20.0 percent; health care, 4.1 percent; and entertainment, 5.5 percent (see *www.bls.gov/csxhome.htm*). The National Survey of America's Families (NSAF) collected data on child care expenditures in 1997 that can be compared with the SIPP, although the comparisons are not exact because of differences in survey design. The percentage of families with an employed mother and a child under age thirteen who paid for care in the NSAF was 48 percent, and average monthly expenditure for payers was $286. The corresponding figures for families in which the youngest child was under age five were 60 percent and $325 (Gianarelli and Barsimantov 2000).

7. It is possible to use the CPS to track the number of child care workers over time, but changes in survey design limit the comparability of the data over time. In 1977, 0.485 percent of all women between eighteen and sixty-four were child care workers, for a total of about 304,000. This percentage increased fairly steadily to 1.371 percent in 1991, for a total of 1,063,000 women. In 1992, when the CPS was redesigned, 0.659 percent of women were child care workers, or only 734,000. The corresponding figures in 1998 were 0.527 percent, or 644,000. It is unclear what feature of the survey design accounts for the abrupt change between 1991 and 1992, and which design produces more accurate estimates.

8. See Kisker et al. (1991, ch. 6) for further details. The PCS subsample on which these comparisons are based differs from the overall PCS sample in order to make it comparable with the NDCS sample.

CHAPTER 3

1. An example that illustrates this approach is to assume that Q is the Early Childhood Environment Rating Scale (ECERS) score described in chapter 2. ECERS scores range from 1 to 7. Suppose $\alpha = 1$ and $\beta = 0.5$. Then $P = 1 + 0.5Q$. The price of an hour of child care with an ECERS rating of 2 would be $2.00, and the price of an hour of care with an ECERS rating of 5 would be $3.50.

2. Some relatives charge a fee for child care (see chapter 2). A model could be developed to account for such behavior, but it is relatively rare, so I do not present such a model here. See Blau (1993) and Connelly (1992b) for models of the decision to be a child care worker.

3. A provider who does not care at all about profit nevertheless faces a break-even constraint: revenue cannot exceed cost in the long run, accounting for the reduction in cost provided by donations and subsidies. Nonprofit providers also face a constraint on the amount of profit they can earn and retain their tax-exempt status.

4. With constant returns to scale, an individual provider can increase output at constant cost. But when many providers attempt to increase output at the same time, they increase the demand for teachers. This tends to drive up the wages of teachers, leading to increased input costs and rising average cost as output ex-

pands. If the supply of teachers (and other inputs) is flexible enough so that output can expand without driving up labor and other costs, then the market supply curve is horizontal.

CHAPTER 4

1. A multinomial logit model of the discrete choices is estimated jointly with linear models of group size and staff-child ratio and a binomial logit model of training, using a random effects estimator to allow for correlation among the discrete and continuous outcomes. See Blau and Hagy (1998) for details.

2. To be more precise, let $P_{ij} = \alpha_j + \beta Q_{ij} + \varepsilon_{ij}$ be the price charged by center i in site j, and Q_{ij} the quality of care provided by center i in site j. A statistical disturbance ε_{ij} is included to account for unobserved factors that affect price. I let the intercept α_j differ by site and restrict the slope coefficient β to be the same across sites. I do not have data on quality, so suppose that quality is determined by $Q_{ij} = \gamma + \delta X_{ij} + \eta_{ij}$, where X_{ij} is a set of quality determinants such as group size, teacher training, and so forth, and η_{ij} is a disturbance. The parameters γ and δ are assumed to be the same across sites, because this equation reflects the "technology" of producing quality, which is not site-specific. Substituting the equation for Q_{ij} into the price equation and collecting terms yields the version of the price equation I estimate: $P_{ij} = (\alpha_j + \beta\gamma) + \beta\delta X_{ij} + (\varepsilon_{ij} + \beta\eta_{ij}) = a_j + bX_{ij} + c_{ij}$. After estimating this equation, I assign all households in site j a price of $\hat{P}_j = \hat{a}_j + \hat{b}\overline{X}$, where a ^ denotes an estimate and $\overline{X}$ is the overall (not site-specific) mean of X. Thus, the only source of variation in the price is the site-specific intercept.

3. In the model of chapter 3, the wage rate is taken as given by the individual. In practice, individuals can influence their wage rates by investing in skills, working longer, and putting forth greater effort. Also, the NCCS, like most surveys, does not provide a measure of the wage rate that would have been earned by a nonworker had the individual chosen to be employed. But this piece of information is needed in order to estimate the impact of wages on child care decisions. To deal with both of these problems, I estimate a statistical model of wage rates and use the model to assign a "predicted" wage rate to each individual in the sample, workers and nonworkers alike. If the variables used to explain wages are not subject to influence by the individual (for example, age, race, national origin), and if the wages earned by workers with a given set of observed characteristics are representative of the wages that nonworkers with the same set of characteristics would have earned had they worked, then predicted wages solve both problems. They eliminate the kind of wage variation that we should not use, according to the theory, to explain child care demand—variation in wages caused by choices made by the worker. And they provide an estimate of the wage rate for nonworkers. For this approach to be useful, the variables included in the wage equation must be chosen carefully, and the hypothesis that the wages earned by workers are representative of the wages that nonworkers would have earned had they worked must be tested. If the hypothesis is rejected, some method to control for the nonrepresentative nature of the sample of workers must be employed.

4. As noted earlier, the appropriate income variable to use is nonwage income, excluding sources of income that are directly related to labor supply. However, the only data available to measure household income other than the mother's wage rate are the spouse's annual earnings. A significant number of observations were missing data on the spouse's earnings. For these cases I predicted earnings using a regression model. See Blau and Hagy (1998) for details.

5. The elasticity concept is used throughout the empirical chapters. It is a standard tool for reporting effect sizes in a way that is not affected by units of measurement and therefore lends itself to comparisons of results across studies. An elasticity is the ratio of percentage changes of two variables. If a 1 percent increase in the price of a service causes a 0.5 percent decrease in the quantity of the service demanded, then the price elasticity of demand for the service is $-0.5/1.0 = -0.5$. If a 10 percent increase in the price of a service causes a 5 percent decrease in the quantity of the service demanded, then the price elasticity of demand for the service is $-5/10 = -.5$.

6. This estimate is at the low end of the range of estimates in the literature, but of the same order of magnitude as the estimates in other studies using similar methods, such as Ribar (1995) and Tekin (2001). Other studies that have estimated the elasticity of employment of mothers with respect to the price of child care include Anderson and Levine (2000), Blau and Robins (1988, 1991), Connelly and Kimmel (1999), Connelly (1992a), Fronstin and Wissoker (1995), Han and Waldfogel (1999), Hotz and Kilburn (1994), Kimmel (1998), Michalopoulos and Robins (1999), Powell (1997), Ribar (1992), and U.S. General Accounting Office (1994b). See Blau (2000a), Connelly (1991), Gelbach (1999), and Ross (1998) for surveys of this literature.

7. The parameter estimates of the model are used to compute the predicted proportion of families who would use each type of child care, first assigning a price of $1.50 to each family, and then assigning a price of $0.00 to each family. The absolute (and percentage) differences in these proportions are shown in the table. See Blau and Hagy (1998) for further details.

8. The elasticity of employment with respect to the price of child care may differ across groups. Kimmel's (1998) results indicate quite different elasticities for married and single mothers, but Anderson and Levine (2000) and Connelly and Kimmel (1999) produce estimates that are much closer for the two groups. If the elasticities differ substantially by the level of income, then estimates for the population as a whole could be misleading if applied to the low-income population. Estimates produced by Anderson and Levine (2000), Fronstin and Wissoker (1995), and U.S. General Accounting Office (1994b) all show larger elasticities for low-income groups. This suggests that the elasticity for low-income mothers could be substantially larger in absolute value than the $-.20$ I found.

9. Chaplin et al. (1999) provide a detailed comparison of results from different studies of the demand for child care. Briefly, the elasticity of demand for paid care with respect to the price of care estimated by Blau and Robins (1988) is identical to mine ($-.34$), and Ribar's (1995) estimate of $-.25$ is close as well. Chaplin et al. estimate a price elasticity of demand for center care of $-.40$ compared to $-.24$ in my results; .23 for family day care compared to $-.34$ in my

results; and $-.016$ for relative care versus $-.12$ for other nonparental care in my results. My estimate of the elasticity of demand for hours of child care with respect to the mother's wage rate is small: $.01$. Ribar (1992) and Hotz and Kilburn (1994) report much larger effects: 1.41 and 2.16, respectively. My estimate of the elasticity of demand for paid care with respect to the mother's wage rate is $.67$, versus $.14$ in Ribar (1995). My estimate of the elasticity of demand for hours of child care with respect to the spouse's earnings is a very small $-.032$, compared to $-.84$ and -2.39 for working and nonworking mothers in Hotz and Kilburn (1994).

10. The NICHD Study of Early Child Care (SECC) contains measures of quality similar to the ECERS for all types of child care, not just centers. These data were made available to researchers recently, but too late for use in this book.

11. When both the dependent and independent variables in an equation are in logarithms, the coefficient on the independent variable is a direct estimate of the elasticity.

12. See *156.40.88.3/publications/pubs/early—child—care.htm*, and *public.rti.org/secc/ home.cfm*, for information about the Study of Early Child Care.

CHAPTER 5

1. Labor is the most important input in terms of cost, and there is little information available about the prices of other inputs, so I focus primarily on the effect of the price of teacher labor.

2. This restriction is imposed for two reasons: first, the wage rates of all labor types are needed to estimate the cost function, and if a center does not employ one of the labor types, then the wage rate for that type is unobserved for that center. Second, economic theory implies that a center that does not use any labor of a particular type will respond differently to a change in the wage rate of that type of labor than a center that does use labor of that type. For more details on this and other technical aspects of the analysis, see Blau and Mocan (2000).

3. Sixty-two percent of nonprofits and 5 percent of for-profit centers use donated space.

4. Wages are averaged over all staff with a given level of education. The center's total expenditure on fringe benefits is divided by total staff hours to measure the average hourly value of fringe benefits.

5. When computed separately by state, the quality supply elasticity appears to be larger in the lower-quality states, Colorado and North Carolina (not shown in the table).

6. However, changes over time in the mix of child care by type (center, family day care, and so on) could cause divergence between trends in child care labor supply and child care supply. Day care centers have the highest child-staff ratios, and if more care is provided in centers over time, then a given change in the number of child care workers would be associated with a different change in the number of children in care over time.

7. No data on the value of fringe benefits are available in the survey used for this analysis.

8. The total number of hours worked in child care, H, can be expressed as the proportion of women who work in child care, C, multiplied by the average number of hours worked per child care worker, $\overline{H}$: $H = C\overline{H}$. The percentage change in H caused by a wage change is approximately the sum of the percentage changes in C and $\overline{H}$: $\%\Delta H = \%\Delta C + \%\Delta\overline{H}$, where $\%\Delta$ indicates percentage change. Dividing through both sides by the percentage change in the wage, W, gives the result stated in the text, since an elasticity is just the percentage change in one variable divided by the percentage change in another variable: $(\%\Delta H/\%\Delta W) = (\%\Delta C/\%\Delta W) + (\%\Delta\overline{H}/\%\Delta W)$.

9. The child care wage data are available back to 1977, but I use 1983 as the base year because prior to 1983 there were too few prekindergarten teachers to include in the sample.

10. This assumes that capital and labor are not substitutes in the production of child care. It seems plausible that day care centers would be able to fairly easily substitute one type of labor for another but would not be easily able to substitute capital for labor.

11. The basis for the calculation is simple supply-demand analysis. Let $Log(Q_S) = \alpha log(W) + Log(X)$, and $Log(Q_D) = \beta log(W) + Log(Y)$, where Q_S is the quantity of child care labor supplied, Q_D is the quantity demanded, W is the child care wage, α is the supply elasticity (1.15), β is the demand elasticity $(-.238)$, X is a factor that causes supply to shift (for example, increased immigration), and Y is a factor that causes demand to shift (greater employment of mothers). In equilibrium, $Q_S = Q_D$, and we can solve for the percentage effect on child care wages of a given percentage demand shift as $\Delta Log(W) = [1/(\alpha - \beta)] \times \Delta Log(Y) = [1/(1.15 - [-.238])] \times \Delta Log(Y) = .72 \times \Delta Log(Y)$. The observed demand shift $\Delta Log(Y) = 24$ percent, so the predicted wage increase is $.72 \times 24$ percent $= 17$ percent.

CHAPTER 6

1. The NICHD SECC contains data on price and quality for child care arrangements of all types in ten sites. The data currently available to researchers cover children through age thirty-six months. These data should be useful for analyzing the price-quality relationship for relative care, baby-sitters, and family day care. The data were made available to researchers too late for inclusion here.

2. Another approach is to use data collected from consumers on the amount paid for child care and the characteristics of the care, including the inputs. This has the advantage of sampling from all types of care in the proportions in which they are actually used by consumers. See Blau (1991) and Waite, Leibowitz, and Witsberger (1991) for analysis of this type.

3. For example, I estimate models of the form $Log(P) = \alpha + \beta Log(Q)$, with β constrained to be the same across all zip codes within a town, while α is allowed to differ by zip code.

4. The results in the first row were also reported in chapter 5 (table 5.3) and used there to estimate the supply of quality.

5. The fit of the model was substantially improved with the inclusion of county dummies compared to state dummies or no geographic controls, similar to the case of centers.

CHAPTER 7

1. The only exception is that if a variable is uncorrelated with other factors and omitted from the analysis, then no bias results. This is why randomized assignment experiments are so useful: by design, assignment to the "treatment" of interest is uncorrelated with all other explanatory variables, so the latter can be omitted without causing bias.

2. Some studies violate the fourth condition by not presenting coefficient estimates or in some cases even the signs of the estimated effects of the inputs (for example, Howes et al. 1998; Howes and Rubenstein 1981; Kontos and Fiene 1987; Phillips, McCartney, and Scarr 1987; Smith and Connolly 1986). Without this information, we cannot determine the quantitative magnitude of the effects of interest.

3. The studies to which I refer include Burchinal et al. (1996), Clarke-Stewart and Gruber (1984), Dunn (1993b), Holloway and Reichart-Erickson (1988), Howes et al. (1988), Kontos, Hsu, and Dunn (1994), McCartney (1984), Parcel and Menaghan (1990), and Smith et al. (1989). Most of these studies examined multiple child outcomes. The studies that found statistically significant effects of the inputs usually found such effects for a minority of the outcomes examined.

4. See Vandell and Wolfe (2000) for a review. Studies include Deater-Deckard, Pinkerton, and Scarr (1996), Dunn (1993b), Field (1991), Hestenes, Kontos, and Bryan (1993), Howes (1988, 1990), Howes and Olenick (1986), Howes and Rubenstein (1981), Kontos (1994), Lamb et al. (1988), Peterson and Peterson (1986), Phillips et al. (1987), Vandell and Powers (1983), and Vandell, Henderson, and Wilson (1988).

5. See Arnett (1989), Berk (1985), Bronson, Tivnan, and Seppanen (1995), Clarke-Stewart (1987), Dunn (1993a), Holloway and Reichart-Erickson (1988), Howes (1983), Kontos et al. (1994), Kontos et al. (1995), and Phillips et al. (1987), Phillips, Howes, and Whitebook (1991), and Scarr, Eisenberg, and Deater-Deckard (1994).

6. Another new regulation was the requirement that every day care center have at least one staff person per twenty children with a CDA or equivalent credential. However, this change did not take effect until 1996, after the last data collection point of the study.

7. The stratification was on client income, urban-rural location, and profit-nonprofit status.

8. Twenty of the centers in the sample in 1992 dropped out of the study in 1994 and were replaced with eighteen newly sampled centers. Twenty-two centers in

the 1994 sample dropped out of the study and were replaced with twenty-two newly sampled centers in the 1996 wave.

9. I used data from the National Child Care Staffing Study (NCCSS) to do a similar analysis of the effects of inputs on classroom quality, comparing results using between-center and within-center variation (Blau 1997). The results were very similar to the CQOS results, indicating that the latter are not a fluke. Note that in both the CQOS and the NCCSS the sample is limited to day care centers.

10. There were too few cases with PPVT scores in adjacent surveys to estimate this specification for the PPVT score.

CHAPTER 8

1. Information dissemination and training of child care providers are other forms of government policy toward child care. Government efforts in these areas are much smaller than in subsidies and regulation, and there is little information available for systematic analysis of these efforts. I discuss the potential of government to take a broader role in information dissemination in chapter 10. Another government policy is direct provision of child care. I treat this as a form of subsidy.

2. Some smaller programs omitted from the table are listed in U.S. General Accounting Office (1994a) and Robins (1991). A number of states offer their own tax credits for child care, but they generally provide small benefits.

3. These figures were derived as follows from U.S. Department of Labor (1999a, table 3). Forty-five percent, 37 percent, and 21 percent of professional-technical, clerical-sales, and blue-collar–service employees, respectively, were eligible for reimbursement plans. From table 183, 90 percent, 93 percent, and 91 percent of reimbursement accounts of professional-technical, clerical-sales, and blue-collar–service employees, respectively, covered dependent care expenses. Multiplying the appropriate pairs of numbers gives the figures in the text. From U.S. Department of Labor (1999b, table 3), 18 percent, 16 percent, and 7 percent of professional-technical, clerical-sales, and blue-collar–service employees, respectively, were eligible for reimbursement plans. From table 87, 90 percent, 82 percent, and 75 percent of reimbursement accounts of professional-technical, clerical-sales, and blue-collar–service employees, respectively, covered dependent care expenses. Nine percent of full-time employees in state and local government were eligible for subsidized employer-provided child care benefits in 1994, and 64 percent of such employees had access to child care reimbursement accounts (U.S. Department of Labor 1994).

4. Three of the previous programs (Aid to Families with Dependent Children—Child Care [AFDC-CC], Transitional Child Care [TCC], and At-Risk Child Care [ARCC]) were authorized and funded by the Social Security Act under Title IV-A. They were replaced by the child care block grant of the Temporary Assistance for Needy Families (TANF) program, the cash assistance welfare program created by the PRWORA in 1996 to replace AFDC and funded by the Social Security Act. PRWORA also reauthorized and revised the Child Care and Development Block Grant (CCDBG) with its own funding. Finally, it stipulated

that both the new TANF child care block grant and the CCDBG be administered by the CCDBG program. The combined program is called the CCDF, and it consists of the two separately authorized funding streams, administered jointly and subject to the same rules (Pitegoff and Bream 1997).

5. See Administration for Children and Families (1998a) for details of state CCDF subsidy programs, and the final rule issued by the U.S. Department of Health and Human Services (1998).

6. Head Start served 822,316 children in fiscal year 1998, compared to an estimate of 4.775 million children under age six in poverty in calendar year 1998 (Delaker 1999, table 2). However, 96 percent of children in Head Start are age three to five (the other 4 percent are served by Early Head Start, a relatively new program). Assuming that half the children under age six are three to five years old yields 34.4 percent as the percentage of three- to five-year-old children in poverty who are served by Head Start. Looking at table 8.2, the CCDF appears to be well funded on a per-child basis, but it is likely that the number of children listed is an underestimate. Many states spend part of their CCDF funds on their own state-specific child care programs, and data on children served by these programs may not be included in the lower panel but are included in the upper panel.

7. Fuchs (1989) and others have argued that children are a significant barrier to economic equality for women, because mothers are expected to assume the burden of child-rearing, and that child-centered policies are an effective way to help women achieve economic equality with men. This could be interpreted as a rationale for child care subsidies, but Fuchs explicitly states that child allowances are the kind of policy he has in mind (41). A child allowance—a cash subsidy for children that is not restricted in its use—is not the same as a child care subsidy. The distinction is discussed in more detail in chapter 10.

8. Employment may also be considered a desirable goal for its own sake, aside from any future benefits it brings. It may increase self-esteem and provide children with a good role model.

9. Evidence summarized by Currie (2001) suggests that the benefits of high-quality preschool programs are larger for the most disadvantaged children than for other children. If the magnitude of the externalities and information problems that are the source of market imperfections is proportional to the gains from high-quality care, then this would suggest that subsidies be targeted to disadvantaged children.

10. Regulations can deal with information problems to some extent, by ensuring that all providers offer care of some minimum quality. This is discussed in chapter 9.

11. See *nccic.org/ccpartnerships/profiles/georgia.htm* for information about Georgia's prekindergarten program.

12. Another difficulty with most randomized trials is that some of the people in the treatment group do not accept the offer of services, and some of the people in the control group find the same services elsewhere. This does not invalidate the randomization but does affect the interpretation of the nature of the "treatment"

and its effects. (For a detailed discussion and analysis of this issue, see Heckman, Hohmann, and Smith 2000.) Other demonstrations and experiments that included child care subsidies were the Teenage Parent Demonstration (Kisker, Rangarajan, and Boller 1998), New Chance (Quint, Bos, and Polit 1997), GAIN in California (Riccio, Friedlander, and Freedman 1994), the National Evaluation of Welfare-to-Work Strategies, formerly known as the JOBS program (Hamilton et al. 1997), the Minnesota Family Investment Program (Miller et al. 1997), the Florida Family Transition Program (Bloom et al. 1999), and the Gary, Seattle, and Denver Income Maintenance Experiments. The GAIN demonstration excluded children under age six. Granger and Cytron (1999) report that the effects of the Teenage Parent Demonstration and of New Chance (which was also targeted at teenage mothers) on the use of center-based child care were smaller than in New Hope and often statistically insignificant. Robins and Spiegelman (1978) estimate that eligibility for a child care subsidy in the Seattle and Denver Income Maintenance Experiments increased the use of market child care by eighteen percentage points in Seattle and by fourteen percentage points in Denver. Results for child care use in the other demonstrations are not available.

13. Meyer and Rosenbaum (1999) use a time series of cross-sections from the Current Population Survey to examine the association between state child care spending, other policy variables, and employment of single mothers. They cannot determine whether any given mother in their sample actually received a child care subsidy, so this is an indirect approach to analyzing subsidy effects.

14. Gelbach reports that his estimation strategy performed poorly for single mothers with a five-year-old child and another child younger than five.

15. The elasticity estimate of $-.20$ applies to mothers of preschool-age children, but subsidies are not broken down by the age of the child. I assume that the proportion of employment-related child care subsidies going to families with preschool-age children is the same as the proportion of total child care expenditures incurred by families with preschool-age children. This proportion was 73.6 percent in 1995, and the amount of expenditure was $26.2 billion (Smith 2000). From table 8.2, total employment-related child care subsidies were $6.554 billion in 1995 ($7.163 billion measured in 1999 dollars, converted to 1995 dollars by dividing by 1.093; see the note to table 8.2). If 73.6 percent of these subsidies went to families with preschool-age children, then their subsidy amount was $4.823 billion, which amounted to 15.5 percent of the total amount of $31.2 billion spent on preschool-age child care ($26.2 billion in private expenditures plus $4.823 billion in public expenditures). Thinking of the removal of the subsidy as equivalent to a price increase to families of 15.5 percent, the labor force participation rate of mothers of preschool-age children, which was 62.3 percent in 1995, would have been 3.1 percent lower had the subsidies not been in place (a 15.5 percent increase in price multiplied by an elasticity of $-.20$). Thus, the labor force participation rate would have been 60.4 percent instead of 62.3 percent, a decrease of 355,000 of the total number of mothers of preschool-age children in 1995, 18.7 million.

16. A recent report of the Advisory Committee on Head Start Research and Evalua-

tion (1999) strongly recommended a randomized assignment evaluation of Head Start.

CHAPTER 9

1. Market power refers to the ability of a firm to exploit a dominant market position by raising its price above its marginal cost. This is a concern in industries dominated by a few large firms, and the arguments in favor of regulation in such industries are much more widely accepted by economists.

2. Federal interagency day care requirements (FIDCRs) were developed in the 1960s to standardize the requirements for receiving federal funding for child care services. These requirements were eliminated in 1981. Head Start imposes uniform federal standards that providers must meet to qualify for funding, and Title I-A also uses the Head Start standards. Hayes, Palmer, and Zaslow (1990, appendix B) describe the FIDCR. Head Start program standards are available at: *www2.acf.dhhs.gov/programs/hsb/regs/regs/rg__index.htm.*

3. Other models of occupational licensing and minimum quality standards are of less relevance to child care because they are based on the assumption that a seller's product quality is fixed and cannot be modified in response to regulations. In such a model, a potential seller's only response to the imposition of a regulation is the decision to exit the market or to not enter in the first place (see Leland 1979).

4. The model could easily be reinterpreted to apply to group size and child-staff ratio standards as well, with similar implications. The model would have to be altered in an analysis of group size and child-staff-ratio standards, however, to account for the reversibility of these inputs (training investments are not reversible).

5. A standard interpretation of "positive net benefits" in this context is that consumers who gain from regulation could compensate the consumers who lose and still come out ahead. Shapiro also discusses an alternative to licensing: certification, in which sellers who meet a specified level of human capital investment are certified by the government (five stars instead of three or four in North Carolina, for example). He shows that there are some circumstances in which certification is preferable to licensing, and other circumstances in which the reverse is true.

6. It has been suggested that providers might care about the quality of care they offer *relative* to the average in their market (Chipty and Witte 1997, based on Ronnen 1991). In this case, if the regulation is binding on some providers, and as a result the average level of quality is affected, then providers that are not directly affected by the regulation might choose to alter their quality in response to a regulation.

7. U.S. General Accounting Office (2000a) documents the licensing enforcement budgets and caseloads of the states. In most states the budget is small relative to the number of providers.

8. This is a general concern in the analysis of the effects of regulations. For a discussion, see Joskow and Rose (1989, 1459–61).

9. Previous analyses of the effects of child care regulations have relied exclusively on cross-state variation. See Chipty (1995), Chipty and Witte (1997), Gormley (1991), Hofferth and Chaplin (1998), Hotz and Kilburn (1994), Lowenberg and Tinnin (1992), and Rose-Ackerman (1983).

10. This percentage is computed from table 9.2 as "exactly meet" divided by the sum of "exceed" and "exactly meet." A more liberal definition of compliance counts a room that is within one unit on either side of the regulation (for California and Connecticut) or a room that is within the range of the multiple regulations (in the cases of Colorado and North Carolina) as being exactly in compliance. This boosts the rates of exact compliance to 7 to 19 percent for measures other than enrolled, and to 23 to 26 percent for enrolled.

11. This percentage is computed from table 9.2 as "exactly meet" divided by the sum of "exactly meet" and "violate."

12. These are the only regulations that vary by child age. Later in the chapter, I report on analyses of the effects of other child care regulations with the CPS.

13. I use the child-staff ratio regulation because two of the states do not regulate group size.

CHAPTER 10

1. Other authors have discussed general principles for the reform of child care policy but have not made specific reform proposals. See Hayes, Palmer, and Zaslow (1990, ch. 10) and Gomby and her colleagues (1996). Hayes, Palmer, and Zaslow do offer some specific recommendations, including the expansion of Head Start. Gormley (1995) makes a number of child care policy recommendations that are generally similar in style and intent to those of the economists. Sawhill and Thomas (2000) propose several child care policy reforms that are designed to encourage employment and do not have any quality-related features.

2. Other elements of his overall strategy to achieve these goals include paid parental leave and support for increased accreditation and professionalization of child care.

3. This proposal is part of a larger plan that includes subsidized health insurance, a strengthened child support enforcement system, and other elements.

4. Positive balances in the account at the time of retirement would be transferred to a worker's Social Security account, and negative balances would be deducted from the worker's Social Security account. This would require some restructuring of the Social Security system.

5. Kahn and Kamerman (1987) propose a school-based child care system, in less detail than Zigler and Finn-Stevenson.

6. They propose a network of support and outreach services for family day care providers who care for children up to age three, but this is not a major or well-developed part of their proposal. They recognize that their plan does not specifically provide for the care of children before age three, but they state that care for such children can be addressed by paid parental leave.

7. I used the CQOS data to compute the average cost per child of care in day care centers with an ECERS score of 5 or more. This was approximately $5,000 in 1993. The cost figure includes the imputed value of donated space and volunteer labor. After adjusting for inflation, this amounts to $5,765 (in 1999 dollars). I add an extra $235 per child to account for the higher real salary that will be needed to attract substantial numbers of well-qualified providers to the field. The $6,000 figure I use here can be compared to the $6,000 estimate of the cost of high-quality care used by Barnett (1993a); that estimate is equivalent to $6,918 in 1999 dollars after adjusting for inflation, and to the $5,403 cost per child of Head Start in 1998.

8. I do not account for the tax revenue implications of any possible labor supply effects of the new policy.

9. The cost of accreditation is assumed to be $1,000, which is the maximum fee charged by the NAEYC for the accreditation process (see *www.naeyc.org/accreditation/faq_1.htm*). This is incurred every three years. In 2000, there were an estimated 106,000 licensed day care centers (Children's Foundation 2000). I arbitrarily assume that there will be 150,000 day care centers in the new system, 50,000 of which would incur the accreditation cost per year, at a cost of $50 million. I add another $25 million per year for accreditation of family day care homes and baby-sitters. The cost of producing and distributing the informational booklet and video is estimated at $10 per child, with an estimated 3.5 million children born per year.

10. The CCDF child care subsidy benefits are quite large in both states, but it should be recalled that only a small fraction of eligible families actually receive these benefits (11 percent in Alabama, 5 percent in Connecticut).

11. For information about state child care initiatives, see *cpmcnet.columbia.edu/dept/nccp/main5.html* and *www.gao.gov.news.items/he00011.pdf*. See Abt Associates (2000) for a more detailed discussion of state child care policy in selected states.

References

Abt Associates. 2000. "National Study of Child Care for Low-Income Families: State and Community Substudy, Interim Report." Cambridge, Mass. (November).

Adams, Gina, Karen Schulman, and Nancy Ebb. 1998. "Locked Doors: States Struggling to Meet the Child Care Needs of Low-Income Working Families." Washington: Children's Defense Fund (March).

Administration for Children and Families. 1995. "Federal Child Care Programs in FY1995." Available at: *www.acf.dhhs.gov/programs/ccb/data/1995.htm*.

———. 1998a. "Child Care Development and Block Grant Report of State Plans." Washington (March). Available at: *www.acf.dhhs.gov/programs/ccb/programs/plan/index.htm*.

———. 1998b. "State Spending Under the Child Care Block Grant." Washington (November). Available at: *www.acf.dhhs.gov/news/press/1998/cc97fund.htm*.

———. 1999. "Access to Child Care for Low-Income Working Families." Washington. Available at: *www.acf.dhhs.gov/news/ccreport.htm*.

———. 2000a. "New Statistics Show Only Small Percentage of Eligible Families Receive Child Care Help." *HHS News* (December 6). Available at: *www.acf.dhhs.gov/news/ccstudy.htm*.

———. 2000b. "TANF Program: Third Annual Report to Congress." Available at: *www.acf.dhhs.gov/programs/opre/annual3.pdf*.

Advisory Committee on Head Start Research and Evaluation, U.S. Department of Health and Human Services. 1999. "A Recommended Framework for Studying the Impact of Head Start Programs." Available at: *www.acf.dhhs.gov/programs/hsreac/oct99/textrpt.htm*.

Anderson, Patricia M., and Philip B. Levine. 2000. "Child Care and Mothers' Employment Decisions." In *Finding Jobs: Work and Welfare Reform*, edited by Rebecca M. Blank and David Card. New York: Russell Sage Foundation.

Arnett, Jeffrey. 1989. "Caregivers in Day Care Centers: Does Training Matter?" *Journal of Applied Developmental Psychology* 10: 541–52.

Barnett, W. Steven. 1992. "Benefits of Compensatory Preschool Education." *Journal of Human Resources* 27(2): 279–312.

———. 1993a. "New Wine in Old Bottles: Increasing Coherence in Early Childhood Care and Education Policy." *Early Childhood Research Quarterly* 8(4): 519–58.

———. 1993b. "Benefit-Cost Analysis of Preschool Education: Findings from a Twenty-five-Year Follow-up." *American Journal of Orthopsychiatry* 64(4): 500–8.

———. 1995. "Long-term Effects of Early Childhood Programs on Cognitive and School Outcomes." *The Future of Children* 5(3): 25–50.

Baydar, Nazli, and Jeanne Brooks-Gunn. 1991. "Effects of Maternal Employment and Child-Care Arrangements on Preschoolers' Cognitive and Behavioral Outcomes: Evidence from the Children of the National Longitudinal Survey." *Developmental Psychology* 27(6): 932–45.

Belsky, Jay, and David Eggebeen. 1991. "Early and Extensive Maternal Employment and Young Children's Socioemotional Development: Children of the National Longitudinal Survey of Youth." *Journal of Marriage and the Family* 53(4): 1083–98.

Berger, Mark C., and Dan A. Black. 1992. "Child Care Subsidies, Quality of Care, and the Labor Supply of Low-Income Single Mothers." *Review of Economics and Statistics* 74(4): 635–42.

Bergmann, Barbara. 1996. *Saving Our Children from Poverty: What the United States Can Learn from France.* New York: Russell Sage Foundation.

Berk, Laura E. 1985. "Relationship of Caregiver Education to Child-oriented Attitudes, Job Satisfaction, and Behaviors Toward Children." *Child Care Quarterly* 14(2): 103–29.

Blau, David M. 1991. "The Quality of Child Care: An Economic Perspective." In *The Economics of Child Care,* edited by David M. Blau. New York: Russell Sage Foundation.

———. 1992. "The Child Care Labor Market." *Journal of Human Resources* 27(1): 9–39.

———. 1993. "The Supply of Child Care Labor." *Journal of Labor Economics* 11(2): 324–47.

———. 1997. "The Production of Quality in Child Care Centers." *Journal of Human Resources* 32(2): 354–87.

———. 1999. "The Effect of Child Care Characteristics on Child Development." *Journal of Human Resources* 34(4): 786–822.

———. 2000a. "Child Care Subsidy Programs." Working Paper 7806. Cambridge, Mass.: National Bureau of Economics (*www.nber.org*). Forthcoming in an NBER volume edited by Robert Moffitt.

———. 2000b. "The Production of Quality in Child Care Centers: Another Look." *Applied Developmental Science* 4(3): 136–48.

Blau, David M., and Alison P. Hagy. 1998. "The Demand for Quality in Child Care." *Journal of Political Economy* 106(1): 104–46.

Blau, David M., and H. Naci Mocan. 2000. "The Supply of Quality in Child Care Centers." Chapel Hill: University of North Carolina (August). Unpublished paper.

Blau, David M., and Philip K. Robins. 1988. "Child Care Costs and Family Labor Supply." *Review of Economics and Statistics* 70(3): 374–81.

———. 1991. "Child Care Demand and Labor Supply of Young Mothers over Time." *Demography* 28(3): 333–52.

Blau, Francine D., and Adam J. Grossberg. 1992. "Maternal Labor Supply and Children's Cognitive Development." *Review of Economics and Statistics* 74: 474–81.

Bloom, Dan, Mary Farrell, James J. Kemple, and Nandita Verma. 1999. "The Family Transition Program: Implementation and Three-Year Impacts of Florida's Initial Time-Limited Welfare Program." New York: Manpower Demonstration Research Corporation (April).

Bos, Johannes M., Aletha C. Huston, Robert C. Granger, Greg J. Duncan, Thomas W. Brock, and Vonnie C. McCloyd. 1999. "New Hope for People with Low Incomes: Two-Year Results of a Program to Reduce Poverty and Reform Welfare." New York: Manpower Demonstration Research Corporation (August).

Broberg, Anders G., Holger Wessels, Michael E. Lamb, and C. Phillip Hwang. 1997. "Effects of Day Care on the Development of Cognitive Abilities in Eight-Year-Olds: A Longitudinal Study." *Developmental Psychology* 33(1): 62–69.

Bronson, Martha B., Terrance Tivnan, and Patricia S. Seppanen. 1995. "Relations

Between Teacher and Classroom Activity Variables and the Classroom Behaviors of Prekindergarten Children in Chapter 1 Funded Programs." *Journal of Applied Developmental Psychology* 16: 253–82.

Bryant, Donna M., Margaret Burchinal, Lisa B. Lau, and Joseph J. Sparling. 1994. "Family and Classroom Correlates of Head Start Children's Developmental Outcomes." *Early Childhood Research Quarterly* 9: 289–309.

Burchinal, Margaret B., Joanne E. Roberts, Laura A. Nabors, and Donna M. Bryant. 1996. "Quality of Center Care and Infant Cognitive and Language Development." *Child Development* 67(2): 606–20.

Campbell, Frances A., Elizabeth P. Pungello, Shari Miller-Johnson, Margaret Burchinal, and Craig T. Ramey. In press. "The Development of Cognitive and Academic Abilities: Growth Curves from an Early Childhood Educational Experiment," *Developmental Psychology.*

Campbell, Frances A., and Craig T. Ramey. 1994. "Effects of Early Intervention on Intellectual and Academic Achievement: A Follow-up Study of Children from Low-Income Families." *Child Development* 65(2): 684–98.

Capizzano, Jeffrey, Gina Adams, and Freya Sonenstein. 2000. "Child Care Arrangements for Children Under Five: Variation Across States." Assessing the New Federalism Series B, B-7. Washington: Urban Institute (March).

Caspar, Lynne M. 1995. "What Does It Cost to Mind Our Preschoolers?" *Current Population Reports,* series P70, no. 52 (September). Washington: U.S. Government Printing Office for the U.S. Bureau of the Census. Available at: *www.census.gov/population/www/socdemo/childcare.html.*

———. 1996. "Who's Minding Our Preschoolers?: Fall 1993." *Current Population Reports,* series P70, no. 53 (March). Washington: U.S. Government Printing Office for the U.S. Bureau of the Census. Available at: *www.census.gov/population/www/socdemo/childcare.html.*

———. 1997. "Who's Minding Our Preschoolers?: Fall 1994 Update." *Current Population Reports,* series P70, no. 62 (November). Washington: U.S. Government Printing Office for the U.S. Bureau of the Census. Available at: *www.census.gov/population/www/socdemo/childcare.html.*

Caughy, Margaret O'Brien, Janet A. DiPietro, and Donna M. Strobino. 1994. "Day-Care Participation as a Protective Factor in the Cognitive Development of Low-Income Children." *Child Development* 65(2): 457–71.

Center for Career Development in Early Care and Education. 1998. "1997 State Child Care Licensing Regulations at a Glance." Boston: Wheelock College.

Chaplin, Duncan D., Philip K. Robins, Sandra L. Hofferth, Douglas A. Wissoker, and Paul Fronstin. 1999. "The Price Elasticity of Child Care Demand: A Sensitivity Analysis." Working Paper. Washington: Urban Institute.

Children's Foundation. 2000. "Child Care Center Licensing Study Summary Data." Washington, D.C. Available at: *www.childrensfoundation.net/centerssum.htm.*

Chipty, Tasneem. 1995. "Economic Effects of Quality Regulation in the Day Care Industry." *American Economic Review* 85(2): 419–24.

Chipty, Tasneem, and Ann Dryden Witte. 1997. "An Empirical Investigation of Firms' Responses to Minimum Standards Regulations." Working Paper 6104. Cambridge, Mass.: National Bureau of Economic Research.

Clarke-Stewart, K. Alison. 1987. "Predicting Child Development from Child Care Forms and Features: The Chicago Study." In *Quality in Child Care: What Does*

Research Tell Us?, edited by Deborah A. Phillips. Washington: National Association for the Education of Young Children.

Clarke-Stewart, K. Alison, and Christian P. Gruber. 1984. "Day Care Forms and Features." In *The Child and the Day Care Setting: Qualitative Variations and Development*, edited by Ricardo C. Ainslie. New York: Praeger Press.

Committee on Ways and Means, U.S. House of Representatives. 1998. *1998 Green Book.* Washington: U.S. Government Printing Office.

———. 2000. *2000 Green Book.* Washington: U.S. Government Printing Office.

Connelly, Rachel. 1991. "The Importance of Child Care Costs to Women's Decision Making." In *The Economics of Child Care*, edited by David M. Blau. New York: Russell Sage Foundation.

———. 1992a. "The Effects of Child Care Costs on Married Women's Labor Force Participation." *Review of Economics and Statistics* 74(1): 83–90.

———. 1992b. "Self-employment and Providing Child Care: Employment Strategies for Mothers with Young Children." *Demography* 29(1): 17–30.

Connelly, Rachel, and Jean Kimmel. 1999. "Marital Status and Full-time/Part-time Work Status in Child Care Choices." Working Paper 99–58. Kalamazoo, Mich.: Upjohn Institute (September).

Council of Economic Advisers. 1997. "The Economics of Child Care." Washington.

Cryer, Debby, and Margaret Burchinal. 1995. "Parents as Child Care Consumers." In *Cost, Quality, and Child Outcomes in Child Care Centers: Technical Report*, edited by Suzanne W. Helburn. Denver: Department of Economics, Center for Research in Economic and Social Policy, University of Colorado (June).

Cryer, Debby, Ellen S. Peisner-Feinberg, Mary L. Culkin, Leslie Phillipsen, and Jean Rustici. 1995. "Design of Study." In *Cost, Quality, and Child Outcomes in Child Care Centers: Technical Report*, edited by Suzanne W. Helburn. Denver: Department of Economics, Center for Research in Economic and Social Policy, University of Colorado.

Cryer, Debby, Wolfgang Tietze, Margaret Burchinal, Teresa Leal, and Jesus Palacios. 1999. "Predicting Process Quality from Structural Quality in Preschool Programs: A Cross-Country Comparison." *Early Childhood Research Quarterly* 14(3): 339–61.

Currie, Janet. 2001. "Early Childhood Intervention Programs: What Do We Know?" *Journal of Economic Perspectives* 15(2): 213–38.

———. 1995. "Does Head Start Make a Difference?" *American Economic Review* 85(3): 341–64.

Currie, Janet, and Duncan Thomas. 1999. "Does Head Start Help Hispanic Children?" *Journal of Public Economics* 74(2): 235–62.

Dalaker, Joseph L. 1999. "Poverty in the United States, 1998." *Current Population Reports*, Series P60-207, U.S. Census Bureau. Washington: U.S. Government Printing Office. Available at: *www.census.gov/prod/99pubs/P60-207.pdf.*

Deater-Deckard, Kirby, Relana Pinkerton, and Sandra Scarr. 1996. "Child Care Quality and Children's Behavioral Adjustment: A Four-Year Longitudinal Study." *Journal of Child Psychology and Psychiatry* 37(8): 937–48.

Desai, Sonalde, P. Lindsay Chase-Lansdale, and Robert T. Michael. 1989. "Mother or Market?: Effects of Maternal Employment on the Intellectual Ability of Four-Year-Old Children." *Demography* 26(4): 545–61.

Doherty-Derkowski, Gillian. 1995. *Quality Matters: Excellence in Early Childhood Programs.* New York: Addison-Wesley.

Duncan, Greg J., and Christina Gibson. 2000. "Selection and Attrition in the NICHD Child Care Study's Analyses of the Impacts of Child Care Quality on Child Outcomes." Northwestern University (July). Unpublished paper.

Dunn, Lorraine. 1993a. "Ratio and Group Size in Day Care Programs." *Child Care and Youth Forum* 22(3): 193–226.

———. 1993b. "Proximal and Distal Features of Day Care Quality and Children's Development." *Early Childhood Research Quarterly* 8: 167–92.

Field, Tiffany M. 1980. "Preschool Play: Effects of Teacher-Child Ratios and Organization of Classroom Space." *Child Study Journal* 10(3): 191–205.

———. 1991. "Quality Infant Day Care and Grade School Behavior and Performance." *Child Development* 62: 863–70.

Fronstin, Paul, and Doug Wissoker. 1995. "The Effects of the Availability of Low-Cost Child Care on the Labor Supply of Low-Income Women." Working Paper. Washington, D.C.: Urban Institute (January).

Fuchs, Victor R. 1989. "Women's Quest for Economic Equality." *Journal of Economic Perspectives* 3(1): 25–42.

Fuller, Bruce, Sharon L. Kagan, Gretchen Caspary, Nancy Cohen, Desiree French, Laura Gascue, Africa Hands, James Mensing, Jan McCarthy, Gege Kreischer, Jude Carroll, and Kristen Cool. 2000. "Remember the Children: Mothers Balance Work and Child Care Under Welfare Reform." Berkeley: University of California. Unpublished paper.

Fuller, Bruce, Stephen W. Raudenbush, Li-Ming Wei, and Susan D. Holloway. 1993. "Can Government Raise Child Care Quality?: The Influence of Family Demand, Poverty, and Policy." *Educational Evaluation and Policy Analysis* 15(3): 255–78.

Gamoran, Adam, Robert D. Mare, and Lynne Bethke. 1999. "Effects of Nonmaternal Child Care on Inequality in Cognitive Skills." Discussion Paper 1186–99. Madison: Institute for Research on Poverty, University of Wisconsin.

Gelbach, Jonah. 1999. "How Large an Effect Do Child Care Costs Have on Single Mothers' Labor Supply?: Evidence Using Access to Free Public Schooling." Working Paper. College Park: Department of Economics, University of Maryland (December).

Gianarelli, Linda, and James Barsimantov. 2000. "Child Care Expenses of America's Families." Washington, D.C.: Urban Institute Occasional Paper Number 40. Available at: *newfederalism.urban.org/pdf/occa40.pdf*.

Gladden, Tricia, and Christopher Taber. 2000. "Wage Progression Among Less-Skilled Workers." In *Finding Jobs: Work and Welfare Reform*, edited by David Card and Rebecca Blank. New York: Russell Sage Foundation.

Goelman, Hillel, and Alan Pence. 1988. "Children in Three Types of Day Care: Daily Experiences, Quality of Care, and Developmental Outcomes." *Early Childhood Development and Care* 33: 67–76.

Gomby, Deanna S., Nora Krantzler, Mary B. Larner, Carol S. Stevenson, Donna L. Terman, and Richard E. Behrman. 1996. "Financing Child Care: Analysis and Recommendations." *The Future of Children* 6(2): 5–25.

Gormley, William T. 1991. "State Regulations and the Availability of Child Care Services." *Journal of Policy Analysis and Management* 10(1): 78–95.

———. 1995. *Everybody's Children: Child Care as a Public Problem.* Washington: Brookings Institution.

Granger, Robert C., and Rachel Cytron. 1999. "Teenage Parent Programs: A Synthesis of the Long-term Effects of the New Chance Demonstration, Ohio's Learning, Earning, and Parenting Program, and the Teenage Parent Demonstration." *Evaluation Review* 23(2): 107–45.

Greenstein, Theodore N. 1993. "Maternal Employment and Child Behavioral Outcomes: A Household Economics Analysis." *Journal of Family Issues* 14(3, September): 323–54.

Hamilton, Gayle, Thomas Brock, Mary Farrell, Daniel Friedlander, and Kristen Harknett. 1997. "The National Evaluation of Welfare-to-Work Strategies: Evaluating Two Welfare-to-Work Approaches: Two-Year Findings on the Labor Force Attachment and Human Capital Development Programs in Three Sites." New York: Manpower Demonstration Research Corporation (December).

Han, Wen-Jui, and Jane Waldfogel. 1999. "The Effect of Child Care Costs on the Employment of Single and Married Mothers: Evidence from the Current Population Survey." Working Paper. New York: School of Social Work, Columbia University (July).

Han, Wen-Jui, Jane Waldfogel, and Jeanne Brooks-Gunn. 1999. "Long-run Effects of Early and Extensive Maternal Employment on Children's Achievement and Behavior." Paper presented at the annual meeting of the Population Association of America (March).

Harms, Thelma, and Richard Clifford. 1980. *Early Childhood Environment Rating Scale.* New York: Teachers College Press.

Harms, Thelma, Debby Cryer, and Richard Clifford. 1990. *Infant-Toddler Environment Rating Scale.* New York: Teachers College Press.

Hayes, Cheryl D., John L. Palmer, and Martha L. Zaslow, eds. 1990. *Who Cares for America's Children?: Child Care Policy for the 1990s.* Washington, D.C.: National Academy Press.

Head Start. 2001. "2001 Head Start Fact Sheet." Available at: *www2.acf.dhhs.gov/programs/hsb/about/fact2001.htm.*

Heckman, James J. 1979. "Sample Selection Bias as a Specification Error." *Econometrica* 47(1): 153–62.

Heckman, James J., Neil Hohmann, and Jeffrey Smith. 2000. "Substitution and Dropout Bias in Social Experiments: A Study of an Influential Social Experiment." *Quarterly Journal of Economics* 115(2): 651–94.

Helburn, Suzanne W., ed. 1995. *Cost, Quality, and Child Outcomes in Child Care Centers: Technical Report.* Denver: Department of Economics, University of Colorado.

Hestenes, Linda, Susan Kontos, and Yvonne Bryan. 1993. "Children's Emotional Expression in Child Care Centers Varying in Quality." *Early Childhood Research Quarterly* 8: 295–307.

Hofferth, Sandra, L., April Brayfield, Sharon Deich, and Pamela Holcomb. 1991. "National Child Care Survey, 1990." Report 91–5. Washington, D.C.: Urban Institute.

Hofferth, Sandra L., and Duncan D. Chaplin. 1998. "State Regulations and Child Care Choice." *Population Research and Policy Review* 17: 111–40.

Holloway, Susan, and Marina Reichart-Erickson. 1988. "The Relationship of Day Care Quality to Children's Free-Play Behavior and Social Problem-Solving Skills." *Early Childhood Research Quarterly* 3: 39–53.

Hotz, V. Joseph, and M. Rebecca Kilburn. 1994. "Regulating Child Care: The Effects of State Regulations on Child Care Demand and Its Costs." Working Paper. Santa Monica, Calif.: RAND.

Howes, Carollee. 1983. "Caregiver Behavior in Center and Family Day Care." *Journal of Applied Developmental Psychology* 4: 99–107.

———. 1988. "Relations Between Early Child Care and Schooling." *Developmental Psychology* 24: 53–57.

———. 1990. "Can the Age of Entry into Child Care and the Quality of Child Care Predict Adjustment in Kindergarten?" *Developmental Psychology* 26: 292–303.

Howes, Carollee, Ellen Galinsky, Marybeth Shinn, Leyla Gulcur, Margaret Clements, Annette Sibley, Martha Abbott-Shim, and Jan McCarthy. 1998. *The Florida Child Care Quality Improvement Study: 1996 Report.* New York: Families and Work Institute.

Howes, Carollee, and Michael Olenick. 1986. "Family and Child Care Influences on Toddler's Compliance." *Child Development* 57: 202–16.

Howes, Carollee, Carol Rodning, Darlene C. Galluzzo, and Lisbeth Myers. 1988. "Attachment and Child Care: Relationships with Mother and Caregiver." *Early Childhood Research Quarterly* 3: 403–16.

Howes, Carollee, and Judith L. Rubenstein. 1981. "Toddler Peer Behavior in Two Types of Day Care." *Infant Behavior and Development* 4: 387–93.

———. 1985. "Determinants of Toddlers' Experience in Day Care: Age of Entry and Quality of Setting." *Child Care Quarterly* 14(2): 140–51.

Jacobs, Eva E., ed. 1999. *Handbook of Labor Statistics,* 3rd ed. Lanham, Md.: Bernan Press.

Joint Committee on Taxation, U.S. Congress. 1999. JCS-13-99. "Estimates of Federal Tax Expenditures for Fiscal Years 2000–2004." Committee Print JCS-13-99 (December 22). Washington: U.S. Government Printing Office. Available at: *www.house.gov/jct/s-13-99.pdf.*

———. 2000. "Description of Revenue Provisions Contained in the President's Fiscal Year 2001 Budget Proposal." Committee print JCS-2-00 (March 6). Washington: U.S. Government Printing Office.

Joskow, Paul, and Nancy Rose. 1989. "Effects of Economic Regulation." In *Handbook of Industrial Organization,* vol. 2, edited by Richard Scmalense and Robert D. Willig. New York: North Holland.

Kagan, Sharon L., and Nancy Cohen. 1996. "A Vision for a Quality Early Care and Education System." In *Reinventing Early Care and Education: A Vision for a Quality System,* edited by Sharon Kagan and Nancy Cohen. San Francisco: Jossey-Bass.

Kahn, Alfred, and Sheila Kamerman. 1987. *Child Care: Facing the Hard Choices.* Dover, Mass.: Auburn House.

Karoly, Lynn A., Peter W. Greenwood, Susan S. Everingham, Jill Houbé, M. Rebecca Kilburn, C. Peter Rydell, Matthew Sanders, and James Chiesa. 1998. "Investing in Our Children: What We Know and Don't Know About the Costs and Benefits of Early Childhood Interventions." Report MR-898-TCWF. Santa Monica, Calif.: RAND.

Kimmel, Jean. 1998. "Child Care Costs as a Barrier to Employment for Single and Married Mothers." *Review of Economics and Statistics* 80(2): 287–99.

Kisker, Ellen E., Sandra L. Hofferth, Deborah A. Phillips, and Elizabeth Farquhar. 1991. "A Profile of Child Care Settings: Early Education and Care in 1990." Report prepared for U.S. Department of Education. Princeton, N.J.: Mathematica Policy Research.

Kisker, Ellen E., Anu Rangarajan, and Kimberly Boller. 1998. "Moving into Adulthood: Were the Impacts of Mandatory Programs for Welfare-Dependent Teenage Parents Sustained After the Programs Ended?" Princeton, N.J.: Mathematica Policy Research (February).

Kontos, Susan. 1991. "Child Care Quality, Family Background, and Children's Development." *Early Childhood Research Quarterly* 6: 249–62.

———. 1994. "The Ecology of Family Day Care." *Early Childhood Research Quarterly* 9: 87–110.

Kontos, Susan, and Richard Fiene. 1987. "Child Care Quality, Compliance with Regulations, and Children's Development: The Pennsylvania Study." In *Quality in Child Care: What Does Research Tell Us?*, edited by Deborah A. Phillips. Washington: National Association for the Education of Young Children.

Kontos, Susan, Carollee Howes, Marybeth Shinn, and Ellen Galinsky. 1995. *Quality in Family Child Care and Relative Care.* New York: Teachers College Press.

Kontos, Susan, Hui-Chin Hsu, and Lorraine Dunn. 1994. "Children's Cognitive and Social Competence in Child Care Centers and Family Day Care Homes." *Journal of Applied Developmental Psychology* 15: 387–411.

Korenman, Sanders, Jane E. Miller, and John E. Sjaastad. 1995. "Long-term Poverty and Child Development in the United States: Results from the NLSY." *Child and Youth Services Review* 17(12): 127–55.

Lamb, Michael E. 1998. "Nonparental Child Care: Context, Quality, Correlates, and Consequences." In *Child Psychology in Practice*, edited by Irving E. Sigel and K. Ann Renninger, vol 4. In *Handbook of Child Psychology*, 5th ed., William Damon, series editor. New York: Wiley.

Lamb, Michael E., C. Phillip Hwang, Anders G. Broberg, and Fred L. Bookstein. 1988. "The Effects of Out-of-Home Care on the Development of Social Competence in Sweden: A Longitudinal Study." *Early Childhood Research Quarterly* 3: 379–402.

Leland, Hayne. 1979. "Quacks, Lemons, and Licensing: A Theory of Minimum Quality Standards." Journal of Political Economy 87: 1328–46.

Love, John M., Peter Z. Schochet, and Alicia L. Meckstroth. 1996. "Are They in Any Real Danger?: What Research Does—And Doesn't—Tell Us About Child Care Quality and Children's Well-being." Princeton, N.J.: Mathematica Policy Research (May).

Lowenberg, Anton D., and Thomas D. Tinnin. 1992. "Professional Versus Consumer Interests in Regulation: The Case of the U.S. Child Care Industry." *Applied Economics* 24: 571–80.

Magenheim, Ellen B. 1995. "Information, Prices, and Competition in the Child Care Market: What Role Should Government Play?" In *Readings in Public Policy*, edited by J. M. Pogodzinksi. Cambridge, Mass.: Blackwell.

Marcon, Rebecca A. 1999. "Differential Impact of Preschool Models on Development and Early Learning of Inner-City Children: A Three-Cohort Study." *Developmental Psychology* 35(2): 358–75.

McCartney, Kathleen. 1984. "Effect of Quality of Day Care Environment on Children's Language Development." *Developmental Psychology* 20: 244–60.

Meyer, Bruce D., and Dan T. Rosenbaum. 1999. "Welfare, the Earned Income Tax Credit, and the Labor Supply of Single Mothers." Working Paper 7363. Cambridge, Mass.: National Bureau of Economic Research (September).

Meyers, Marcia K., Theresa Heintze, and Douglas A. Wolf. 2000. "Child Care Subsidies and the Employment of Welfare Recipients." Working Paper. New York: School of Social Work, Columbia University (August).

Michalopoulos, Charles, and Philip K. Robins. 1999. "Employment and Child-Care Choices in Canada and the United States." New York: Manpower Demonstration Research Corporation (August).

Michalopoulos, Charles, Philip K. Robins, and Irwin Garfinkel. 1992. "A Structural Model of Labor Supply and Child Care Demand." *Journal of Human Resources* 27(1): 166–203.

Miller, Cynthia, Virginia Knox, Patricia Auspos, Jo Anna Hunter-Means, and Alan Orenstein. 1997. "Making Welfare Work and Work Pay: Implementation and Eighteen-Month Impacts of the Minnesota Family Investment Program." New York: Manpower Demonstration Research Corporation (September).

Mitchell, Anne, Emily Cooperstein, and Mary Larner. 1992. "Child Care Choices, Consumer Education, and Low-Income Families." New York: National Center for Children in Poverty, Columbia University.

Mocan, H. Naci, Margaret Burchinal, John R. Morris, and Suzanne W. Helburn. 1995. "Models of Quality in Center Child Care." In *Cost, Quality, and Child Outcomes in Child Care Centers: Technical Report,* edited by Suzanne W. Helburn. Denver: Department of Economics, Center for Research in Economic and Social Policy, University of Colorado (1995).

Morgan, Gwen, and Sheri Azer. 1997. "A Primer of Child Care Licensing 1997: Its Role in Public Policy." Boston: Wheelock College. Unpublished paper.

Mott, Frank L. 1991. "Developmental Effects of Infant Care: The Mediating Role of Gender and Health." *Journal of Social Issues* 47(2): 139–58.

National Child Care Information Center. 2000. "State Child Care Profiles." Available at: *www.nccic.org/statepro.html.*

National Institute of Child Health and Human Development, Early Child Care Research Network. 1998a. "Early Child Care and Self-control, Compliance, and Problem Behavior at Twenty-four and Thirty-six Months." *Child Development* 69(4): 1145–70.

———. 1998b. "Relations Between Family Predictors and Child Outcomes: Are They Weaker for Children in Child Care?" *Developmental Psychology* 34(5): 1119–28.

———. 2000a. "Characteristics and Quality of Child Care for Toddlers and Preschoolers." *Applied Developmental Science* 4(3): 116–35.

———. 2000b. "Child Care and Children's Peer Interactions at Twenty-four and Thirty-six Months: The NICHD Study of Early Child Care." Working Paper. Pittsburgh: University of Pittsburgh (January).

———. 2000c. "The Relation of Child Care to Cognitive and Language Development." *Child Development* 71(4): 960–80.

Office of Management and Budget. 1996. *Budget of the United States Government, Fiscal Year 1997.* Washington: OMB. Available at: *w3.access.gpo.gov/usbudget/fy1997/ spec.pdf.*

Parcel, Toby L., and Elizabeth G. Menaghan. 1990. "Maternal Working Conditions and Children's Verbal Facility: Studying the Intergenerational Transmission of Inequality from Mothers to Young Children." *Social Psychology Quarterly* 53(2): 132–47.

Peisner-Feinberg, Ellen S., and Margaret R. Burchinal. 1997. "Relations Between Pre-school Children's Child-Care Experiences and Concurrent Development: The Cost, Quality, and Outcomes Study." *Merrill-Palmer Quarterly* 43(3): 451–77.

Peisner-Feinberg, Ellen S., Margaret R. Burchinal, Richard M. Clifford, Noreen Yaze-jian, Mary L. Culkin, Janice Zelazo, Carollee Howes, Patricia Byler, Sharon Lynn Kagan, and Jean Rustici. 1999. "The Children of the Cost, Quality, and Outcomes Study Go to School." Chapel Hill: Frank Porter Graham Child Development Center, University of North Carolina. Available at: *www.fpg.unc.edu/~SCPP/pages/cqes.htm.*

Peterson, Carole, and Richard Peterson. 1986. "Parent-Child Interaction and Day-care: Does Quality of Daycare Matter?" *Journal of Applied Developmental Psychology* 7: 1–15.

Phillips, Deborah, Carollee Howes, and Marcy Whitebook. 1991. "Child Care as an Adult Work Environment." *Journal of Social Issues* 47(2): 49–70.

Phillips, Deborah, Kathleen McCartney, and Sandra Scarr. 1987. "Child-Care Quality and Children's Social Development." *Developmental Psychology* 23(4): 537–43.

Pitegoff, Peter, and Lauren Bream. 1997. "Child Care Policy and the Welfare Reform Act." *Journal of Affordable Housing and Community Development Law* 6(2): 113–30.

Powell, Lisa M. 1997. "The Impact of Child Care Costs on the Labour Supply of Married Mothers: Evidence from Canada." *Canadian Journal of Economics* 30(3): 577–94.

Queralt, Magaly, and Ann Dryden Witte. 1997. "Effects of Regulations, Consumer Information, and Subsidies on Child-Staff Ratios at Child Care Centers." Working Paper 97–2. Miami: Florida International University.

Quint, Janet C., Johannes M. Bos, and Denise F. Polit. 1997. "New Chance: Final Report on a Comprehensive Program for Young Mothers in Poverty and Their Children." New York: Manpower Demonstration Research Corporation (October).

Raikes, Helen. 1998. "Investigating Child Care Subsidy: What Are We Buying?" *Social Policy Report* [Society for Research in Child Development] 12(2): 1–18.

Ribar, David. 1992. "Child Care and the Labor Supply of Married Women." *Journal of Human Resources* 27(1): 134–65.

———. 1995. "A Structural Model of Child Care and the Labor Supply of Married Women." *Journal of Labor Economics* 13(3): 558–97.

Riccio, James, Daniel Friedlander, and Stephen Freedman. 1994. "GAIN: Benefits, Costs, and Three-Year-Impacts of a Welfare-to-Work Program." New York: Man-power Demonstration Research Corporation (September).

Robins, Philip K. 1990. "Federal Financing of Child Care: Alternative Approaches and Economic Implications." *Population and Policy Review* 9(1): 65–90.

———. 1991. " Child Care Policy and Research: An Economist's Perspective." In *The Economics of Child Care,* edited by David Blau. New York: Russell Sage Foundation.

Robins, Philip K., and Robert Spiegelman. 1978. "An Econometric Model of the Demand for Child Care." *Economic Inquiry* 16(January): 83–94.

Ronnen, Uri. 1991. "Minimum Quality Standards, Fixed Costs, and Competition." *Rand Journal of Economics* 22(4): 490–504.

Rose-Ackerman, Susan. 1983. "Unintended Consequences: Regulating the Quality of Subsidized Day Care." *Journal of Policy Analysis and Management* 3(1): 14–30.

Ross, Christine. 1998. "Sustaining Employment Among Low-Income Parents: The

Role of Child Care Costs and Subsidies." Washington: Mathematica Policy Research (December).

Ruhm, Christopher L. 2000. "Parental Employment and Child Cognitive Development." Working Paper 7666. Cambridge, Mass.: National Bureau of Economic Research (April).

Ruopp, Richard, Jeffrey Travers, Frederic Glantz, and Craig Coelen. 1979. *Children at the Center.* Cambridge, Mass.: Abt Books.

Sawhill, Isabel V., and Adam Thomas. 2000. "A Hand Up for the Bottom Third: Toward a New Agenda for Low-Income Working Families." Washington: Brookings Institution.

Scarr, Sandra, Marlene Eisenberg, and Kirby Deater-Deckard. 1994. "Measurement of Quality in Child Care Centers." *Early Childhood Research Quarterly* 9(June): 131–51.

Shapiro, Carl. 1986. "Investment, Moral Hazard, and Occupational Licensing." *Review of Economics Studies* 53: 843–62.

Smith, Anne B., Bruce W. McMillan, Shelley Kennedy, and Brenda Ratcliffe. 1989. "The Effect of Improving Preschool Teacher-Child Ratios: An 'Experiment in Nature.'" *Early Child Development and Care* 41: 123–38.

Smith, Kristin. 2000. "Who's Minding the Kids?: Child Care Arrangements, Fall 1995." *Current Population Reports,* series P70, no. 70. Washington: U.S. Government Printing Office for the U.S. Bureau of the Census (October). Available at: *www.census.gov/population/www/socdemo/childcare.html.*

Smith, Peter K., and Kevin J. Connolly. 1986. "Experimental Studies of the Preschool Environment: The Sheffield Project." *Advances in Early Childhood Education* 4: 27–66.

Sonenstein, Freya L. 1991. "The Child Care Preferences of Parents with Young Children." In *Parental Leave and Child Care: Setting a Research and Policy Agenda,* edited by Janet S. Hyde and Marilyn J. Essex. Philadelphia: Temple University Press.

Stoney, Louise. 1998. "Looking into New Mirrors: Lessons for Early Childhood Finance and System-Building." Vienna, Va.: National Child Care Information Center (October). Available at: *nccic.org/pubs/mirrors/highed.html.*

Studer, Marlena. 1992. "Quality of Center Care and Preschool Cognitive Outcomes: Differences by Family Income." *Sociological Studies of Child Development* 5: 49–72.

Tekin, Erdal. 2001. "An Analysis of Single Mothers' Child Care, Employment, and Welfare Choices." Chapel Hill: Department of Economics, University of North Carolina (May). Unpublished doctoral dissertation.

U.S. Bureau of the Census. 1997. *Census of Services.* Available at: *www.census.gov/epcd/www/econ97.html.*

U.S. Department of Agriculture. 2001. "Child and Adult Care Food Program." Available at: *www.fns.usda.gov/cnd/Care/CACFP/cacfpfaqs.htm#HowmuchdoesCACFP.*

U.S. Department of Education. 1996. "Serving Preschool Children." Available at: *www.ed.gov/legislation/ESEA/Title—I/preschoo.html.*

U.S. Department of Health and Human Services. 1998. "Final Rule for Federal CCDF Guidelines and Requirements." *Federal Register* (July 24). Available at: *www.acf.dhhs.gov/programs/ccb/policy/fr072498.pdf.*

———. Various years. "TANF-AFDC Data Reports and Analyses." Available at: *www.acf.dhss.gov/programs/opre/director.htm.*

U.S. Department of Labor. 1994. *Reports on Benefits in State and Local Governments.* Washington: Bureau of Labor Statistics. Available at: *stats.bls.gov/news.release/ebs2.toc.htm.*

————. 1998. "Issues in Labor Statistics." Summary 98–9. Washington: U.S. Department of Labor (August).

————. 1999a. "Employee Benefits in Small Private Establishments, 1996." Bureau of Labor Statistics Bulletin 2507. Washington: U.S. Department of Labor (April).

————. 1999b. "Employee Benefits in Medium and Large Private Establishments, 1997." Bureau of Labor Statistics Bulletin 2517. Washington: U.S. Department of Labor (September).

————. Various years. *Handbook of Labor Statistics*. Washington: U.S. Department of Labor.

U.S. General Accounting Office. 1994a. "Early Childhood Programs: Multiple Programs and Overlapping Target Groups." Report GAO/HEHS-95-4FS. Washington: U.S. GAO (October).

————. 1994b. "Child Care Subsidies Increase the Likelihood That Low-Income Mothers Will Work." Report GAO/HEHS-95-20. Washington: U.S. GAO (December).

————. 1998. "Welfare Reform: States' Efforts to Expand Child Care Programs." Report GAO/HEHS-98-27. Washington: U.S. GAO (January).

————. 1999. "Education and Care: Early Childhood Programs and Services for Low-Income Families." Report GAO/HEHS-00-11. Washington: U.S. GAO (November).

————. 2000a. "Child Care: State Efforts to Enforce Safety and Health Requirements." Report GAO/HEHS-00-28. Washington: U.S. GAO (January).

————. 2000b. "Title I Preschool Education: More Children Served, but Gauging Effect on Preschool Readiness Difficult." Report GAO/HEHS-00-171. Washington: U.S. GAO (September).

U.S. Internal Revenue Service. Various years. *Statistics of Income Bulletin*. Available at: *www.irs.ustreas.gov/prod/tax—stats/soi/cmplt-rpt.html*.

Vandell, Deborah Lowe, V. Kay Henderson, and Kathy S. Wilson. 1988. "A Longitudinal Study of Children with Day Care Experiences of Varying Quality." *Child Development* 59: 1286–92.

Vandell, Deborah Lowe, and Carol S. Powers. 1983. "Day Care Quality and Children's Free-Play Activities." *American Journal of Orthopsychiatry* 53(3): 493–500.

Vandell, Deborah Lowe, and Janaki Ramanan. 1991. "Children of the National Longitudinal Survey of Youth: Choices in After-School Care and Child Development." *Developmental Psychology* 27(4): 637–43.

Vandell, Deborah Lowe, and Barbara Wolfe. 2000. "Child Care Quality: Does It Matter and Does It Need to Be Improved?" Madison: Institute for Research on Poverty, University of Wisconsin. Available at: *aspe.hhs.gov/hsp/ccquality00/ccqual.htm*.

Waite, Linda J., Arleen Leibowitz, and Christina Witsberger. 1991. "What Parents Pay For: Child Care Characteristics, Quality, and Costs." *Journal of Social Issues* 47(2): 33–48.

Waldfogel, Jane. 1999. "Child Care, Women's Employment, and Child Outcomes." Paper presented at the IZA Conference on the Economics of Child Care, Bonn, Germany (November).

Walker, James. 1991. "Public Policy and the Supply of Child Care Services." In *The Economics of Child Care*, edited by David Blau. New York: Russell Sage Foundation.

————. 1996. "Funding Child Rearing: Child Allowance and Parental Leave." *The Future of Children* 6(2): 122–36.

Whitebook, Marcy, Carollee Howes, and Deborah Phillips. 1989. *Who Cares?: Child Care Teachers and the Quality of Care in America: Final Report of the National Care Staffing Study.* Oakland, Calif.: Child Care Employee Project.

Willer, Barbara. 1987. "Quality or Affordability: Trade-offs for Early Childhood Programs?" *Young Children* (September): 41–42.

Zigler, Edward, and Matia Finn-Stevenson. 1999. *Schools of the Twenty-first Century: Linking Child Care and Education.* Boulder, Colo.: Westview Press.

Index

Boldface numbers refer to figures and tables.

Abecedarian Project, 168–69
accreditation, proposal to subsidize, 220–21
Adams, Gina, 9, 233n2
availability of child care: problem of, 6–7; under proposed reforms, 229; shortages as argument for subsidies, 157–58. *See also* supply of child care

Barnett, W. Steven, 168, 170, 216–17, 219
Berger, Mark, 164–66, 168
Bergmann, Barbara, 162, 216–17, 219
Black, Dan, 164–66, 168
Blau, David, 138–40, 145
Bryant, Donna, 143
Burchinal, Margaret, 137, 145, 160, 211

Cappizzano, Jeffrey, 233n2
CCDF. *See* Child Care and Development Fund
CCFP. *See* Child and Adult Care Food Program
Chaplin, Duncan, 207
child allowance, means-tested, proposal for, 220, 223, **225**
Child and Adult Care Food Program (CCFP), **153,** 155, **156,** 216
child care: defined, 17–18; formal and informal defined, 21
Child Care Action Campaign, 10
Child Care and Development Fund (CCDF), 12, 151, **152,** 153–55, **156,** 216
child care market, 43–45; arrangements, variation in, 20–25; characteristics of facilities, 34, **36, 37**–38, **39;** fam-

ily expenditures, 26–27, **28–29;** growth of, 19–21; imperfections as argument for regulation, 179–81; imperfections as argument for subsidies, 159–62; labor force participation of mothers and, 18–19; market equilibrium model of, 57–64; number of children and average income, **224;** price and quality, relationship of (*see* price-quality relationship in the child care market); quality, measuring and data, 38, 40–43, **44** (*see also* quality of child care); supply side, 27, 29–34 (*see also* supply of child care)
child care voucher, means-tested, proposal for, 221–24, **225–26, 228**
child development: employment, tension with, 12–13; quality of care and (*see* quality of care and child development); quality of child care and, 5–6, 11, 209 (*see also* quality of child care); subsidies, impact of, 168–70
Chipty, Tasneem, 207
Cohen, Nancy, 217, 219, 231
consumers of child care: behavior, model of, 48–53; data, model for estimating, 68–72, **85;** experimental demonstration projects, impact on income, 163–164; knowledge and information problems (*see* information); miscellaneous variables, effects of, 79–81; mothers, labor force participation of (*see* employment); price, effects of, 72–77 (*see also* price of child care); quality, demand for, 81–84 (*see also* quality of

consumers of child care (*cont.*)
child care); wages and income, effects of, 77–79
Cooperstein, Emily, 9
Cost, Quality, and Outcomes Study (CQOS): descriptive statistics, 41–43; price-quality relationship, 106–13; quality, consumer demand for, 68, 81–82; quality and child development, 136–38, 145; quality and cost, price and relative weight functions, 89–91; regulations, effect of, 184–200
cost of child care: family expenditures, 26–27, **28–29;** and incentives for improving quality, 209; low-income families (*see* low-income families); proposed new system, 223–24, **225–26,** 227–28; quality and, 7–8, 87–88, 92 (*see also* quality of child care)
CPS. *See* Current Population Survey
CQOS. *See* Cost, Quality and Outcomes Study
Cryer, Debby, 160, 211
Current Population Survey (CPS), 27, 29–34, 204–6
Currie, Janet, 168–70, 241*n*9
Cytron, Rachel, 242*n*12

day care centers: age of child and use of, 79–81; characteristics of, **36;** cost and quality, 87–89; earnings of teachers in (*see* wages); Florida Child Care Quality Improvement Study, 132–34; income elasticity of demand, 77; moral hazard, 160; National Day Care Study (NDCS), 131–32, 146; price elasticity of demand, 72–73; price-quality relationship (*see* price-quality relationship in the child care market); Profile of Child Care Settings, 34, 37; profit and nonprofit, 94–98; quality at, 4–5, 81–82, 87, 94–98; regulation of, 174–78, **194.** *See also* formal child care

DCTC. *See* Dependent Care Tax Credit
demand for child care and mother's employment, 67–68, 83–84; additional variables, effects of, 79–81; data, 68–72; price effects, 72–77; quality and, 81–82; wage and income effects, 77–79
Dependent Care Tax Credit (DCTC), 151, **152,** 155, **156,** 211–12, 216
Doherty-Derkowski, Gillian, 129
Dunn, Lorraine, 129

Early Childhood Environment Rating Scale (ECERS), 4, 40–43, 45–46, 68, 105, 137–38
Earned Income Tax Credit (EITC), 67, 213
Ebb, Nancy, 9
ECERS. *See* Early Childhood Environment Rating Scale
economic models. *See* models of child care
EEPDCE. *See* Exclusion of Employer-Provided Dependent Care Expenses
EITC. *See* Earned Income Tax Credit
elasticity, concept of, 236*n*5
Elementary and Secondary Education Act, Title I-A, 12, **153,** 155, **156,** 216
employment: of child care providers (*see* providers of child care); child care subsidy programs, impact of, 164–67, 211–13; child development, tension with, 12–13; consumer behavior, model of, 48–53; and demand for child care (*see* demand for child care and mother's employment); experimental demonstration projects, impact of, 163–64; mothers of young children, 18, **19,** 20–25, **71;** price effects on, 72–77; price of child care and elasticity of, 236*n*8; subsidies and price effects on, 167–68; and use of child care by type, **70**
equilibrium: concept of, 58–59; markets and, 60–64, 105

equity, as argument for subsidies, 162, 213–14
Exclusion of Employer-Provided Dependent Care Expenses (EEPDCE), 150–51, **152,** 155, **156,** 211–12, 216

families, single-parent, 233n3
family day care homes and relatives: age of child and use of, 79–81; characteristics of regulated, **36;** income elasticity of demand, 77; price-quality relationship, 121–23, **122–23;** Profile of Child Care Settings, 34, 37; quality of, 5; regulation of, 174–78. *See also* informal child care
Federal interagency day care requirements (FIDCRs), 243n2
FIDCRs. *See* Federal interagency day care requirements
Finn-Stevenson, Matia, 217–19, 231
Florida Child Care Quality Improvement Study, 132–34
Florida Family Transition Program, 242n12
formal child care: day care centers (*see* day care centers); defined, 21; growth in, 21–25
Fuchs, Victor, 241n7
Fuller, Bruce, 9, 207

GAIN in California project, 242n12
Gelbach, Jonah, 166–67, 242n14
Gladden, Tricia, 158–59, 213
Gormley, William, 207, 244n1
government: availability of child care and, 6–7; regulation of child care (*see* regulation of child care); subsidies of child care (*see* subsidies of child care)
Granger, Robert, 242n12

Hayes, Cheryl, 125, 129, 244n1
Head Start, **153,** 155, **156;** children served through, 241n6; evaluations of, 143, 168–70; limitations of, 12; quality requirement, 161, 216

Heintze, Theresa, 165–66
Helburn, Suzanne, 4
Hofferth, Sandra, 207
Holloway, Susan, 207
Hotz, V. Joseph, 204, 207

Income Maintenance Experiments (Gary, Seattle, and Denver), 242n12
Infant Health and Development Projects, 168
Infant-Toddler Environment Rating Scale (ITERS), 40–43, 45–46
informal child care: defined, 21; family day care homes and relatives (*see* family day care homes and relatives); likelihood of using, 20–25
information: about quality of child care, 83, 160, 211; high-quality child care, proposal to publicize benefits of, 221; licensing as antidote for, 179–81; and principles to guide child care policy, 214–15; problems of, 9, 11–12, 159–60
ITERS. *See* Infant-Toddler Environment Rating Scale

Kagan, Sharon, 217, 219, 231
Kahn, Alfred, 244n5
Kamerman, Sheila, 244n5
Karoly, Lynn, 143, 161, 168, 170
Kilburn, M. Rebecca, 204, 207
Kontos, Susan, 5

Lamb, Michael, 125, 129
Larner, Mary, 9
licensing, 179–81
Love, John, 6, 125, 129
Lowenberg, Anton, 207
low-income families: child care and, 9–10; expenditure on child care, 26–27, **28;** government subsidies targeted at, 12; proposed reforms, impact on, 227–28; self-sufficiency as argument for subsidies, 158–59, 212–13

market failure: as argument for regulation, 179–81; as argument for subsidies, 159–62; problem of child care and, 10–13

market power, defined, 243n1

markets: child care (*see* child care market); equilibrium and, 58–64, 105; and quality of child care, 5, 11

means-tested child allowance, proposal for, 220, 223, **225**

means-tested child care voucher, proposal for, 221–24, **225–26, 228**

Meckstroth, Alicia, 125, 129

Menaghan, Elizabeth, 139

Meyer, Bruce, 242n13

Meyers, Marcia, 165–66

Minnesota Family Investment Program, 242n12

Mitchell, Anne, 9

models of child care, 13–14, 47–48, 64; child care market and equilibrium, 57–64; consumer behavior, 48–53, 68–72; provider behavior, 53–57

moral hazard, 160

NAEYC. *See* National Association for the Education of Young Children

National Association for the Education of Young Children (NAEYC), 126, 174, 220

National Child Care Staffing Study (NCCSS), 41–43, 113–15, 145, 200–203

National Child Care Survey (NCCS), 68, 72, 235n3

National Day Care Study (NDCS), 131–32, 146

National Evaluation of Welfare-to-Work Strategies, 242n12

National Institute of Child Health and Human Development (NICHD): Early Child Care Research Network (NICHD ECCRN), 134–36, 145; Study of Early Child Care (SECC), 134–36

National Longitudinal Survey of Youth (NLSY), 138–43

National Survey of America's Families (NSAF), 233n2, 234n6

NCCS. *See* National Child Care Survey

NCCSS. *See* National Child Care Staffing Study

NDCS. *See* National Day Care Study

New Chance project, 242n12

New Hope program, 163–64

NICHD. *See* National Institute of Child Health and Human Development

NICHD ECCRN. *See* National Institute of Health and Human Development, Early Child Care Research Network

NLSY. *See* National Longitudinal Survey of Youth

NSAF. *See* National Survey of America's Families

Palmer, John, 125, 129, 244n1

Parcel, Toby, 139

PCS. *See* Profile of Child Care Settings

Peisner-Feinberg, Ellen, 137, 145

Perry Preschool Project, 168–70

Personal Responsibility and Work Opportunity Reconciliation Act (PRWORA), 151, 154–55, 213, 240–41n4. *See also* welfare reform

price of child care: determinants of log price in day care centers, **117–18, 120**; determinants of log price in family day care homes, **122–23**; effects on choices, 72–77, 209; and elasticity of demand, 209; employment and subsidies, relationship to, 167–68; quality and, 87–89, 92–94 (*see also* price-quality relationship in the child care market)

price-quality relationship in the child care market, 104–6, 123–24; by city or county, **110–11**; determinants of log price, **117–18, 120, 122–23**; elasticity of, **112, 116**; per week by city, **114–15**; by state, **108–9**; weakness and variability of, data indicating, 106–23

process quality, 125–27

Profile of Child Care Settings (PCS), 34, 37, 68, 71–72, 115–23

providers of child care: accreditation, proposal to subsidize the cost of, 220–21; behavior, model of, 53–57; characteristics of, 31–32, **33;** cost function, 88; earnings (*see* wages); training of, 43, **44,** 145; turnover among, 8, 34, **35;** wages and supply of child care, 99–102

PRWORA. *See* Personal Responsibility and Work Opportunity Reconciliation Act

public policy: and child care quality, 6; cost calculations for proposed reforms, **225–26;** employment and child development, tension between, 12; evidence that should guide, 209–10; income gain for families under proposed reforms, **228;** principles to guide child care, 214–16; proposed reforms, reasons for consideration, 230–32; rationale for child care, 210–14; reform, existing proposals for, 216–20; reform, new proposals for, 15–16, 220–24, **224–26,** 227–30, **228**

quality of care and child development, 125, 144–46, 209; Cost, Quality, and Outcomes Study (CQOS), 136–38; early childhood intervention programs, 143; family environment, impact of, 128; Florida Child Care Quality Improvement Study, 132–34; inputs, estimates of effects on development, **141;** inputs, models of effects on quality, **139;** literature on, 129–31; modelling, issues for, 128–29; National Day Care Study (NDCS), 131–32; National Longitudinal Survey of Youth (NLSY), 138–43; quality, process *vs.* structural, 125–28; Study of Early Child Care (SECC), 134–36

quality of child care: and child development (*see* quality of care and child development); consumer concerns regarding, 83–84; cost effects, 209; determinants of, 209; economic models, accounting for in, 55; as function of price and cost, conclusions regarding, 92–94; as function of price and cost, data regarding, 89–92; as function of price and cost, theory of, 87–89; measuring and data, 38, 40–43, **44,** 81–82, 105–6; price effects, 75–77, 209; priority of, 7–8; problem of, 4–6, 11–13; profit and nonprofit day care centers, relative weight given to, 94–98; "quality' defined, 87; wage effects, 78–79, 82

quantity of child care: child care workers, number of, 234*n*7; determinants of, 98–103. *See also* availability of child care; supply of child care

Queralt, Magaly, 197, 207

race and ethnicity, child care, variation in usage of, 22, **23**

Raikes, Helen, 6

Raudenbush, Stephen, 207

regulation of child care, 173–74; arguments for, 179–81; child-staff and group size regulations in selected states and cities, **196;** compliance with, **194, 201;** effects of, **198–99, 203,** 206–7, 210; effects of, Cost, Quality, and Outcomes Study, 184–200; effects of, Current Population Survey, 204–6; effects of, economic theory, 181–82; effects of, empirical approach, 182–84; effects of, National Child Care Staffing Study, 200–203; existing state regulations, 174, **175–77,** 178–79; Federal interagency day care requirements (FIDCRs), 243*n*2; preschooler-staff ratio, selected states, **185–92;** sup-

regulation of child care (*cont.*)
ply and wages of providers, impact on, **205**
Robins, Philip, 216–17, 242*n*12
Rose-Ackerman, Susan, 207
Rosenbaum, Dan, 242*n*13

Sawhill, Isabel, 244*n*1
Schochet, Peter, 125, 129
Schulman, Karen, 9
SECC. *See* Study of Early Child Care
Shapiro, Carl, 179–81, 243*n*5
single-parent families, 233*n*3
SIPP. *See* Survey of Income and Program Participation
Sonenstein, Freya, 83, 233*n*2
Spiegelman, Robert, 242*n*12
structural quality, 125–27
Studer, Marlena, 139–40
Study of Early Child Care (SECC), 134–36
subsidies of child care: accreditation, proposal to subsidize, 220–21; arguments for, 157–62, 210–14; child development, impact on, 168–70; demand for child care and, 98; effect on employment, 162–68; employment and child development, tension between, 12; employment *vs.* quality goals, 149–50, 171–72; existing policies, 150–55; expenditures, federal and state, 155, **156;** impact on choices, 74; quality and quantity, effects on, 84, 210
supply of child care, 86; Current Population Survey (CPS), 27, 29–34, 204–6; elasticity, 30; providers (*see* providers of child care); quality, relative weight of for profit and nonprofit day care centers, 94–98; quality as a function of price and cost, 87–94; quantity, determinants of, 98–102; responsiveness to demand, 103; subsidies and, 98 (*see also* subsidies of child care). *See also* availability of child care
Survey of Income and Program Participation (SIPP), 19

Taber, Christopher, 158–59, 213
TANF. *See* Temporary Assistance for Needy Families
tax policy: Dependent Care Tax Credit (DCTC), 151, **152,** 155, **156,** 211–12, 216; Earned Income Tax Credit (EITC), 67, 213; Exclusion of Employer-Provided Dependent Care Expenses (EEPDCE), 150–51, **152,** 155, **156,** 211–12, 216
teachers in day care centers. *See* providers of child care
Teenage Parent Demonstration project, 242*n*12
Temporary Assistance for Needy Families (TANF), 154–55, 222
Thomas, Adam, 244*n*1
Thomas, Duncan, 169–70
Tinnin, Thomas, 207
Title 1–A. *See* Elementary and Secondary Education Act, Title 1–A
Title XX Social Services Block Grant (TXX), **153,** 154–55, **156,** 164–65
TXX. *See* Title XX Social Services Block Grant

wages: of child care providers, 8, 11, 29–31, **32;** effects on consumer's choices, 77–79; regulations, impact of, 204–6; and supply of child care workers, 99–102
Waldfogel, Jane, 168
Walker, James, 159–60, 179, 211, 216, 218–19, 223
Wei, Li-Ming, 207
welfare reform: child care and, 10; mothers, movement into labor force, 18; research validity, impact on, 167. *See also* Personal Responsibility and Work Opportunity Reconciliation Act (PRWORA)
Willer, Barbara, 8–9
Witte, Ann Dryden, 197, 207
Wolf, Douglas, 165–66

Zaslow, Martha, 125, 130, 244*n*1
Zigler, Edward, 217–19, 231